THE RAILWAY DATA BOOK
J.N.WESTWOOD

THE RAILWAY DATA BOOK

J.N. WESTWOOD

PSL Patrick Stephens, Cambridge

Title page *A General Motors main line diesel-electric of a type purchased in large numbers by US railroads in the 1950s. These are 'cab units' (that is, with all-over body). In the picture an 'A' unit (with cab) leads a cabless 'B' unit.*

©J. N. Westwood 1983

All rights reserved. No part of this publication may be reproduced, stored in a retrieval system or transmitted, in any form or by any means, electronic, mechanical, photocopying, recording or otherwise, without prior permission in writing from Patrick Stephens Limited.

First published in 1983

British Library Cataloguing in Publication Data

Westwood, J. N.
  Railway data book.
  1. Railway-History-Dictionaries
  I. Title
  385'.03'21   HE1037

ISBN 0-85059-629-7

Photoset in 10 on 11 Times by MJL Typesetting Limited, Hitchin, Herts. Printed in Great Britain on 115 gsm Fineblade coated cartridge, and bound, by The Garden City Press, Letchworth, Herts, for the publishers, Patrick Stephens Limited, Bar Hill, Cambridge, CB3 8EL, England.

Contents

	Introduction	6
Chapter 1	What is a railway?	7
Chapter 2	Railway ownership and control	11
Chapter 3	Entrepreneurs and managers	27
Chapter 4	Track and its terminology	30
Chapter 5	The railway builders	43
Chapter 6	Gauge	46
Chapter 7	Train control	53
Chapter 8	Signals	62
Chapter 9	The measurement of locomotives	82
Chapter 10	The anatomy of the steam locomotive	91
Chapter 11	Steam locomotive trends and trend-setters	102
Chapter 12	Electrification	115
Chapter 13	The electric locomotive	126
Chapter 14	The diesel locomotive	133
Chapter 15	Unorthodox locomotives	142
Chapter 16	Self-propelled trains and multiple units	151
Chapter 17	Locomotive manufacturers	159
Chapter 18	Brakes, couplings and lamps	164
Chapter 19	Locomotive inscriptions	172
Chapter 20	The freight train	176
Chapter 21	The passenger train	186
Chapter 22	Speeds and schedules	201
Chapter 23	A note on statistics	206
Appendix 1	Preserved steam railways	208
Appendix 2	Major railway museums	213
Appendix 3	Railway enthusiast societies	216
	Further reading	217
	Index	221

Introduction

This book is intended to be a general reference work and source of basic information for the railway enthusiast being virtually a concentration of facts, histories and concepts. It should be of especial use to relative newcomers to the fraternity of railway enthusiasts who soon find that there is substantial background information which the older enthusiast has acquired over many decades, and who would like to acquire the same knowledge, but at a faster pace. As the author has painfully discovered while writing this book, the long-standing enthusiast has often forgotten much that he once knew, thanks to concentration for too long on just one or two special fields of interest. For such forgetful characters, this book will also have some value. The text is orientated towards the British enthusiast, but much information is provided about those countries closest to Britain and therefore most likely to be visited. North America is covered to the extent necessary to enable the British reader to read American and Canadian railway publications with some understanding.

Aiming to sketch in the background for new enthusiasts, and to fill some gaps for the older enthusiast, this book obviously cannot say everything. It is hoped that the addresses and book titles mentioned in the text will enable the individual reader to develop further his particular interests.

J. N. Westwood
Bristol 1983

Chapter 1

What is a railway?

The Railway Age began in the 1820s and is still with us. Railways, strictly defined, had existed long before then. If a railway is taken to be a transport technology in which smooth wheels run on smooth rails, with those rails also providing a guiding function, the 18th century was also a railway century, for it was then that horse, gravity or manual industrial railways developed from the much cruder wooden guideways of previous centuries. Typically, these industrial lines carried coal from mine to wharf. Many mines used stationary steam engines for pumping and other purposes, and employed mechanics, so it was only natural that early steam locomotives were built by and for collieries. It was the addition of mechanical traction to the metal wheel rolling along the metal rail which made the technological leap into the transport revolution, transformed first Britain, then other technically advanced countries, and went on to bring outlying territories into economic relations with the older centres of population. This latter process is still continuing, for although the feverish railway-building of the 19th century is now over, railway construction continues in most parts of the world.

Railways may be classified in various ways; for example, by size or by type of traction. However, a common classification is according to function:

Common-carrier railways By far the predominant type of railway, and sometimes referred to as public railways, these carry traffic for the general public. The term *common carrier* had a specific as well as a general meaning, implying a legal obligation to carry whatever traffic was offered, without any picking and choosing. The first common carrier railway is believed to have been the Surrey Iron Railway, near Croydon, England, from 1803 onwards. In the 19th century the big common-carrier railway companies had a virtual monopoly but, with the coming of road and air transport, there was a loss of traffic which, for most railway administrations, has meant financial deficits. Whether a common-carrier railway should give priority to making a profit or providing a social service is a question frequently discussed, and different governments at different times have given different answers. In most countries (even, now, in Britain and North America), railways are regarded as social services which may receive taxpayers' support without raising ideological hackles. However, this has not prevented the closure of many lines and stations where traffic revenue was far below costs. With some exceptions, common-carrier railways are profitable only when they can carry bulk traffic over long distances; freight transits less than 200 miles, especially of non-bulk commodities, are usually

Top *The railway as bulk carrier: a main line passenger train passes 'merry-go-round' coal trains on the Western Region of British Rail* (BR).

Above *A sugar-cane railway in Queensland. Steam traction is still used on these seasonal lines in many parts of the world, although no longer in Australia* (J. van den Broeke).

more suited to highway transport with its cheaper and faster pick-up and delivery operation.

Industrial railways These are lines which are not open to the public, but form part of an industrial process. The early mine railways were of this type and mining industries of most countries still operate their own systems; in Britain the National Coal Board is the biggest railway operator after British Rail. Industrial railways can provide transport within a plant, or they can convey products or raw materials to and from the enterprise. Some such lines, especially those built to carry ores, like the Hammersley Railway in Australia and the Quebec North Shore & Labrador Railway in Canada, may be very long and technically very advanced. Sugar-cane railways, which operate only during the cane-cutting season, and forestry lines, both of which are usually narrow-guage, are technically quite primitive and require little capital investment.

Commuter railways Most of the big railway systems run suburban services around main centres for commuter traffic, and there have been only a few railways built purely for commuters, apart from underground and rapid transit lines. One such railway is the Long Island Railroad, virtually a commuter railway serving the outer suburbs and dormitory towns of New York; Italy,

Japan and Switzerland are among those countries which have a number of small independent commuter railways.

Rapid transit railways This is a diffuse term and under it fall underground and Metro railways. Rapid Transit lines are intended to provide fast and frequent passenger services between close-lying stations in urban areas. Almost always electric, they usually operate underground in the central city areas; however, they are occasionally elevated railways, running on viaducts above street level. The term Light Rail Transit (LRT) refers to urban and suburban lines which use lightweight rolling stock. In some cities, as a first move to reduce street congestion, tramways have been given underground tracks which are sometimes provided with stations suitable for use by the trains which are expected to supersede the tramcars. In Brussels, this new kind of underground line was called the Pre-Metro and this term is likely to survive for use elsewhere.

Inter-urban railways These American railways, now defunct, were fast electric tramcar-type systems linking towns or groups of towns in a defined area. Somewhat similar systems still exist in Belgium (between Ostend and Knokke), Switzerland, Spain, Japan and elsewhere.

Below *The industrial railway: a Bristol fuel distributor uses stand-by steam power to handle its coal traffic.*

Bottom *The North Milan Railway, linking Milan with Lake Como, one of several continental European commuter railways.*

One of the oldest underground railways, the Paris Metro, now modernised with rubber-tyred rolling stock.

Tourist railways The multiplication of steam-operated tourist railways over the last two decades should not obscure the fact that tourist railways have long been in existence. Many of these might be more properly termed entertainment railways, being minimum-gauge lines in parks. But several mountain railways, like the Snowdon Railway in Wales and the Mount Washington line in the USA, were designed purely for tourist traffic, as were long minimum-gauge lines like the Romney, Hythe and Dymchurch in England.

Lastly, two sub-categories:

Military railways are lines built to aid a military campaign, or are lines reserved for the training of railway troops (like the recently closed Longmoor Military Railway in Britain). The term has been wrongly applied to many lines (usually those built by a potential enemy!) which perhaps might be of use in wartime, but have commercial motives as well.

Bridge line is sometimes used to describe railways which do not themselves serve big centres, but are essential links in main traffic flows. Such railways, having none of the expense associated with train assembly, are usually very profitable. Examples are the Berne–Lötschberg–Simplon Railway in Switzerland, channelling international traffic through the Simplon Tunnel, and the Fredericksburg, Richmond & Potomac RR in the USA, a link in the northeast to south trunk route.

Chapter 2

Railway ownership and control

Britain

The British railways were built by private capital, obtained normally by the sale of shares to the public, and initiated by promoters who marshalled support, defended their projects from attacks by other existing or proposed railway companies, and aimed for an Act of Parliament authorising construction. Parliament was concerned with questions of land ownership and railway safety above all else, and there was little impediment to the construction of several lines between the same points, the assumption being that the fittest would survive. Soon, however, the government acted (through the Board of Trade) in favour of technical standardisation, the best-known event being its imposition of a uniform gauge.

Sometimes fierce competition gave way to co-operation, exemplified by the several 'joint railway' companies which were owned and managed by two (sometimes more) of the larger companies as an alternative to each building its own line. Among these were the Somerset & Dorset Joint, Cheshire Lines Committee, and Midland and Great Northern Joint railways. Another alternative was the application by one company for the right to run its trains over the tracks of another to some traffic centre, instead of building its own line. Parliament granted such 'running powers' in many instances. Sometimes these were exercised only for a period, as in the case of the Midland Railway's extension to London over the Great Northern Railway; increasing traffic soon obliged the MR to build its own line, with its new London terminus, St Pancras, across the road from the GNR's Kings Cross.

The Railway Clearing House in London was responsible for the technical and commercial co-ordination of the companies. Among its tasks were the settlement of accounts covering the running of one company's rolling stock over other companies' tracks, and the apportionment of revenue from through passenger tickets, covering more than one company's lines.

Free competition often weakened the strong without proving fatal to the weak. Moreover, it did not automatically guarantee the best possible service, while its duplication of facilities was plainly wasteful. There grew up a movement in favour of state ownership and control, but this was a minority view up to the First World War. In that conflict the government took over the private companies, whose operations were supervised by a Railway Executive Committee (composed of leading railway managers). The Railway Executive did so much better than the private companies in maximising efficiency and capacity that when the railways were handed back to the companies in 1921 it was only for an interlude, during which a reorganisation was engineered by parliament. Thus, on January 1 1923, the so-called Railway Amalgamation took effect with 14 large, and about a hundred small, railway companies in England, Scotland and Wales being merged to form four large companies. Only a very few minor public railways preserved their independence. The four new railways were:

London Midland and Scottish Railway (LMS or LMSR) Its main constituents were the Midland, London & North Western, Lancashire and Yorkshire, Caledonian and Highland railways. It was the largest of the four and at one time claimed to be the world's biggest private company. It was the least successful, organisationally and managerially, of the new companies. There was conflict between cliques made up of former officers of the constituent companies, and the reaction to this in the 1930s was a highly centralised and authoritarian management, with a sometimes mindless application of uniformity. Yet the LMS had its successes despite this. Of the four companies, it was the most consistent in the application of scientific research, and its long sponsorship of diesel yard locomotives brought, eventually, great benefit.

London & North Eastern Railway (LNER) This was the second largest company, formed mainly from the North Eastern, Great Northern, Great Eastern and Great Central railways in England and the North British and Great North of Scotland railways in Scotland. Throughout its life it was financially weak, possibly because the eastern half of Britain was the least prosperous. It was highly decentralised, with the officers of the constituent companies tending to retain considerable power and influence in their localities. It gained great prestige, though little profit, from the exploits of the locomotives designed by its chief mechanical engineer, Nigel Gresley, and, in its selection and training of managerial staff, was well ahead of the other companies.

Great Western Railway (GWR) This, the third largest, was the only company to retain its identity in the Amalgamation. The GWR was one of the original British railways, starting life as the London to Bristol line engineered by Brunel. It grew to link London with South Wales, the Midlands, and the south-west. At the Amalgamation it was joined by a number of small, mainly Welsh, lines, of which the Cambrian, Taff Vale, Barry and Rhymney railways were the most important. It was in many ways a conservative railway after the Amalgamation, but it produced flashes of innovation; for example, its diesel railcar fleet. Its locomotives were distinctive but highly standardised. Staff relations were on a very human level, distinguishing it in particular from the bureaucratic approach of the LMS. It was well-liked both by its staff and by the general public; adept public relations played a part in this. It is the subject of a three-volume history (*History of the Great Western Railway* by E. T. MacDermot and O. S. Nock, revised edition 1982).

Southern Railway (SR) This was the smallest of the four, being basically a combination of the London and South Western, London Brighton and South Coast, and South Eastern & Chatham railways. Unlike the others, it gained most of its revenue from passenger operations. An energetic electrification drive and a special effort in public relations resulted in this company being regarded as the most enterprising and efficient of the four. Its story is told in a revised edition (1982) of C. F. Dendy Marshall's *History of the Southern Railway*. For a short general history of the inter-war railways, M. R. Bonavia's *Four Great Railways* (1980) is recommended.

In the Second World War the railways were again taken over by the government and, on January 1 1948, they were nationalised by the post-war Labour Government, becoming British Railways. Nationalisation was a complete success ideologically, in that it brought a great and key public industry under state ownership. In most other respects the new state railway did not bring the advantages which had been promised. Partly the failure to make good decisions and hold fast to them was a result of inadequacy on the part of administrators and managers. Mainly it resulted from the absence of a satisfactory chain of command and supervisory structure, together with too-frequent changes of government policy. In its first 25 years British Railways endured four major Acts of Parliament making substantial changes to its organisation, and its chairmen had an average term of office of only four years. In 1964 its name was changed (except for legal purposes) to British Rail. Its first decades are chronicled, from the inside, by M. R. Bonavia in *British Rail: the First Twenty-Five Years* (1981).

British Railways inherited from the companies an uneasy future, the wear and tear of wartime having been added to the pre-war difficulties of road transport competition and financial worries. There was no easy way out, a situation which provides golden opportunities for those who believe that reorganisation solves everything. In the beginning, British Railways came under the British Transport Commission which was supposed to replace in some measure the previous private boards of directors, while day-to-day management was entrusted to the Railway Executive, an approximation of the old boards of management. The old company territories were redesignated regions. The Railway Executive and the British Transport Commission lacked both the will and the desire to stay within their intended areas of activity; reciprocal interference resulted in acrimony, foot-dragging and a general lack of co-ordination. In 1953 the Executive was therefore abolished, with an enlarged BTC taking over its functions and acting through area boards. This rearrangement could only work so long as personal relationships were good and often they were not. So, in 1963 after yet another Act of Parliament, the British Railways Board replaced the BTC. It was partly functional and partly directoral, its functional members acting through regional general managers. It did not secure good co-ordination, largely because there was no single authority to manage the regions as a whole. And so, the 1968 Transport Act presented a further reorganisation, which eventually took the form of appointing a Chief Executive who could correspond to the old general managers, and report to the British Railways Board.

In the meantime the regionalisation of BR was not spared reorganisation. Originally there had been six regions (London Midland, Eastern, North Eastern, Western, Scottish and Southern), but in 1965 it was decided to have five instead, the North Eastern being absorbed mainly into the Eastern; there seems every reason to suppose that, had there been only five regions at the start, in about 1965 there would have been a decision to change to six. Over the years there have been periodic readjustments of regional boundaries, but on the whole the regions, except the Scottish, closely follow the old LMS, LNER, GWR and SR boundaries (see map on page 123). Perhaps the largest of the several exceptions has been the transfer of Southern Railway lines west of Exeter to the WR, and of the former GWR lines in the Midlands to the LMR. The regions are subdivided into divisions, of which there were 20 in January 1983.

Government concern with railway deficits, combined with a distrust of rail-

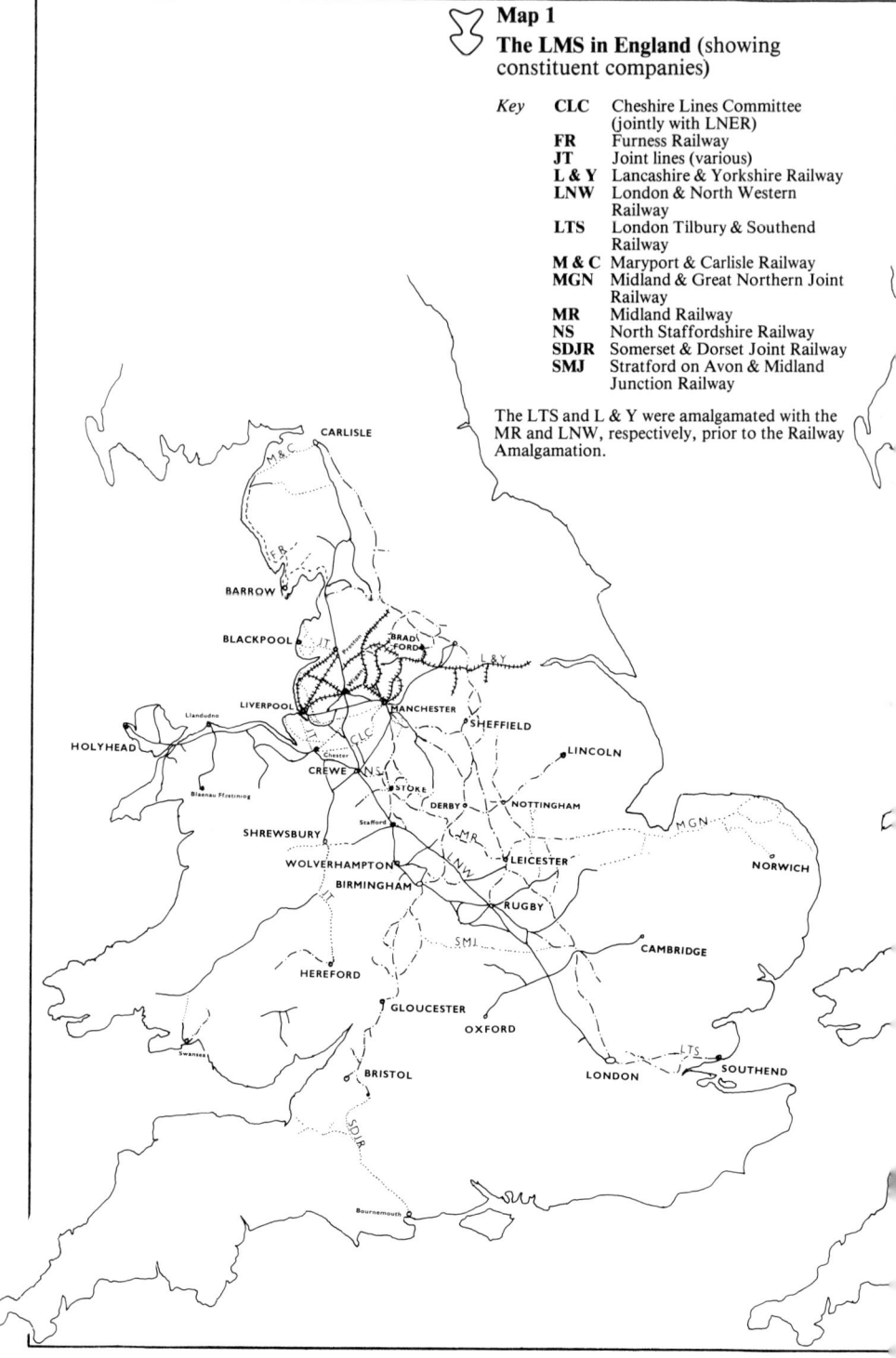

Railway ownership and control

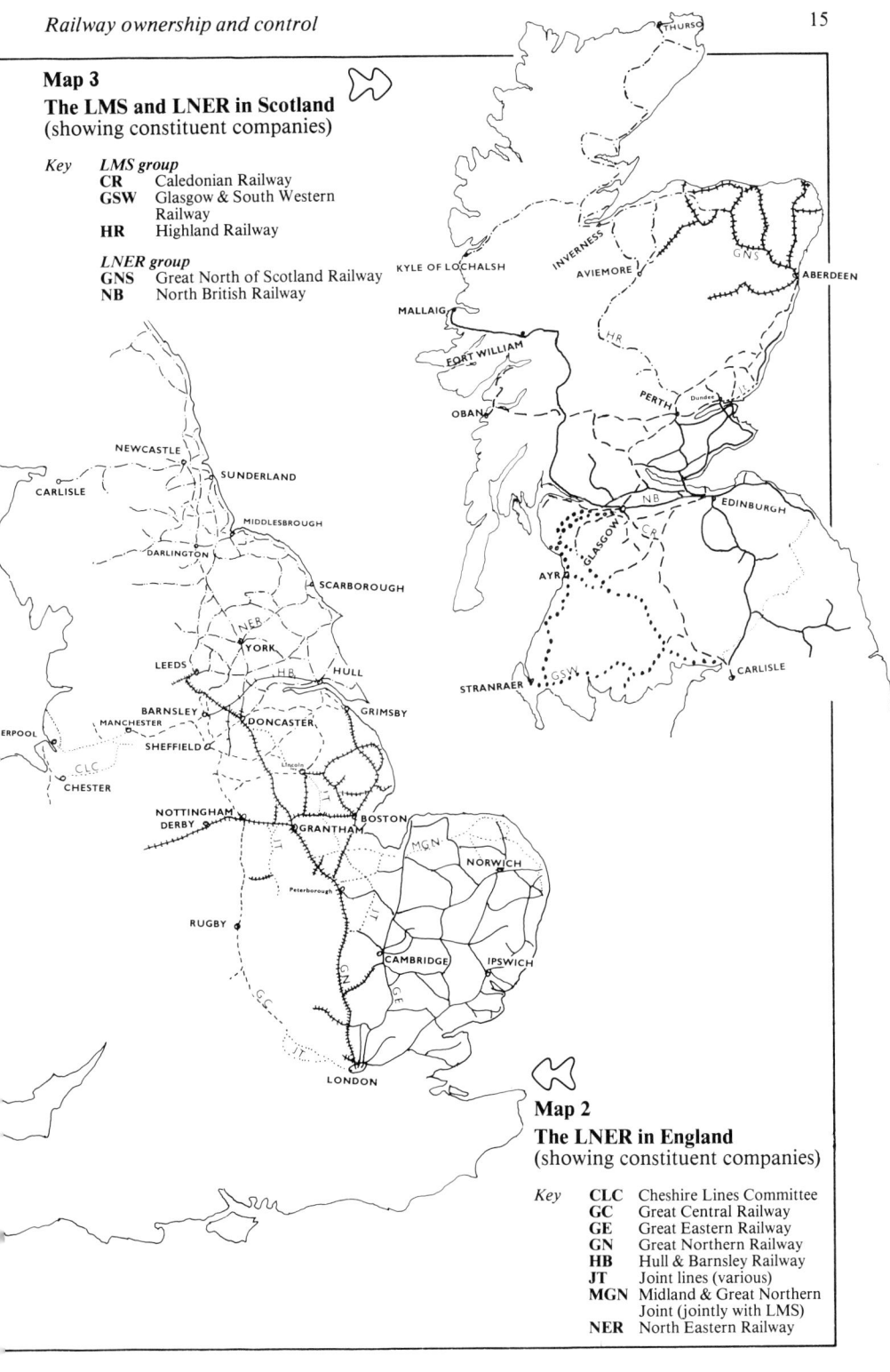

Map 3
The LMS and LNER in Scotland
(showing constituent companies)

Key   **LMS group**
  CR   Caledonian Railway
  GSW Glasgow & South Western Railway
  HR   Highland Railway

  LNER group
  GNS Great North of Scotland Railway
  NB   North British Railway

Map 2
The LNER in England
(showing constituent companies)

Key **CLC** Cheshire Lines Committee
  GC   Great Central Railway
  GE   Great Eastern Railway
  GN   Great Northern Railway
  HB   Hull & Barnsley Railway
  JT   Joint lines (various)
  MGN Midland & Great Northern Joint (jointly with LMS)
  NER North Eastern Railway

The Railway Data Book

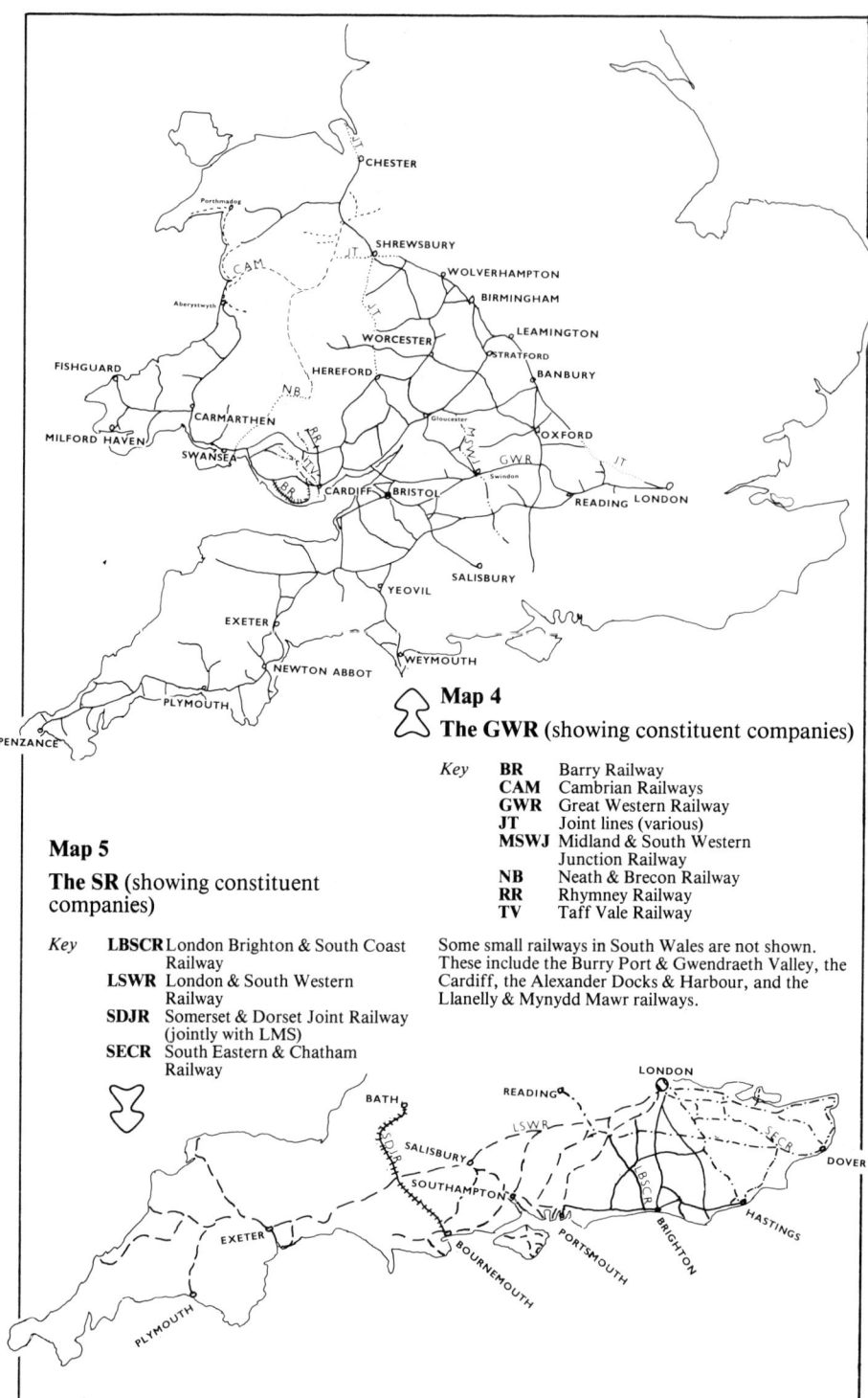

Map 4
The GWR (showing constituent companies)

Key
BR	Barry Railway
CAM	Cambrian Railways
GWR	Great Western Railway
JT	Joint lines (various)
MSWJ	Midland & South Western Junction Railway
NB	Neath & Brecon Railway
RR	Rhymney Railway
TV	Taff Vale Railway

Some small railways in South Wales are not shown. These include the Burry Port & Gwendraeth Valley, the Cardiff, the Alexander Docks & Harbour, and the Llanelly & Mynydd Mawr railways.

Map 5

The SR (showing constituent companies)

Key
LBSCR	London Brighton & South Coast Railway
LSWR	London & South Western Railway
SDJR	Somerset & Dorset Joint Railway (jointly with LMS)
SECR	South Eastern & Chatham Railway

The first British Railways train to leave London's Paddington Station: the 12.05 am train to Birkenhead on January 1 1948.

way management, led to the so-called Beeching Era of 1961–65. Richard Beeching, Technical Director of ICI, was appointed Chairman of the BTC in 1961, charged with finding drastic remedies. His report, *The Reshaping of British Railways*, recommended the elimination of loss-making services, notably branch lines and country passenger trains, and suggested how BR could pursue the traffic for which it was most suitable. As a result of the Beeching proposals, one third of the route mileage and over 4,000 stations were closed.

In the 1970s, governments began to appreciate that the railways could not be expected to provide the services which society demanded, as well as cover their costs. Under the Public Service Obligation (PSO) provisions of the 1974 Railway Act, passenger service subsidies began to be paid to BR for loss-making passenger services over routes where withdrawal of service was not regarded as socially (that is, politically) desirable. Also, in several urban areas, with the aid of government grants, local authorities have set up their own local passenger services, operated, but not financed, by BR. The 1968 Transport Act provided for these latter arrangements by introducing the concept of public transport authorities (PTA), each presiding over a Public Transport Executive (PTE), with the latter providing a co-ordinated road and rail service. In general, the PTEs have created improved transport services in their locality, often effecting that co-ordination of train and bus services which the public had long demanded.

Another sign of the government's willingness to give financial support for the socially beneficial object of shifting some of the transport burden from over-crowded roads to under-used railways is Section 8 of the 1974 Railways Act. In this financial assistance is granted to companies investing in rail facilities, typically private sidings, so as to enable a change to be made from road to rail transport. However, the total assistance received by BR is considerably less, proportionately, than the subsidies enjoyed by most Continental railways.

British Rail is not the only railway owner in Britain. Quite apart from the tourist railways, there are a handful of metropolitan lines owned and operated by local authorities and some industrial railways. Of the latter, the many lines of

A 'MetroTrain' of the South Yorkshire PTE, bearing both the PTE and BR insignia.

the National Coal Board and the British Steel Corporation are the most significant. Of the metropolitan railways, those of London are by far the biggest. The London Passenger Transport Board was formed in 1933 to operate bus, tram and railway routes formerly owned by private companies. It later became the London Transport Executive and owns about 240 miles (385 km) of route, with running powers over 12 miles (19 km) of BR tracks. A smaller but more modern local transit (Metro) system is that of Newcastle, operated by the Tyne and Wear PTE, while the double-track circular underground railway now operated by the Greater Glasgow PTE has a long and sulphurous history.

North America

The US railroads were built by private enterprise and private capital, but with an increasing degree of supervision by the states and the federal government as well as with, sometimes, disguised subsidies at the state and federal level. The most important form of subsidy was the land grant system in which companies were encouraged to build lines west of the Missouri by the offer of enormous tracts of virgin territory. Some of these tracts were later found to be rich in minerals, so several railroads now make more revenue from their lands than from their lines. The US railroad map is still fluid: 19th century phenomena such as mergers and take-overs continue, albeit within a more respectable standard of conduct. Bankruptcy, too, is still a real possibility.

By 1914, by a succession of federal enactments, the railroads were tightly supervised by the Interstate Commerce Commission. The ICC could prevent, among other things, the withdrawal of unprofitable railway services and the reduction of tariffs to favour a big client or a client willing to use more efficient technology (like bigger freightcars). Its consent was required for railway mergers. In cases of bankruptcy it could approve or veto the distribution of the defunct company's assets and it could issue a Directed Service Order compelling the maintenance of train services over all or part of the line concerned but, 'deregulation' of rail transport, and the so-called Stagger's Act of 1980, envisaged a divestment over a period of years of some ICC powers.

Railway ownership and control

Mergers in recent decades have produced, among others: the Burlington Northern, incorporating the Chicago, Burlington & Quincy (CB&Q), the Northern Pacific (NP), Great Northern (GN), and the Spokane, Portland & Seattle (SP&S); the Seaboard Coast Line, incorporating the Atlantic Coast Line (ACL) and Seaboard Air Line (SAL, this being a railroad, despite its name); and the enlarged Norfolk & Western, incorporating the Nickel Plate (NKP), Wabash (WAB) and Virginian (VR) railroads.

Two large systems, the Rock Island RR (in 1975) and the Chicago, Milwaukee, St Paul and Pacific RR (in 1977) have become bankrupt and are being dismembered. Earlier, a similar fate seemed to threaten many of the eastern railroads, and, under federal supervision and with federal financial aid, they were united in the Consolidated Rail Corporation (Conrail) in 1976. The constituents of this new company were the Penn Central, Erie Lackawanna, Central of New Jersey, Lehigh Valley, Lehigh & Hudson River, and Reading railroads. The Penn Central had been a shortlived and unsuccessful merger of the old New York Central, Pennsylvania, and New York New Haven & Hartford railroads.

Another federally created and subsidised company is the National Railroad Passenger Corporation (Amtrak), established in 1971 to take over long-distance passenger services. Amtrak pays the companies over whose tracks its trains operate. But it owns the tracks of the North East Corridor (Boston–New York–Washington) whose use it shares with the freight trains of Conrail. Clause 403(b) of the Amtrak Act provided for federal grants to state governments willing to pay part of the cost of operating trains which could not qualify for fully-subsidised operation by Amtrak. A number of states have taken advantage of this, especially California, whose Department of Transport (CalTrans) has

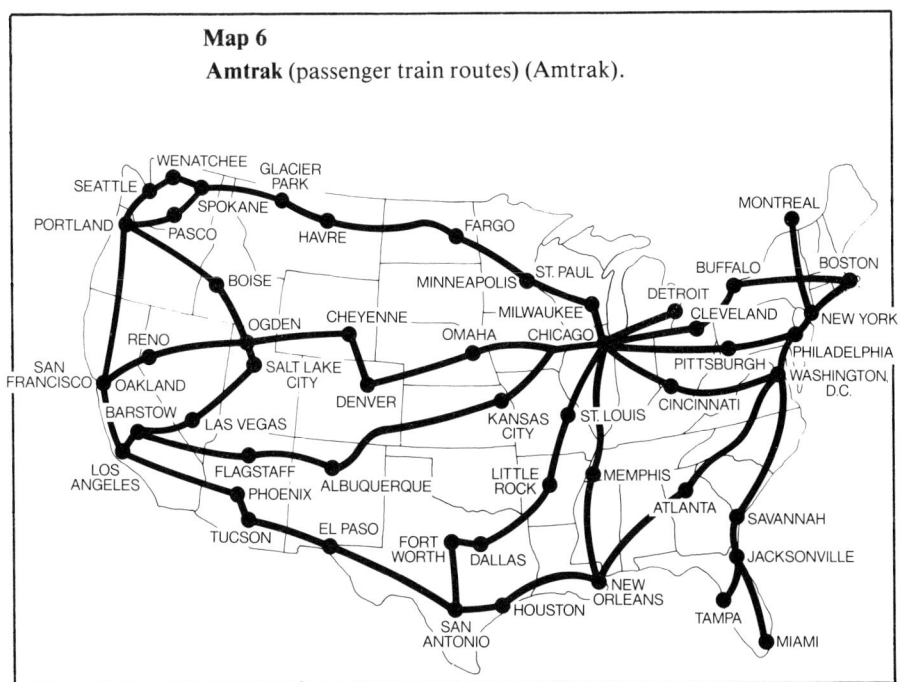

Map 6
Amtrak (passenger train routes) (Amtrak).

sponsored a frequent train service between San Diego and Los Angeles.

In the same spirit as Amtrak, but on a local scale, are the transport authorities which have taken over the responsibility for commuter services in several localities. Among them are New York's Metropolitan Transport Authority which has taken over, among others, the Long Island Railroad, and the Massachusetts Bay Transportation Authority, which is responsible for local passenger services once operated by the Boston & Maine Railroad. The federal Urban Mass Transportation Authority (UMTA) provides capital for new commuter projects, including metro and light rail transit schemes.

There are hundreds of railway companies in the USA, many of them freight-only branches known as Short Lines. Some of the latter are of recent origin, having been established to take over sections of line abandoned by the large railroads. The biggest companies are known as First Class Railroads. From 1956 the ICC defined a Class One Railroad as one with operating revenues of three million dollars or more, all other railroads being classified as Class Two. But the limit has since been raised to gross revenues of 50 million dollars or more; some former Class One companies with long routes but small revenues are now, therefore, excluded. Also excluded are the so-called terminal railroads. The latter, of which the Terminal Railroad of St Louis and the Belt Railroad Company of Chicago are examples, were established by groups of mainline railroads to handle the yard and transit operations of big cities where several railroads converge.

Class One American railroads

Name	Route mileage (miles)	(kilometres)
1 Owned by CSX Corporation		
Baltimore and Ohio (BO)	11,350	18,300
Chesapeake & Ohio (CO)	4,750	7,600
Clinchfield (CRR)	275	450
Louisville & Nashville (LN)	6,575	10,600
Seaboard Coast Line (SCL)	16,300	26,200
Western Maryland (WM)	940	1,500
2 Owned by Norfolk Southern Corporation		
Norfolk & Western (NW)	7,450	12,000
Southern (SR)	10,200	16,400
Alabama Great Southern (AGS)	300	480
Central of Georgia (CofG)	3,300	5,300
Cincinnati, New Orleans & Texas Pacific (CNO&TP)	330	500
3 Owned by Burlington Northern Corporation		
Burlington Northern (BN)	27,450	44,200
Colorado & Southern (CS)	910	1,500
Fort Worth & Denver (FWD)	1,170	1,900
4 Owned by US Steel Corporation		
Bessemer & Lake Erie (B&LE)	200	330
Duluth, Missabe and Iron Range (DM&IR)	940	1,500
Elgin, Joliet & Eastern (EJ&E)	200	300
5 Southern Pacific group		
Southern Pacific (SP)	13,300	21,400
St Louis South Western (SSW)	1,440	2,320

6 Owned by Grand Trunk Western (Canadian National Railways)

Grand Trunk Western (GTW)	1,400	2,250
Detroit, Toledo & Ironton (DTI)	470	750

7 Others

Atchison, Topeka & Santa Fe (ATSF)	11,680	18,800
Boston & Maine (BM)	1,420	2,250
Chicago & North Western (CNW)	8,320	13,400
Consolidated Rail (Conrail) (CR)	16,670	26,800
Delaware & Hudson (DH)	1,700	2,700
Denver & Rio Grande Western (DRGW)	1,860	3,000
Florida East Coast (FEC)	530	850
Illinois Central Gulf (ICG)	8,320	13,400
Kansas City Southern (KCS)	1,620	2,600
Long Island (LIRR)	320	500
Missouri-Kansas-Texas (MKT)	2,180	3,500
Missouri Pacific (MOPAC)	11,600	18,700
Soo Line (SOO)	4,400	7,100
Union Pacific (UP)	9,450	15,200
Western Pacific (WP)	1,300	2,100

This table relates to 1982. The mileages are approximate and are rounded off. In early 1983 it was expected that the CSX companies would be consolidated as Seaboard System RR (SBD); the GTW was hoping to purchase the surviving lines of the bankrupt (Class One) Milwaukee St Paul & Pacific RR; a merger of the UP, WP and Mopac railroads was likely, the new company to be a UP subsidiary known as Pac-Rail; and Guilford Transportation Industries, owner of BM and the smaller Maine Central, was expected to acquire the DH Railroad.

In Canada there are two major companies operating across the continent. Canadian Pacific (16,400 miles or 26,400 km), a private company with interests in most forms of transport, is the oldest, being the builder of the first transcontinental line. Canadian National Railways (24,000 miles or 38,600 km), a crown corporation formed in 1923, absorbed a number of financially-troubled railways, notably the Grand Trunk, Grand Trunk Pacific, the Canadian Northern, and National Transcontinental (the latter being at the time operated by the state Canadian Government Railways, successor of the Intercolonial Railway).

There are also a number of smaller lines, including the British Columbia Railway (formerly Pacific Great Eastern) which is provincially owned, the Ontario Northland, owned by Ontario, and three railways run by mining companies, the Algoma Central, Quebec North Shore and the Cartier railways. Some Labrador constituent companies of the CP and CN retain separate identities. Among these are the CP's Toronto, Hamilton & Buffalo, Quebec Central, and the CN's subsidiaries in the USA (Grand Trunk, Grand Trunk Western, Central Vermont). The Soo Line in the USA is controlled by the CP. The CN absorbed the 3 ft 6 in gauge Newfoundland Government Railways in 1949.

Corresponding to the US Amtrak is V1A Rail, a crown corporation entrusted with the operation of long-distance passenger trains over CN and CP tracks. Locally-financed and administered suburban services are grandly executed around Toronto, by the GO (Greater Ontario) trains running over CN tracks.

Western Europe

All the European states have brought their principal railways under central government control, but a number of lines continue to operate outside the state railway systems. In Switzerland, in particular, there are a large number of local railways, some company-owned and some owned and operated by local governments.

In the Irish Republic, 26 railways, of which the Great Southern & Western was the largest, were amalgamated into one company, Great Southern Railways, in 1925. The Great Northern of Ireland, which was largely a Northern Ireland line, was excluded. Then, in 1945, the GSR was amalgamated with a Dublin bus company to form Coras Impair Eireain (CIE). In Northern Ireland a 1948 Bill established the Ulster Transport Authority (UTA), which united the provincial bus services with two railways. The latter were the Belfast and County Down and the Northern Counties Committee, which was a former outpost of the British Midland Railway and then of the LMS. In 1948 the Great Northern of Ireland was dissolved by splitting it between Eire and Ulster. Later the UTA was itself dissolved, its four remaining lines becoming Northern Ireland Railways.

The French railway network was closely supervised by the state, which provided various incentives to encourage private capital. This supervision ensured that different railways would serve different territories, with main lines converging on Paris. The Est Railway was particularly helped by the state; regarded as of strategic significance, it was expected to have more secondary lines, more loops and more advanced signalling than purely commercial requirements demanded. Apart from the Est, the ancestral companies of the present-day French National Railways (SNCF) were the Nord, serving a prosperous industrial region and easily graded; the Paris–Orleans to Bordeaux and Toulouse; the Paris–Lyon–Méditerranée, which owned the greatest trunk route, from Paris to Lyons and Marseilles; the Midi, which did not approach Paris but served the south-west; and the Ouest to Normandy and Brittany. In 1909 the impoverished Ouest was nationalised and became the main part of the State Railway (Etat), and in 1934 the Paris–Orleans and Midi railways merged. The SNCF, whose capital was 51 per cent state-owned, combined these companies in 1938. Its *Conseil d'Administration* was to act like a board of directors, and its management was in the hands of its *Direction Générale*. It was divided into six administrative regions (Nord, Est, Ouest, Sud-Ouest, Sud-Est and Méditerranée). In 1982 the SNCF became a wholly state-owned company.

In the late 19th century, to stimulate the building of railways in sparsely populated areas, the government encouraged local communities to build their own feeder lines. Many of these 'local interest' or 'departmental' lines were of metre gauge. Just a handful survive, mostly operated by the CFD (*Compagnie des Chemins de Fer Départmentaux*) and the CFTA (*Société Générale de Chemins de Fer et de Transports Automobiles*). Recently, local authorities with government help and financial aid have established transport authorities charged with providing local passenger services. The SNCF handles the operation of these, but the trains have their own distinctive colour schemes. In a class of its own is the *Réseau Exprés Régional* (RER), in which the SNCF and the Paris transport authority (RATP) have combined to create a fast passenger service using both SNCF routes and new RER cross-city underground lines.

In Germany the Deutsche Reichsbahn (DR) was established in 1920 to unite

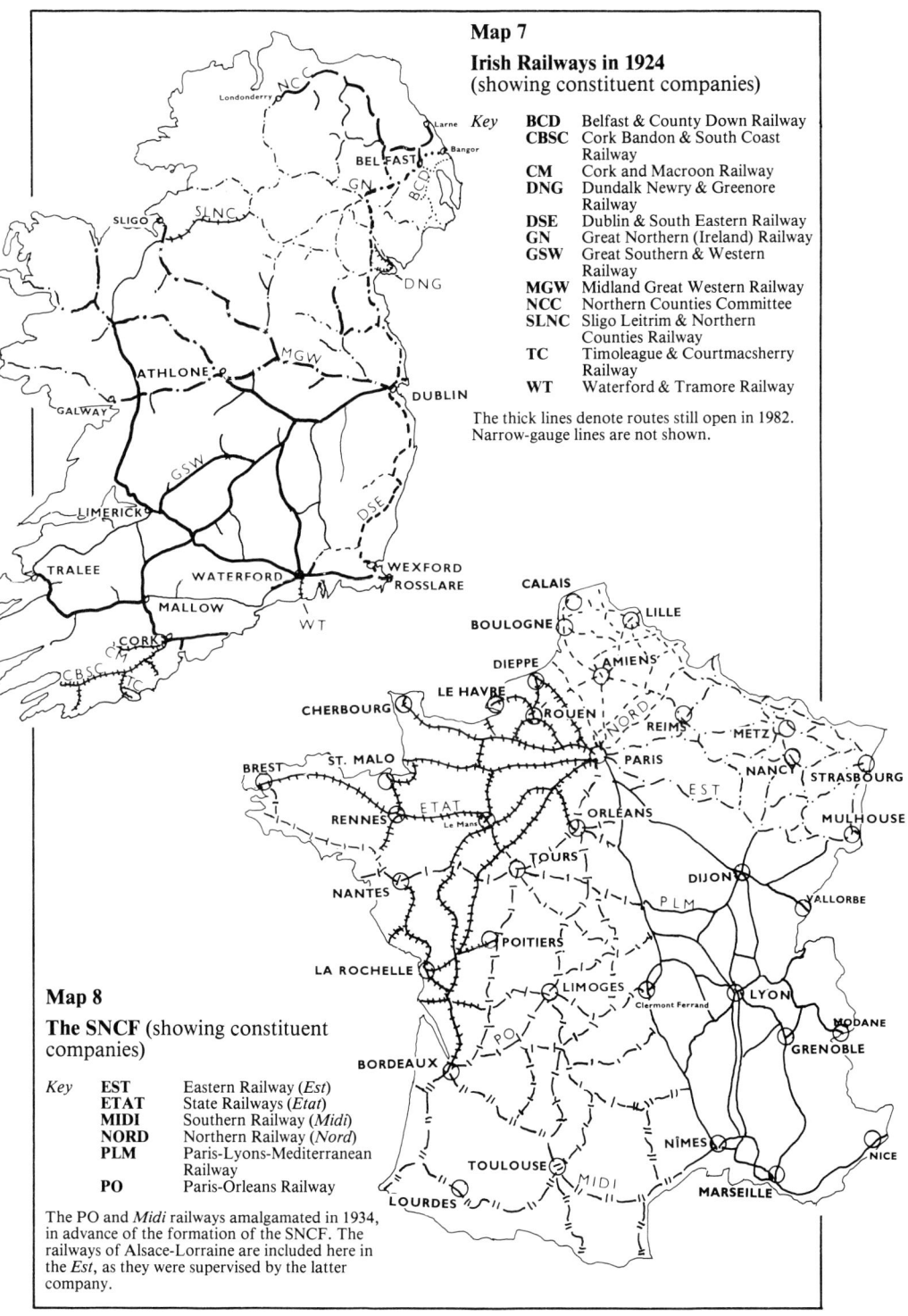

Map 7
Irish Railways in 1924
(showing constituent companies)

Key
BCD	Belfast & County Down Railway
CBSC	Cork Bandon & South Coast Railway
CM	Cork and Macroon Railway
DNG	Dundalk Newry & Greenore Railway
DSE	Dublin & South Eastern Railway
GN	Great Northern (Ireland) Railway
GSW	Great Southern & Western Railway
MGW	Midland Great Western Railway
NCC	Northern Counties Committee
SLNC	Sligo Leitrim & Northern Counties Railway
TC	Timoleague & Courtmacsherry Railway
WT	Waterford & Tramore Railway

The thick lines denote routes still open in 1982. Narrow-gauge lines are not shown.

Map 8

The SNCF (showing constituent companies)

Key
	EST	Eastern Railway (*Est*)
	ETAT	State Railways (*Etat*)
	MIDI	Southern Railway (*Midi*)
	NORD	Northern Railway (*Nord*)
	PLM	Paris-Lyons-Mediterranean Railway
	PO	Paris-Orleans Railway

The PO and *Midi* railways amalgamated in 1934, in advance of the formation of the SNCF. The railways of Alsace-Lorraine are included here in the *Est*, as they were supervised by the latter company.

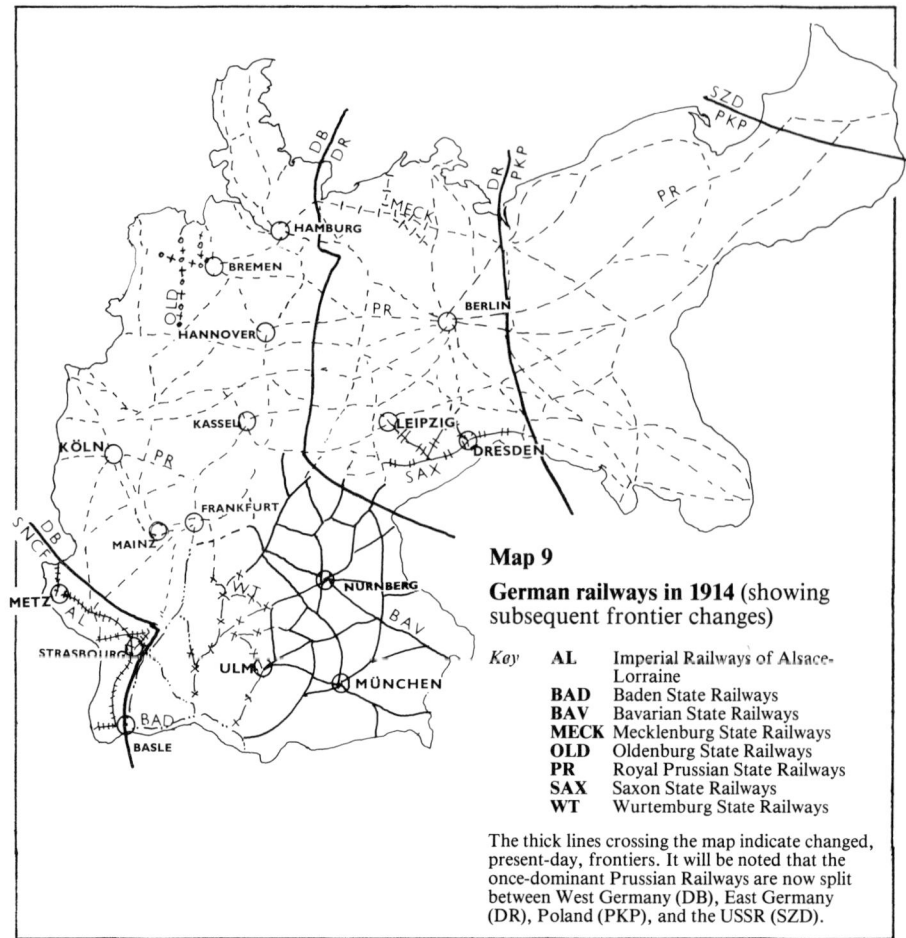

Map 9

German railways in 1914 (showing subsequent frontier changes)

Key		
	AL	Imperial Railways of Alsace-Lorraine
	BAD	Baden State Railways
	BAV	Bavarian State Railways
	MECK	Mecklenburg State Railways
	OLD	Oldenburg State Railways
	PR	Royal Prussian State Railways
	SAX	Saxon State Railways
	WT	Wurtemburg State Railways

The thick lines crossing the map indicate changed, present-day, frontiers. It will be noted that the once-dominant Prussian Railways are now split between West Germany (DB), East Germany (DR), Poland (PKP), and the USSR (SZD).

the railways of the former states into a single system. In 1924 the victorious powers of the First World War forced through a reorganisation by which the DR became a mixed private and state enterprise with its board containing nominees of the Western Allies and with a permanent non-German, watchdog, official. In the 1930s the old position was restored and, at the close of that decade, the DR temporarily absorbed the Austrian State Railways. The postwar split into two Germanys has entailed the establishment of the Deutsche Bundesbahn (DB) with its headquarters at Frankfurt in West Germany, while the DR title has been retained by the railways in East Germany. In West Germany, inner-city, mainly underground, railways are known as *U-bahnen*, while the *S-bahnen* are joint enterprises of local authorities and the DB, providing suburban services.

Belgium was notable in that its first main lines were state enterprises, but later the network was divided between state and private railways. State ownership made large strides in the beginning of the 20th century and, in 1926, the state railway was established, becoming Belgian National Railways (SNCB). Earlier, a separate corporation, the SNCV, had supervised the dense network of local metre-gauge light railways. Almost all the latter have fallen victim to road transport, but the SNCV still exists, although it is intended to merge it into the SNCB.

In the Netherlands, the state sponsored two large companies, in 1890, to take over the ten or so main railways. These two, the State Railway and the Netherlands Railway, were brought together in 1938 to form the Netherlands Railway Company (NS) in which the state holds all shares.

Main European railways

Name	Abbreviation	RIV/RIC No (see below)	Gauge	Route (km)	Route (miles)
Albanian State Railways	ASR*	21	standard	230	142
Austrian Federal Railways	OBB	81	standard	5,900	36,640
Belgian National Railways	SNCB	88	standard	4,000	2,470
Berne–Lötschberg–Simplon Railway	BLS	63	standard	120	75
British Rail	BR	70	standard	17,600	10,930
Bulgarian State Railways	BDZ	52	standard	4,300	2,670
Czechoslovak State Railways	CSD	54	standard	13,000	8,075
Danish State Railways	DSB	86	standard	2,450	1,520
Finnish State Railways	VR	10	5 ft	100	3,785
French National Railways	SNCF	87	standard	34,350	2,133
German State Railway	DR	50	standard	14,200	8,820
German Federal Railway	DB	80	standard	28,400	17,360
Hellenic Railways	CH	73	standard and metre	1,650	1,025
Hungarian State Railways	MAV	55	standard	8,150	5,060
Irish Transport Company	CIE		5 ft 3 in	2,000	1,240
Italian State Railways	FS	83	standard	16,200	10,060
Luxembourg Railways	CFL	82	standard	250	155
Netherlands State Railways	NS	84	standard	2,850	1,770
Northern Ireland Railways	NIR		5 ft 3 in	320	200
Norwegian State Railways	NSB	76	standard	4,200	2,610
Polish State Railways	PKP	51	standard	24,000	14,900
Portuguese State Railway	CP	94	5 ft 6 in and metre	3,500	2,175
Rhaetian Railway	RhB		metre	360	225
Roumanian State Railways	CFR	53	standard	11,000	6,830
Spanish National Railways	RENFE	71	5 ft 6 in	13,350	8,290
Swiss Federal Railways	SBB/CFF/FFS	85	standard	3,000	1,860
Soviet Railways	SZD*	20	5 ft	140,000	86,940
Yugoslav State Railways	JZ	72	standard	11,500	7,140

*Abbreviation used only internationally.
Route mileage figures are approximations, the kilometres having been rounded off before conversion into miles, and include all gauges.

International railway co-operation

The International Union of Railways (UIC) was founded in 1922, primarily for the co-ordination of international services. Although it has member-railways from more than 60 countries, its main influence is in continental western

Europe. It now approves standard designs for equipment, including rails and rolling stock, designed by the associated ORE engineering research organisation. Such equipment has been adopted by several west European railways.

Inter-railway conventions on standards for rolling stock in international service are formalised in the RIV (freight) and RIC (passenger vehicles) agreements. Vehicles which conform carry the RIV or RIC inscription (see chapters 20 and 21). A few railways, including British Rail, subscribe to RIV but not RIC.

Australian railway abbreviations

ANR	Australian National Railways
CR	Commonwealth Railways (now ANR)
NSWGR	New South Wales Government Railways (now SRA)
QR	Queensland Government Railways
SAR	South Australian Government Railways (now State Transport Authority)
SRA	State Railway Authority of New South Wales
TGR	Tasmanian Government Railways (now part of ANR)
VR	Victorian Railways (Vicrail)
WAGR	Western Australian Government Railways (Westrail)

Indian railway abbreviations

(Pre-Independence)

ABR	Assam–Bengal Railway
BNR	Bengal–Nagpur Railway
BBCI	Bombay Baroda & Central India Railway
EIR	East Indian Railway
GIPR	Great Indian Peninsula Railway
MSMR	Madras and Southern Mahratta Railway
NSR	Nizam's State Railway
NWR	North Western Railway
SIR	South Indian Railway

(Post Independence)

CR	Central Railway
ER	Eastern Railway
NER	North Eastern Railway
NR	Northern Railway
NFR	North Eastern Frontier Railway
SCR	South Central Railway
SER	South Eastern Railway
SR	Southern Railway
WR	Western Railway

Chapter 3

Entrepreneurs and managers

Most of the world's railways were conceived and managed by men long forgotten, but from the hundreds of promoters and thousands of managers a handful, for reasons not always connected with their competence or integrity, are remembered. Some promoters remain in public memory because of their rascality, but even the most depraved of the railway 'kings' and 'barons' had an impact on railway development which was not entirely negative. The following list includes some of the best-known of the promoters, as well as a handful of men who can be regarded as great administrators, either as chairmen of boards or as general managers answerable to those boards.

James Allport A Birmingham man, Allport — after a varied railway career — became general manager of the Midland Railway in 1853. He provided Third class accommodation on the better trains and, in 1875, began a wholly beneficial revolution by abolishing Second class and transferring Third class passengers to the former Second class accommodation.

Lord Ashfield Appointed first chairman of the London Passenger Transport Board in 1933, Lord Ashfield successfully created the unified system which, by the late 1930s, was taken as a model of how urban and underground railways should be organised. He had gained his city transport experience by working for several American streetcar administrations in his youth.

John Aspinall One of the few mechanical engineers to become a notable railway administrator (Daniel Gooch of the GWR and Alfred Belpaire of the Belgian State Railway were two others), Aspinall designed some highly competent locomotives for the Lancashire and Yorkshire Railway and he then became general manager of that company, pioneering the electrification of suburban lines from 1904 onwards.

Sam Fay One of the great British railway managers, Fay began on the London & South Western Railway but in 1902 became general manager of the Great Central, bringing that railway modernisation and public esteem. His achievement and charm led to further public service and a knighthood.

Jay Gould A financial manipulator who, at one time, was said to control half the railways in the US southwest, Gould first provoked public disgust in 1872 when he successfully and unscrupulously contested with another railway baron, Vanderbilt, for control of the Erie Railroad.

James Hill A Canadian who became one of the great American railway barons, Hill was more scrupulous than his associates. Although he later was involved in several insalubrious conflicts, his lasting monument was the Great

Northern Railroad, a transcontinental railway which he successfully completed and managed.

George Hudson The most celebrated, and notorious, of the British railway kings, Hudson started as a York draper, but soon moved into railway speculation. His greatest achievement was the creation of the Midland Railway from a series of shorter lines, but his financial irresponsibility and fraudulant conduct eventually brought his downfall.

King Leopold I Literally a railway king, Leopold, as the first monarch of the new state of Belgium, urged railway construction as a means of unifying his nation in an advanced technological endeavour. It was under his pressure that Belgium created the world's first planned system of state railways.

Friedrich List More an academic than an entrepreneur, List urged the creation of a German railway system after he had successfully built a coal railway in the USA. He engineered the first German line from Nuremburg to Fürth, and later the Dresden–Leipzig main line.

Henry Meiggs An American railway promoter responsible for several South American lines, including the high-altitude Central of Peru Railway, Meiggs had the rare combination of financial acumen and compassion towards his fellow men.

John Pierpont Morgan A Wall Street financier, Morgan's financial and moral strength enabled him to impose a degree of order and honesty on conflicting railroad magnates. Controlling many railroads, or holding strong blocks of shares in them, he was able to encourage railroad mergers; the Southern RR was one of his creations.

Richard Moon The LNWR, like the LMS into which it was merged, was a line whose human relationships were on a master-and-coolie basis. Moon, as chairman of the company, was in this tradition, but he was a conscientious administrator who achieved high profits which he largely ploughed back to make the LNWR one of the best-endowed of the British railways.

Emile and Isaac Péreire The Péreire brothers were French financiers who energetically pushed forward proposals for the early French railways and whose *Crédit Mobilier* bank competed with the Rothschilds in promoting railways throughout continental Europe.

Josiah Stamp In the decade preceding his death from bombing in the Second World War, Stamp headed the LMS Railway, in which he created the office of President for himself. He had a cheese-paring attitude, and the LMS was not a happy railway, but he largely succeeded in bringing order and corporate spirit into a concern which had demonstrated little of these virtues hitherto.

Henry Thornton An American railroad superintendent who was appointed general manager of Britain's Great Eastern Railway in 1914, Thornton distinguished himself in that role. But his great achievement came in the 1920s when, as president of the newly-formed Canadian National Railways, he turned it from being initially poor and unpopular into a strong and respected public enterprise.

Cornelius Vanderbilt A former steamboat operator, Vanderbilt became the most celebrated of the American railway barons. He was an authoritarian who imposed efficiency, as he saw it, on his lines, and was the virtual creator of the New York Central RR.

Herbert Walker As chairman of the newly-formed Southern Railway in the 1920s, Walker, by genuine innovation (notably electrification) and adept public relations, changed the SR from a collection of small and not over-friendly railways into an enterprise both profitable and popular.

Edward Watkins As chairman of the Great Central, Watkins was the initiator of the GCR's London extension in 1899 (the last main line to London). He was almost simultaneously (1866–94) chairman of the South Eastern Railway and also of the Grand Trunk Railway in Canada, where his aggressive personality was of benefit to neither shareholders nor clients.

William Van Horne After a career in US railroads, Van Horne became general manager of the uncompleted Canadian Pacific Railway and, with great political skill and energy, ensured that it did indeed reach the Pacific by an all-Canadian route.

Chapter 4

Track and its terminology

Both by fact and by definition, the vital element of a railway is the rail itself. This has to both bear and guide the wheels rolling over it, presenting a surface which as far as possible is frictionless, stable and long-lasting. The term *permanent way* relates to the rails and to the fittings and formations which are required to fix and support the rails; it arose to distinguish the final track from the temporary line of rails laid down by contractors to assist with the construction work. The track is laid on ballast, which serves as a buffer and transmits the load to the underlying earthwork — the *formation*.

Most routes are *single-track* or *double-track*, but *multiple track* is often encountered and, over longer distances, is traditionally four-track. However, a third track is sometimes laid when, because of gradients, trains take longer to move in one direction. Modern signalling methods, enabling trains to run in either direction on each of the two tracks, can enhance the capacity of a double-track line.

In Britain, on double-track, the track carrying trains in the direction of London is known as the *up* line, with the other being called the *down* line. In other countries, including North America, one track is called northbound and the other southbound (or eastbound and westbound). Some countries, including the USSR, name one track *even* and the other *odd*; the train numbers correspond so that, for example, the fastest train on the route is called Train No 1 in the odd direction and returns as Train No 2 in the even direction.

Rail

Steel rail, which replaced iron in the late 19th century, was longer-lasting and less liable to fracture, although more expensive than iron. The hardness and hard-wearing properties of steel rail depend on the amount of carbon in the metal; the greater the carbon, the harder the rail but, unfortunately, increasing hardness is accompanied by increasing brittleness.

Rail types may nowadays be broadly divided into *flat-bottom* and *bull-head*. The latter is carried in *chairs* bolted to the sleepers and is held tightly to the chair by wedges known as *keys*, which are traditionally of hardwood although patented metal designs are common. Early variants of rail included *bridge-rail*, in which the running surface was broad and hollow. *Reversible* rail had identical cross-sections at the top and bottom and was intended to be inverted when the top rail-head was worn-out. This two-for-the-price-of-one idea was, however, unsuccessful, because of the impression left on the bottom surface by the constant hammering against the chairs under passing trains.

Flat-bottom rail was developed in the 1830s, in Britain by Vignoles and in the USA by R. Stevens. It could be fixed directly to the sleepers by means of spikes, and was therefore cheaper and easier to lay than bull-head rail. Nowadays, because flat-bottom rail is better supported than bull-head it is, weight for weight, rather stronger and it can be made of steel with a lower carbon content. Flat-bottom rail was generally adopted right at the dawn of the railway age in North America, but this was not the case in Europe. Britain was notably late in changing over, the final decision being made only in the 1950s. Inevitably, much bull-head track is still in use on British Rail.

With steel of equal qualities, the load-bearing capacity and the longevity of a rail depend on its cross-sectional size; that is, on its weight. In Britain and America, rail weight is expressed in pounds per yard and in Europe in kilograms per metre. Over the decades, weights have progressively increased. In North America, where axleweights of 30 tons or more are permitted, rails of 136 lb/yd (67 kg/m) or even heavier are in main line use. In Britain, where 25-ton axleloads are accepted on main tracks, 113 lb (56 kg) rail is purchased, although lighter rails will continue in service for many years. In continental Europe there is again a great variety, but an 'international' rail designed for the International Railways Union and known as UIC60 is a move towards standardisation; this weighs 60 kg/m (121 lb/yd). Quality of manufacture is very important. Proper and uniform cooling of rails is vital, but even with the best-made rails some invisible fissures may be present. These may enlarge in use and can be detected only by electrical or ultrasonic devices.

The standard length of British rails is 60 ft (18.3 m), although 45 ft (13.7 m) rails can still be seen in sidings. The traditional beat of the four-axle passenger car as it passes over the rail joints on unwelded track is absent in North America, where the rail joints are staggered rather than being alongside each other as in Britain and elsewhere.

The battering which a rail end receives can be observed as a slow-moving wheel passes over a rail joint, depressing one rail end and thereby giving a hard knock as it mounts the next. As speeds increase this impact increases disproportionately. For this reason many solutions have been proposed for the joining of rail ends with a view to maximum rigidity. The *fishplate* was invented in the early days of railways; it is a metal plate bolted to each side of the rail at a joint. Contrary to what might have been expected, a rail joint placed directly over two sleepers (*fully-supported*) proved to be no more rigid than one where the joint was midway between two sleepers (*fully-suspended*). A compromise, tried in inter-war Britain, was a partly-supported joint, the sleepers being brought closer together by means of a shorter (2-bolt) fishplate; however, the traditional British 4-bolt fishplate was finally accepted as the best compromise.

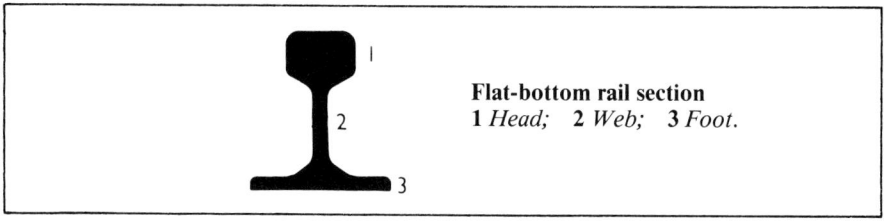

Flat-bottom rail section
1 *Head;* 2 *Web;* 3 *Foot.*

The technology of continuous welded rail (*cwr*) has lately advanced so far that most main lines are, or soon will be, relatively joint-less. The main problem with welding rails into long continuous lengths is that of expansion. In Britain, with 60 ft rails, the difference between maximum and minimum temperatures is such that the length of rail can vary by about half an inch (13 mm), and an appropriate gap is therefore left at the joints. With welded rail, the rigidity has to be such that the rail cannot bend vertically or horizontally in hot weather. The weight of the track itself is sufficient to prevent upward movement, while heavy ballasting, 10-12 in (254 mm-305 mm) deep with good shoulders, inhibits lateral displacement. In addition, welded track is distressed after laying; that is, the rails are mechanically or thermally stretched and fixed so that at a temperature typical of a hot sunny day they are stress-free. Typically, welded rail is laid in lengths of from 600-900 ft (183-274 m), and special joints ('adjustment switches') are used between the lengths to permit a very limited longitudinal creep as temperatures vary. Welded track reduces maintenance expenses by about half and can increase rail life by as much as 30 per cent. High-speed trains in the modern sense would have been close to impractical with unwelded rail; they would have been accompanied by enormous track and vehicle maintenance costs, and traction energy demand would have been about ten per cent greater. On the other hand, cwr demands very careful laying and supervision, and in its early years some serious accidents were caused by high-temperature buckling.

Sleepers

In the very early days of railways the rails were fixed to stone blocks but soon softwood supports were used instead. These sleepers, called more logically cross-ties in America, soon showed their superiority over rival solutions like Brunel's longitudinal beams placed beneath the full length of the rails (although such longitudinal support continued to be used on bridges). To delay the advance of rot, sleepers were soon treated with chemical impregnation under pressure. Zinc chloride was used initially, but creosote soon proved superior although, in Second World War Germany, there was a reversion to the former. Softwood sleepers do decay despite impregnation and, in European conditions, last from ten to 25 years. Since sleeper replacement is expensive in labour and line capacity, relief is sometimes sought by the use of hardwood sleepers (British Rail once favoured jarrah). However, this problem has been solved by the development of really good prestressed concrete sleepers, the life of the latter being, it is thought, 50 years or more.

Although on some of the world's railways, flat-bottom rail is still spiked directly to the sleepers, usually a soleplate (baseplate) is now interposed. The

Background photograph *A characteristic length of North American main line, with heavy rail attached with plain spikes to the baseplates, the latter being spiked to timber crossties (Association of American Railroads).*

Inset above *Bull-head rail, with two-bolt fishplates, showing (at left) a key which has worked loose from its chair. The wire bridging the rail-joint is an electrical bond which secures an unimpaired train detection circuit. The sleepers supporting the joint are normally placed closer together.*

Inset left *BR 110-1b flat-bottom rail. Concrete sleepers are shown, with two different types of fastening. The elastic clip on the right is of the Pandrol type.*

later may be spiked or screwed to the sleeper. However, with concrete sleepers, a seat for the rail can be integrally cast, which makes things easier. Instead of plain spikes, various 'elastic spikes' have been designed for fastening the rails and discussion of their relative merits seems endless.

The roadbed

The quality of ballast is of crucial importance for the stability of the track. It assists drainage but its main role is to distribute the load transmitted by the sleepers under a passing train. Hard rocks of between 3/5 and $2^{2}/_{5}$ in (15–60 mm) are ideal; under pressure these grip together tightly, forming a kind of crude lattice structure which distributes the load outwards as well as downwards. In some countries, like the USSR, where good stone is not easily obtainable, all kinds of substitutes have been sought. Sand is commonly used, despite its inadequacies (leading to speed restrictions and high maintenance expense). Lately Soviet Railways have been laying asbestos wastes as ballast. In some circumstances, tracks may be laid without benefit of ballast or indeed of any proper formation. Such lines are inevitably temporary, and include military frontline railways and forestry lines. New railways in 19th century America were usually laid in a similarly elementary fashion, in the expectation that the revenues of a new line would soon pay for an upgrading of the track.

The foundation on which the ballast is laid is generally created by the earthworks which are undertaken, as part of railway construction, with the aim of keeping gradients and curvature as moderate as possible. Since soils bear loads less readily when wet, proper drainage is the most important part of the formation preparation and maintenance. *Blanketing* is the technique sometimes used to prevent excessive water penetration and consists of a layer of sand or stone dust immediately beneath the ballast. The blanket slopes downwards to each side of the track, encouraging water to run down into drains which are located along both edges of the ballast. Nowadays a plastic sheet is sandwiched in the blanket.

Switches and crossings

Lengths of unbroken line are known as *plain line*, as opposed to that other element of track, switches and crossings (*s & c*), whose function is to permit the diversion of a train from one track to another. Despite the complex appearance of some s & c work, it is composed of three basic elements: *switches*, acute angle crossings (*common crossings*) and obtuse angle crossings (*diamond crossings*). The combination of switch and crossing constitutes a *turnout*, or, more popularly, *points*. A *trailing point* is one where the direction of travel is such that trains converge, whereas a *facing point* enables trains to diverge. The latter is more mishap-sensitive than the former; a train passing over wrongly-set trailing points pushes the movable blades into the correct position. Hence, in most countries, facing points are equipped with extra safety devices. The sharpness of the divergence provided by s & c installations determines the maximum speed of trains passing over them, and most railways have several standard angles. On British Rail, for example, there are eight such standard angles. Because rails are necessarily interrupted in these layouts, there are rail ends which are exposed to the impact of wheels. Rails of exceptionally high manganese content (12 per cent or more) are therefore used for busy crossings; such rails are very expensive but are long-wearing.

Switches are operated mechanically or electrically on most main lines in Europe, including Britain, their control being centralised in the signalling installations. Hand-thrown switches, operated by yard or train personnel, are still used, because more convenient, in many yards. In North America, where trains often have to run into remotely located loops, the hand-thrown switch is still common, traditionally being operated by a member of the train crew.

A distinct variety of switch is the *catch point* which consists of a switch without, usually, any rail lead from it. Its purpose is to derail any vehicle which is out of proper control and likely to come into collision with a train on the main running line. In Britain the government required sidings leading to a running line to be so equipped, so that a vehicle overrunning the siding exit signal would

Left *A BR adjustment switch separating two lengths of continuous welded rail. The two bars are to inhibit sleeper creep at this sensitive point.*

Right *A 'double slip', or double compound switch. This is a versatile but costly layout, known in Germany as the 'English switch'* (M. Deane).

Left *Two sets of catch points in South Wales. The ringed signal was used by the GWR for freight-only lines; similar signals on the SR controlled the entry to freight yards* (M. Deane).

Below *Check rails installed on a sharp curve* (M. Deane).

Bottom *Protective rails at New Westminster, British Columbia. The line here has a check rail alongside the inner running rail, with guard rails in the middle.*

be derailed before it reached the running line. On steep gradients, trailing catch points — held by springs so as to be permanently set in the diverging position except when ascending trains are passing over them — are intended to intercept any breakaway portion of a train before it can collide with a following train. Sometimes catch points lead to a trap road (*catch siding*) where the errant vehicles might be brought to a halt by a buffer stop, an upturning of the final length of rail, or a sand-drag. These devices have been especially prevalent in Britain because of the late survival there of unbraked or partially braked freight trains and of weak chain couplings.

Another device, used somewhat more freely in Britain than elsewhere, is the *check rail*. This is an additional rail laid alongside and inside one or both of the running rails. The distance between the check and running rail is about 1⅘ in (45 mm), just enough to create a flangeway for the moving wheel. Check rails are used with crossings to ensure that the wheel successfully jumps the gap in the running rail. Another common use is on sharp curves where there is a propensity for wheels to climb up and over the rail on the outside of the curve. Fixing a check rail to the inside running rail holds the flanges of the inside wheels, thereby preventing the outer wheels moving across the outside rail. Check rails are often used on bridges, and the approaches to bridges, to make derailment less likely. Also on bridges may be seen *guard rails* of various types. A common variety is a pair of additional rails laid inside the running rails; the purpose of these is to hold derailed vehicles to the line of the track and thus prevent them falling off the bridge or viaduct.

Gradients and curves

Railway builders always sought to minimise curves and gradients. This is somewhat less important with diesel and, especially, electric locomotives, which are less susceptible to gradients, and whose shorter rigid wheelbase eases their passage through curves. Gradients are traditionally moderated by earthworks, with the spoil removed from cuttings in high areas used to construct embankments in low areas. These earthworks, and tunnelling where necessary, may make the building of easily-graded lines quite expensive. Many pioneer railways, especially in North America, were accordingly heavily graded and, more recently, the French high-speed line south-east from Paris was planned with severe gradients in the knowledge that the electric TGV trains could easily master such inclines. This not only reduced the costs of earthworks but avoided much of the curved track required by lines designed to remain on a constant level.

Gradients are measured in two ways. In British-style practice the measure is the horizontal distance required to raise the level of the line by one unit. Thus a line which rises or falls by 2 ft over 500 ft is said to be inclined at 1 in 250. At the trackside, wherever the gradient changes, a gradient post indicates the incline in each direction. Elsewhere, including North America, it is customary to define the gradient in terms of the rise per 100 ft. Thus a 1 in 50 gradient would be described as 2 per cent, and a 1 in 250 as ·4 per cent. In general, grades steeper than 1 in 200 were regarded as stiff in steam days, although much depended on their length and curvature. On main lines, the hardest British grade is the 1 in 37 of the Lickey Incline at Bromsgrove, although Dainton Bank in Devon includes a short stretch of 1 in 36. On the tourist Welshpool and Llanfair Railway there is a gradient of 1 in 27. In Switzerland, on the Rhaetian Railways, there are

gradients as steep as 1 in 14, which may be taken as the limit for adhesion railways (that is, lines not using a rack or cable haulage system). The term *ruling gradient* refers to the limiting gradient in a given section; it therefore excludes grades for which assisting locomotives are customarily provided, and is used to calculate the loads which locomotives are allowed to haul.

Curves are also measured in two ways. In the USA and elsewhere the angle is measured between two lines drawn from the centre of the imaginary circle to two points 100 ft apart on the imaginary circumference (that is, the curve). In America straight track is known as *tangent*. In Britain it is the radius of the imaginary circle which is measured; this is now expressed usually in metres rather than chains. *Superelevation*, or *cant*, on curves is the raising of the outside rail to a higher level than the inside, so as to counteract the centrifugal forces created by the motion of a train on a curved path. Since not all trains move at the same speed, a compromise level of superelevation has to be chosen. The faster trains are not therefore fully compensated, and tolerate what is known as a *cant deficiency*. The chosen speed, known as the *equilibrium speed*, is usually that of a typical passenger train at that point. In order that the superelevation may be introduced gradually, *transition curves* (curves of progressively changing radius) are used to introduce and terminate the *main curve*, or *circular curve* (which is a curve of constant radius). Transition curves may also join the two parts of a *compound curve* (two circular curves of the same direction having different radii) and *reverse curves* (two circular curves of opposing direction). Negative (and hence potentially perilous) cant can occur at a turnout where the diverging line curves in the opposite direction to the canted main line.

Curves are a frequent source of speed restrictions. When the curve is so sharp that a speed below that of the general speed limit of that section of route is required, a permanent speed restriction is imposed. A major cause of fast rail wear is wheel flanges cutting against the inside surface of the railhead on curves. Here again speed is an important factor, but it is the radius of curvature which is the main element. The problem is often alleviated by the fitting of various kinds of rail lubricators. Typically these use the weight of a passing train to actuate finely-adjusted pumps which deposit a drop of oil on the rail inside surface, to be picked up and spread by the wheel flanges.

Track and its terminology 39

Rack railways

Where gradients are too steep for normal steam locomotives, assistance can be provided by cables powered by stationary steam engines. This form of traction, which in the early 19th century seemed to be a strong competitor of the steam locomotive, has now all but died out. Other solutions are the several varieties of railway in which a central rail is gripped by additional driving wheels on the locomotive. In the Fell System, horizontal wheels beneath the locomotive grip the central rail; the Snaefell Mountain Railway, in the Isle of Man, still uses this system, although only for braking. In the later Riggenbach System a serrated rack or cog rail is laid between the running rails and the special locomotives have powered cog wheels which engage in these. The Abt System is a development of the Riggenbach, with the rack slots machined to provide a better fit, and usually with a double row of cogs.

Left *A rail lubricator as used by British Rail.*

Right *The Brienz-Rothorn rack railway. This Swiss Abt-system line is still in operation, with steam traction* (M. Deane).

Right *A German rack railway, the Drachenfels (now closed). This used the Riggenbach system* (M. Deane).

A steam rack locomotive of the Riggenbach system. The sloping boiler ensures that the water does not uncover the firebox on steep grades. Diesel rack locomotives have replaced steam traction on several rack railways (M. Deane).

Track maintenance

At one time, in Britain and several other countries, every mile of track was patrolled each day by a local worker known variously as a trackwalker, platelayer, or ganger. His duty was to observe any developing defects and either to rectify them or report them. With modern track this routine has become less rigorous, but in Britain at least visual, on-foot, inspection is carried out at frequent intervals, depending on the type of line, with branches inspected weekly and high speed lines four times weekly. In Britain the permanent way is divided into regions, divisions, districts, areas and sections and each assistant section supervisor is required to walk his section every fortnight, and every section supervisor every month, to check up on the work of the regular patrolman. Permanent way staff also periodically ride over their sections in locomotives and trains. In addition, there is mechanical inspection, typically with Matisa track recording trolleys (known as 'Neptunes' in Britain). As these move along the track they record, in particular, discrepancies in the heights of rails which impart *twist* to the track, thereby disturbing the stability of moving vehicles. They deposit a red (Immediate) or yellow (Urgent) drop of paint at points where such twist is excessive. These machines have replaced the less convenient Hallade track recorders, although the Hallade system is used in a handful of passenger-train vehicles which can inspect the track at much higher speeds than the Neptunes. Another mechanical aid is the electric, or ultrasonic, flaw detector which can, when carefully used, detect hidden cracks inside rails. In the USA the Sperry self-propelled track inspection vehicle performs the same task.

Rail fractures usually develop slowly, but the affected rails have to be replaced immediately. Most rails fall due for replacement when wear has reduced their weight by about 10 per cent. Thus the rate of replacement depends very much on circumstances; a sharply curved rail carrying an exceptionally intense traffic might last less than a year whereas a straight rail, in a route where traffic is light and speeds low, could last for several decades. Rails removed from main lines are usually re-used on secondary routes. Typically, their worn ends are removed and they are then welded to similarly shortened pieces. All railways, except the most primitive, divide their trackage into categories, reserving new rails for the lines carrying the heaviest and fastest traffic. In Britain, for example, a route is classified by letter and number: the letters from A to D cover four descending speed ranges, and the numbers 1 to 4 ascending tonnage series. Thus the highest category, A4, carries trains moving at over 100 mph with traffic in excess of an annual 18 million tons.

Because of post-war labour shortages and high cost, and because of the need to limit as far as possible the period of *possession*, when lines are closed to traffic in order that the permanent way engineers can work undisturbed, mechanical devices have been rapidly superseding the traditional manual methods of work. Tamping machines raise depressed rails to their designed height and pack ballast tightly beneath the sleepers to ensure that this height is maintained. Lining machines slew back track which has shifted laterally, a common phenomenon on curves. Ballast-cleaning machines cut beneath the sleepers, removing the ballast and screening it, returning the stone to the track after shedding the dirt; fresh ballast is usually then added to make up the loss.

Track relaying machines have not entirely replaced the old and arduous manual methods, but apart from being cheaper to use, they are really the only practical means of relaying modern heavy-duty track with concrete sleepers and welded rail. The predominant method is to work with *track panels* as the basic unit; these are 60 ft preassembled rail-and-sleeper lengths. The relaying machine removes the old track and replaces it with these panels. After the new track has had time to settle down, its rails are sometimes replaced with long welded rails in a separate operation. With modern machines it was becoming possible in the 1970s to relay a mile (1,609 m) of track in 10 hours. However, as in all track maintenance work, highly detailed and meticulous planning was required.

Tunnels and bridges

Tunnels and bridges also come within the responsibility of the civil engineer. Most tunnel-building was achieved in the 19th century, but new tunnels are still being built. The process is somewhat faster than in the past, but the old perils of unforeseen water or unsuitable strata still remain. Britain's longest, the Severn Tunnel, was set back for years because an unforeseen underground stream was encountered. Even earlier, the Kilsby Tunnel of the London & Birmingham Railway was held up by the presence of an unsuspected unstable formation. Tunnel maintenance consists mainly of inspections and piecemeal patching of the brick linings, and of removal of loosened rock from unlined tunnels.

The modern tendency in bridge construction is to move away from the old steel constructions towards concrete designs, which are virtually corrosion-free and hence cheaper to maintain. However, the majority of railway bridges are still of steel girder construction. A considerable mileage of most railways is accounted for by bridgework, and this is especially true in Britain and Europe, where it has been customary to provide bridges at road crossings. In America the *level crossing*, or *grade crossing*, was and is much more common and, unlike in Europe, is frequently unprotected by gates, the minimal warning being a white diagonal cross by the roadside, although at busy locations this may be supplemented by swinging red lights and bells when a train is approaching. In Britain heavy full-length gates, moved by the signalman or by a crossing keeper, were general, although these are now being superseded by the continental style lifting barrier or half barrier.

The construction and maintenance of British track is described in full detail by a textbook published in updated editions from time to time by the Permanent Way Institution: *British Railway Track*.

The loading gauge

The maximum permissible size of rolling stock varies from country to country and also within countries. In Britain, height and width restrictions are more limited than on other standard-gauge railways, a penalty of Britain's pioneering role in railway building. Moreover, because of the adoption of different limits by different companies, there still exist lines in Britain with far-from-standard clearances. Lines of the former Great Western Railway, originally broad gauge, have wider clearances than other lines, while there still exists, on the Tonbridge–Hastings line, tunnels whose meagre width necessitates the use of specially-built rolling stock. Diagrams showing these limitations (often known, loosely, as loading gauges and, more precisely, as diagrams of maximum moving dimensions) are necessarily rigidly enforced.

In continental Europe, a Berne Conference Standard has brought a measure of standardisation but here, as elsewhere, the existence of non-standard structures like tunnels and bridges means that total standardisation is a very long process. Fortunately, because the through running of rolling stock was accepted early, freightcars in Britain, America and Europe were designed to run over entire networks. However, with locomotives, this was usually considered unnecessary.

Chapter 5

The railway builders

It is surprising how fast the profession of civil engineer expanded to meet the demands of the railway age. True, some of the early engineers, like George Stephenson, were untrained and learned the business partly through costly mistakes. Others were former military engineers. But, by mid-century, there was no shortage of experienced talent. Many of the more successful engineers went on to become contractors, tendering for the construction of lines and employing their own engineers and sub-contractors. Among the thousands of civil engineers used by the railways, a few names stand out: the following list is so short as to omit many praiseworthy engineers and moreover it includes some whose fame was not earned by competence. A much more complete listing can be found in *A Biographical Dictionary of Railway Engineers* by John Marshall (1978).

Benjamin Baker Baker participated in the building of several London underground lines and was responsible for the practice of placing stations on a plateau to aid braking and acceleration. He was the designer of the cantilever Forth Bridge which was opened in 1890.

Peter Barlow Builder of much of the South Eastern Railway, Barlow is best remembered for his concept of building tube railways through London's clay. He bored the first such line, the Tower Subway, in 1870.

William Barlow Brother of Peter, William Barlow built much of the Midland Railway, including the extra-wide St Pancras Station train shed. His patented Barlow Rail with its curious cross-section was used for some years by a few railways.

Thomas Bouch A capable Scottish engineer, Bouch's cheese-paring and his failure to properly supervise work in progress led to his downfall when the Tay Bridge succumbed to gales in 1879.

Thomas Brassey Best-known and probably the most influential of the British railway contractors, Brassey began as a civil engineer under Locke, helping in the construction of lines between Birmingham and Warrington (Grand Junction Railway), London and Southampton, Chester and Crewe, and others. As a contractor, he built the Paris to Le Havre and other lines and, in partnership with Peto and Betts, many other railways all over the world, including the Canadian Grand Trunk.

Isambard Brunel Perhaps the most celebrated and certainly the most idealised and idolised of the British engineers, Brunel had many interests. Foremost among his railway work was the engineering of the Great Western Railway from

London to Bristol and, later, of railways like the Bristol & Exeter and South Devon which were associated with the GWR. His Box Tunnel (near Bath) and his unusual Tamar Bridge at Saltash are still in use, but his technically superior broad gauge and his technically unsuccessful atmospheric propulsion system (for the South Devon Railway) did not survive.

Frederik Conrad Conrad engineered the first Dutch main line, from Rotterdam to Amsterdam, in the 1840s. This line was notable for the number of waterways which it crossed and the unstable nature of the ground upon which it was laid.

Lewis Cubitt More an architect than an engineer, Cubitt's works include Kings Cross Station (1851).

William Cubitt The uncle of Lewis Cubitt, William Cubit had many fields of interest (including treadmills, which he seems to have invented). His work on the London to Dover line included the Shakespeare Cliff Tunnel and associated blasting operation. He was consulting engineer of the GNR from 1844. His son, **Joseph Cubitt**, followed in his footsteps and was responsible, among many other things, for the Blackfriars Bridge over the Thames.

Alexander Eiffel The Eiffel Tower demonstrates its designer's mastery of iron and steel construction, which he employed for a number of great railway bridges in Central France, Spain and Portugal.

Sandford Fleming A Scottish immigrant to Canada, Fleming surveyed many of the great Canadian main lines. The Yellowhead Pass route (now CNR) and the Kicking Horse Pass route (CPR) were surveyed by him.

John Fowler Best-known for his engineering of London's Metropolitan Railway, Fowler also had a large share in the building of the Forth Bridge in partnership with Benjamin Baker.

Charles Fox After helping with the London & Birmingham Railway in the 1830s, Fox specialised in the design of large station roofs and, among others, designed those at Paddington and Birmingham New Street stations. Best-known for his work on the Crystal Palace (1851), Fox also devoted much energy to the study and advocacy of narrow-gauge railways, especially for India. His firm, Sir Charles Fox & Sons, undertook many railways in Britain and overseas.

Karl von Ghega Ghega was an engineer of the first Austrian steam railway in the 1830s and is best known for his engineering of the trunk line over the Semmering Pass which remains one of the most outstanding railway works of all time.

John Hawkshaw Probably the most prolific of the Victorian civil engineers, Hawkshaw devoted only part of his time to railway work. He surveyed and built much of the Lancashire & Yorkshire Railway and brought the difficult Severn Tunnel to a successful conclusion in 1887.

Benjamin Latrobe Latrobe built much of the Baltimore & Ohio Railroad in the 1830s and 1840s. His Thomas Viaduct, still standing, was the first stone-built railway viaduct in the USA.

Jospeh Locke Beginning with the Liverpool & Manchester Railway, Locke participated in or directed the building of many important lines, mainly in Britain but sometimes abroad. His Lancaster and Carlisle line of the 1840s, now part of the West Coast Main Line, illustrates his propensity for avoidance of heavy works, including tunnels, thereby reducing construction costs but accepting steep gradients.

Ralph Modjeski A Polish immigrant to the USA, Modjeski in the first two decades of this century built a number of outstanding railway bridges. His train-carrying Benjamin Franklin Bridge at Philadelphia is celebrated for its long suspended span.

Samuel Peto Best-known as a contractor, when he usually worked in partnership with men like Brassey and Betts, Peto built much of the Great Western Railway's network in the Midlands and several railways in Canada and Australia. In the Crimean War he built the Balaklava Railway to supply the allied troops.

John Rastrick Apart from building some steam locomotives, Rastrick surveyed and built early English railways, of which the 1841 London–Brighton line was the most important.

Robert Stephenson Beginning as assistant to his father, **George Stephenson**, whose education did not really fit him to civil engineering, Robert Stephenson undertook many railway projects of lasting importance, including the London & Birmingham Railway in the 1830s. His bridges and viaducts include the Royal Border Bridge at Berwick and the Newcastle High Level Bridge, but his great tubular bridges over the Menai Strait and at Montreal have not survived.

Charles Vignoles One of the several railway engineers who began their career in the army, Vignoles was engaged in railway work for 40 years (1825–65). He was engineer or consultant for many foreign railways, especially in Russia, but also in France, Germany, Switzerland, Spain and Brazil. He devised the British version of the flat-bottom rail in 1837; this rail is still sometimes known as the Vignoles Rail.

Thomas Walker One of those civil engineers who never quite received their due because they worked under other engineers, Thomas Walker did much of the work on the Grand Trunk Railway for Brassey, on the Metropolitan Railway for Peto, and on the East London Railway and the Severn Tunnel for Hawkshaw.

George Whistler A former army engineer, Whistler undertook the engineering of several southern US lines in the 1820s and 1830s and, in the 1840s, was responsible for the construction of the Petersburg–Moscow Railway. He was married to 'Whistler's Mother'.

John Whitton Designer and engineer of much of New South Wales' railway network, Whitton's great achievement was the famous zigzag alignment of the route through the Blue Mountains at Lithgow. Both this, and his Hawkesbury River Bridge, have since been superseded.

Chapter 6

Gauge

Railway gauge is the distance between the inner faces of the rails, measured at the running edge on straight track. On curved track, depending on the sharpness of the curve, a few extra millimetres are added to provide the necessary sideplay; for example, on a curve of 350 metres (1,150 ft) radius, there might be an increase of the gauge by 15 mm (⅗ in). Traditionally, the gauge is checked periodically, especially when new track is laid, by a special instrument. However, with modern track on concrete sleepers, this check has lost its importance. In recent years some railways have reduced their gauge by a few millimetres. This is because the existing sideplay was felt to be excessive for fast freight trains and was a potential cause of freightcar derailments. Thus, from 1966, standard gauge in Britain began to be 4 ft 8⅗ in (1,432 mm) instead of 4 ft 8½ in (1,435 mm), and in the USSR the nominal 5 ft (1,524 mm) gauge is really 4 ft 11⅞ in (1,520 mm) on main lines.

The term *standard gauge* can be ambiguous. Inside a given state it can mean the particular gauge chosen for the main railways, but in a worldwide context it refers to the 4 ft 8½ in (1,435 mm) gauge which is the nominal standard in Britain, continental Europe, North America and in other countries. *Broad gauge* refers, usually, to lines wider than 4 ft 8½ in, while *narrow gauge* can be ambiguous in the same way as standard gauge: it usually describes lines of 3 ft (914 mm) or smaller but can sometimes refer to lines smaller than the prevailing gauge in a given country. For example, 3 ft 6 in (1,067 mm) gauge may be narrow gauge in Canada but standard gauge in South Africa. Lines of less than 1 ft 6 in (460 mm) are popularly known as miniature railways, although their proponents prefer the term *minimum gauge*.

An advantage of the broad gauge, particularly with steam traction, is that it simplifies the design of powerful locomotives because there is more space between the frames. Other claimed advantages of the wider gauges often derive less from the distance between the rails as from the circumstance that broad gauge lines are usually built with wider clearances. But this is not always so, for example, in the 1930s the British railway companies' vehicles typically had a maximum width of 9 ft 6 in (2,895 mm) whereas South African Railways, whose gauge was 1 ft 2½ in (368 mm) narrower, could operate vehicles 6 in (152 mm) wider than that. In other words, the effect of the gauge on the carrying capacity of vehicles is influenced by the ratio of permissible vehicle width to gauge. For example, in India the 5 ft 6 in (1,676 mm) gauge has a ratio of almost 2:1, but the metre gauge (3 ft 3⅜ in) has 2.7:1 and the 2 ft 6 in (762 mm) gauge has 3:1.

In practice, the narrow gauges do usually offer less capacity but the difference between say, 5 ft 6 in and 4 ft 8½ in, or between the latter and metre gauge, is either negligible or a consequence of factors other than gauge, of which lineside clearances is the most important. The claim advanced in the 19th century — that the broader gauges enhanced stability and thereby permitted higher speeds — might have been sound in theory but has not proved realistic in practice; after all, the broader gauge systems in India, Spain and Russia have not been noted for high speeds.

The great advantage of the narrow gauges is that they are much cheaper to build and this has meant in the past that between small or less prosperous centres there was a choice between a narrow-gauge railway, or no railway at all. In difficult terrain, this cost advantage was especially clear-cut because the narrow-gauge line, with its permissible short radius of curvature, could follow winding valleys without the excavation and earthworks demanded by a broader gauge. On average, the capital cost of a metre-gauge line, with its locomotives and rolling stock, is only half that of a 5 ft 6 in gauge line. True narrow-gauge lines (less than 3 ft or 914 mm) are even cheaper, but if traffic develops fast they may prove too small, and in many countries narrow-gauge lines were built with the intention of upgrading them to the broader gauge should traffic develop as hoped. However, the coming of the motor vehicle changed the picture and throughout the world it was the narrow-gauge lines which first felt the effect of highway competition. In a sense, though, this was a measure of success, for it was these low-cost lines which developed their hinterlands to the point that roadbuilding became worth while.

It is to George Stephenson's credit that at a time when the steam railway was regarded merely as an interesting device of purely local significance, he realised the importance of standardising the gauge so that, one day, trains would be able to run from one end of Britain to the other. Less creditable was his choice of gauge, which was not so much chosen as handed down from the north country colliery lines on which Stephenson began his career. This gauge was 4 ft 8 in, although Stephenson added an extra half-inch because he found his vehicles needed a little more sideplay. Thus 4 ft 8½ in became the 'standard gauge', first in Britain and later in other parts of the world, even though it was not based on any scientific enquiry. But it had the advantage, perhaps, of being an acceptable compromise which was neither exceptionally narrow nor exceptionally broad.

The 'Battle of the Gauges' was fought in Britain between the protagonists of Stephenson's 4 ft 8½ in gauge and Brunel's Great Western Railway, which had been laid to a gauge of 7 ft 0¼ in (2,140 mm). The inconvenience of two gauges in one small country had soon become apparent to railway-users. Thackeray's short story, *Jeames on the Gauge Question*, and the work of several artists and journalists pressed hard on the theme of the notorious break of gauge at Gloucester, and parliament's eventual decision, embodied in the Gauge Act of 1846, to make 4 ft 8½ in the maximum gauge in England, Wales and Scotland, was almost inevitable. Trials held to enlighten the parliamentary commissioners had seemed to show that the GWR gauge was technically superior, but it was more expensive to build and was already considerably outdistanced in terms of mileage by the Stephenson lines. In retrospect, it seems likely that its superior technical performance was due not so much to its gauge as to superior engineering in general. It was only in 1892 that the last broad-gauge line of the GWR was converted to standard gauge; the time and money which conversion required probably justified the government's 1846 decision that the gauge with the greatest mileage should be standardised.

In Ireland the 5 ft 3 in (1,600 mm) gauge was standardised, although in the poorer areas the 3 ft gauge was adopted. The latter lines succumbed early to highway competition so that 5 ft 3 in is now firmly established. Elsewhere in Britain, true narrow-gauge lines continued to be built for short-distance traffic in isolated areas. Many of these were in Wales, where the first public narrow-gauge line, the Ffestiniog Railway of 1 ft 11½ in (600 mm) gauge, had been opened for slate traffic in 1836. The few minimum-gauge railways of 15 in (380 mm) which have survived depend on tourist traffic, although in the late 19th century Sir Arthur Heywood built several lines to this gauge to demonstrate their suitability for agricultural and other uses (see his book, *Minimum Gauge Railways*, of 1898).

In America the early railway builders rarely thought about gauge standardisation; as in Britain, this came later and sometimes expensively. In Canada, for example, although the first lines had been built to Stephenson's gauge, the Portland to Montreal railway was planned to be built on the 5 ft 6 in gauge, probably because this company's first two locomotives had been purchased from a Scottish railway which formerly had been of that gauge. For three decades from 1851 this became the official standard gauge for Canada, despite the difficulties involved with the exchange of traffic with US railroads. Only in 1870 was the 4 ft 8½ in gauge re-established.

In the USA the 4 ft 8½ in gauge predominated, largely because several early railroads bought their locomotives from England, but there were long stretches of 5 ft gauge, especially in the south. There was also a 4 ft 10 in (1,473 mm) gauge line interposed between Philadelphia and Washington, the inconvenience of this for the New York to Washington route being mitigated by the use of 'compromise cars' with extra-wide wheel treads which could run on both gauges. The 4 ft 10 in gauge was also found elsewhere in New Jersey, and in Ohio. The Erie Railroad, from New York to Lake Erie, took pride in its 6 ft (1,830 mm) gauge, and the Missouri Pacific Railroad was originally 5 ft 6 in.

The first transcontinental line was intended to be of 5 ft gauge but, at the last minute, in 1862, President Lincoln changed this to 4 ft 8½ in, making it inevitable that all the main lines would eventually convert to Stephenson's gauge. The

Mixed gauge in Yucatan. On the right stands a standard-gauge locomotive, while a 3 ft gauge engine prepares to leave on the left.

Checking the gauge. This check is most often necessary on curved track carrying heavy axleloads at high speeds.

Erie conformed by 1880 and by the end of the 1880s almost all railroads had changed to the standard gauge. One exception was the Denver & Rio Grande Railroad, serving mountainous Colorado, which was of 3 ft gauge. This company did eventually convert to standard gauge but retained the original gauge for a few long branches, sections of which still survive as tourist railways. This 3 ft gauge also appeared in other countries, notably South America, where American engineers and capital were used to build railways. It also became popular in Ireland, and a section still survives in the Isle of Man. Despite the existence of this gauge, a second narrow gauge also became popular in rural areas of the USA. This was the 2 ft (610 mm) gauge, especially widespread in Maine.

In most countries outside the USA and Britain, the governments exercised strict control over the gauge right from the beginning, but this did not always avoid the introduction of non-standard gauges. India is a notorious example of this. Here the administration was well aware of the dangers of a British-style battle of the gauges and laid down that the standard gauge was to be 5 ft 6 in. But after the main lines had been built it was found that there was insufficient traffic potential to justify the capital cost of secondary lines. So it was decided to create a secondary network with a cheaper gauge. At first the 'Empire' standard of 3 ft 6 in was proposed but, as the Indian government was at the time contemplating metrication (an idea which it soon abandoned), the metre gauge was chosen instead. By the time the British left India in 1947 the metre gauge and broad gauge networks were of equal length. Some experts had advocated a 2 ft 9 in (840 mm) gauge but the military had objected because this would have precluded cavalry horses travelling two abreast. Yet it was not long before true narrow-gauge lines were built to provide transport in districts, especially in north-west India, where even the metre gauge was too expensive. Here again the military had a decisive influence; the 2 ft gauge being superseded by the 2 ft 6 in gauge because the latter was widely in use in other parts of the Empire, thereby guaranteeing reinforcements of rolling stock in time of war.

The British government had tried to ensure that the Australian colonies would choose the same gauge for their first lines, but long delays in communications with London, and the coincidental appointment of new engineers by the colonies, produced enough confusion to result in Victoria and South Australia adopting the Irish gauge of 5 ft 3 in while New South Wales chose 4 ft 8½ in. Queensland, Western Australia and Tasmania then chose 3 ft 6 in for reasons of economy. As the Australian economy and railway network developed, these discrepancies became expensive and inconvenient and, just as in the USA, the choice of the 4 ft 8½ in gauge (for the Trans Australia Railway) signified that that gauge would be the future Australian standard. Since then, however, little has been done towards standardisation, apart from the provision of new 4 ft 8½ in tracks which now make it possible for trains to run from New South Wales to Melbourne and Perth. The Argentinian railways, largely British-financed and British-engineered, suffer from a similar situation, with three main gauges.

In France the government had stipulated 4 ft 8½ in as the standard gauge but, as in India and elsewhere, it was soon discovered that smaller centres could obtain railway communication only by means of cheaper, narrower-gauge lines. Legislation was passed to enable 'lines of local interest' to be built and an extensive mileage of metre-gauge railways developed, the government taking care that these could not join up to provide competition for the main line companies. Some of these metre-gauge lines still exist, carrying freight only, while a few lengths have been restored as tourist lines.

In Germany, while the main lines were built to the 4 ft 8½ in gauge, different states sponsored narrower gauge lines within their own frontiers, of 2 ft 6 in, 2 ft 7 in (785 mm), 2 ft 11 in (900 mm) and metre gauge; several of these are still in operation. The first Dutch railway was of the unusual and inexplicable 6 ft

On the Welsh narrow gauge. Locomotive coal is transhipped from the standard to the narrow gauge on the Welshpool & Llanfair Railway, shortly before the latter's abandonment by British Railways (M. Deane).

4½ in (1,945 mm) gauge and the subsequent Dutch Rhenish Railway was of 2 metre (6 ft 7 in) gauge; both were soon converted to standard gauge.

Russia's first two lines were of 6 ft and 4 ft 8½ in gauge, but the subsequent lines were of 5 ft gauge. British journalists liked to report that this gauge was chosen to make invasion by the standard-gauge West difficult, but it had in fact been chosen by an American engineer, Whistler, who was familiar with 5 ft gauge lines in the USA. Although 5 ft was to remain the standard gauge in Russia, it was not long before narrow-gauge lines were also built. One of these, to Archangel, was overloaded with traffic in the First World War and was converted to mixed narrow and 5 ft gauge by the laying of additional rail; for a time the original narrow-gauge locomotives hauled 5 ft gauge trains.

Although it is passengers, resentful of the necessity of changing trains, who complain loudest of break-of-gauge problems, it is freight traffic which suffers most. Where traffic is large, transhipment sheds are built, in which a central platform is flanked by a line of each gauge. This across-the-platform transhipment is relatively fast, but inevitably transit times are lengthened and the utilisation rate of rolling stock falls. Moreoever, transhipment demands extra man-hours and provides additional opportunity for pilferage. The laying of one, occasionally two, additional rails creates a mixed-gauge track over which trains of two, occasionally three, gauges may run, and this expedient is quite common around junctions and traffic centres, but is of little help for long-distance traffic. Construction of an additional line to provide single-gauge running is feasible where traffic is heavy, as in Australia, but this is an expensive remedy.

Another approach is to design means whereby rolling stock can move over more than one gauge. One such device is the transporter truck, still used on central European narrow-gauge lines. This is a low narrow-gauge flat wagon carrying a set of rails on to which a standard-gauge freightcar can be moved, enabling the larger vehicle to begin or end its trip on a narrow-gauge line. A more sophisticated solution is to design rolling stock with interchangeable wheelsets which are changed at break-of-gauge stations. Soviet passenger vehicles run to many of the European capitals in this way, their wheelsets being changed at the Soviet frontier, while fruit from Spain arrives in London in refrigerated cars with variable gauge wheelsets.

The part played by personal or emotional factors in questions of gauge should not be underestimated. That the 5 ft 3 in gauge exists as a main line standard in some countries can be attributed largely to expatriate Irish engineers, who naturally felt happiest with the gauge of their home railways. In India there is a slow process of re-gauging the busiest metre-gauge routes, and local politicians make great efforts to persuade the railway administration to re-gauge those sections of line serving their own constituencies; a metre- or narrow-gauge town in India is almost regarded as the equivalent of the 'one-horse town' in 19th century America. The Nigerian government has recently decreed that the entire railway system is to be re-gauged from 3 ft 6 in to 4 ft 8½ in, a change for which there is little technical justification but which may have some psychological importance for a run-down and discredited railway system about to embark on a rehabilitation plan. In Japan the new high-speed lines of the *Shinkansen* were built to the 4 ft 8½ in gauge rather than to the Japanese standard 3 ft 6 in; this emphasised the distinctiveness of the new service and may have assisted the export drive of Japanese rolling stock manufacturers.

Although the number of gauges in existence has diminished over recent decades, and despite the different technical characteristics of each gauge, there are undoubtedly many more gauges than are really needed. The metre gauge is the world's second most important gauge, followed by 3 ft 6 in, and there is only about 2 in difference between these. Moreover, the 3 ft gauge is very little different while, as a legacy of Italian and French colonial administration, there exist a 3 ft 1⅝ in (950 mm) gauge in Ethiopia and a 3 ft 5⅜ in (1,050 mm) standard in the Middle East. A similar proliferation exists with the narrow gauge, even if the 1 ft 11½ in and 2 ft gauges are treated as one. In Britain alone there are the 2 ft, 2 ft 3 in (686 mm), 2 ft 6 in, and 2 ft 8½ in (825 mm) gauges, as well as the 2 ft 7½ in (800 mm) favoured in Switzerland and adopted for the Snowdon Mountain Railway.

Outline of world railway gauges

Standard (4 ft 8½ in or 1,435 mm)	Europe (except Ireland, Spain, Portugal, USSR and Finland), Australia (ANR and SRA), North Africa, Israel, Iraq, Iran, China, South Korea, Japan (some lines), Peru, Venezuela, NE Argentina, Uruguay, Paraguay, Mexico, USA, Canada.
5 ft 6 in or 1,676 mm	Spain, Portugal, India, Pakistan, Sri Lanka, Bangladesh, Argentina, Chile.
5 ft 3 in or 1,600 mm	Ireland, Australia (SAR and VR), Brazil.
5 ft or 1,524 mm	USSR, Finland.
3 ft 6 in or 1,067 mm	Australia (QR, WAGR, TGR, parts of South Australia), New Zealand, Southern Africa, Ghana, Nigeria, Sudan, Indonesia, Japan, USSR (Sakhalin), Newfoundland, Ecuador.
3 ft 5½ in or 1,050 mm	Jordan, Syria, Lebanon.
3 ft 3 ⅜ in or 1 metre	East Africa, South East Asia, India, Pakistan, Bangladesh, Burma, Bolivia, Brazil, Chile, Iraq, Portugal, Greece, Switzerland, Argentina.
3 ft or 914 mm	Colombia, Peru.
2 ft 5½ in to 2 ft 6 in or 750 to 762 mm	India, Sri Lanka, Austria, Yugoslavia, Poland, Czechoslovakia, Germany (East), Roumania.
1 ft 11½ in to 2 ft 0 in or 600 to 610 mm	India, Pakistan, South Africa.

Narrow-gauge railways in Britain

3 ft (914 mm)	Isle of Man Railway, Manx Electric Railway.
2 ft 8½ in (820 mm)	Volk's Electric Railway (Brighton).
2 ft 7½ in (800 mm)	Snowdon Mountain Railway.
2 ft 6 in (762 mm)	Sittingbourne & Kemsley Light Railway, Welshpool & Llanfair Railway.
2 ft 3 in (686 mm)	Talyllyn Railway.
2 ft (610 mm)	Brecon Mountain Railway, Leighton Buzzard Light Railway.
1 ft 11½ in (600 mm)	Bala Lake Railway, Ffestiniog Railway, Lincolnshire Coast Light Railway, Llanberis Lake Railway, Vale of Rheidol Railway (BR).

Chapter 7

Train control

The movement of trains is controlled by messages conveyed by lineside signals or by written or electronic instructions, and by the setting of points or switches. Procedures and equipment for these purposes have been in a continuous state of development to enhance safety and to permit the greatest possible number of trains per length of track. The following account of the salient methods is limited to essentials.

One engine in steam (OES) As the Single Line Staff system, this was one of the earliest systems to be used in Britain, and was favoured on branch lines. A wooden staff, unique for the particular section of line, was provided as a tangible symbol of a locomotive's right to proceed. Since there was only one staff there could only be one train on the line. This system had the disadvantage that a following train could not proceed until the staff had been brought back by a train in the opposite direction. To improve this situation, the staff and ticket system was sometimes adopted, in which the signalman or stationmaster would himself hold the staff, on whose authority he would issue a ticket to authorise trains to proceed (but not return) through the section, sending the staff forward with the last train in that direction. In Britain the one engine in steam system is still used on low-traffic lines, but is now known as *one train working*.

The train order system This is still widely used in North America on lines with low or medium traffic, and is current elsewhere in the world, including a few lines in Europe. In Britain it was once used by some lines, notably by the Highland Railway with its long single-track main line, but fell out of favour after some serious accidents. In North America, under this system, trains run according to timetables, and they are time-spaced at least five minutes apart. Control is exercised by a central despatcher acting through operators with whom he is in touch by telegraph. Arrangements for extra trains, and for revised schedules for delayed regular trains, are made by the despatcher and communicated to the appropriate operator, who makes out train orders which are handed to the crews of the trains involved.

Meticulous discipline and rigid procedures are essential for this system. It is, moreover, time-consuming. For example, a train which is unexpectedly halted within a section, and might therefore be overtaken, has to be protected by a flagman, who walks back and places two detonators (torpedoes) on the track and ignites a five-minute red flare (fusee) before walking back to rejoin his train as it moves off. The system is used mainly on single track, and there is an elaborate system of precedence ('superiority') which determines which of two opposing trains will be instructed to take a siding or loop to allow the other, the superior train, to pass.

The block system Whereas the train order system relies on a separation of trains by time, the block system is based on separation by space interval. It became practicable as soon as the telegraph was sufficiently developed to permit communication between neighbouring signalmen or train operators. In this system the line is broken up into sections, or blocks, and only one train may be in a block at one time. Blockposts (signal-boxes in Britain, block stations or interlocking towers in North America) are located at the divisions between blocks to control, by signals, the passage of a train from one block to another. Various telegraphic codes are used so that the blockposts controlling adjacent blocks can quickly pass messages such as 'Is line clear?', 'Train entering block'. In Britain these messages are communicated by bell codes, which may often be overheard by bystanders. The commonest codes used on British Rail are as follows:

British signal-box bell codes

Number of rings	Description
1	Attention for following message
4	Is line clear for Class 1 train?
3 pause 1	Is line clear for Class 2 train?
1 pause 3 pause 1	Is line clear for Class 3 train?
3 pause 1 pause 1	Is line clear for Class 4 train?
4 pause 1	Is line clear for fully-fitted freight train?
5	Is line clear for other Class 6 trains?
1 pause 2 pause 2	Is line clear for Class 7 train?
3 pause 2	Is line clear for Class 8 train?
1 pause 4	Is line clear for unfitted freight (Class 9) train?
2 pause 3	Is line clear for light engine or engines?
2	Train entering section
5 pause 2	Train out of section

There are many other codes for particular purposes and emergencies. In addition, on electrified lines outside the Southern Region, special codes for 'Is line clear?' are used for electric trains (4 pause 2 for fast electric passenger trains, 3 pause 1 pause 2 for ordinary electric trains).

A signal-box on double track has four block instruments. The latter are indicators whose three-position needles show whether there is a train on line, or the line is clear or the line is 'blocked' (the latter is the normal position, signifying that entry to the line is closed). Each of the four indicators relates to one of the four block sections with which the signal-box is concerned. A signalman, seeking to pass a train into the next block, will send the appropriate 'Is line clear?' bellcode to the next signal-box, controlling entry to that block. The latter will acknowledge and, if line is clear, will 'peg' its appropriate block instrument to the Line is Clear indication; this is automatically repeated on the corresponding block instrument in the offering signal-box. If the line is not clear, the needle will be allowed to stay in the Line Blocked position. If the train is accepted, when it passes out of the first block into the second the originating

Train control 55

Inside a 12-lever signal box (Midsomer Norton on the now-closed Somerset & Dorset Joint Railway). Three block instruments are shown; that on the extreme left is out of use, with its operating handle removed (M. Deane).

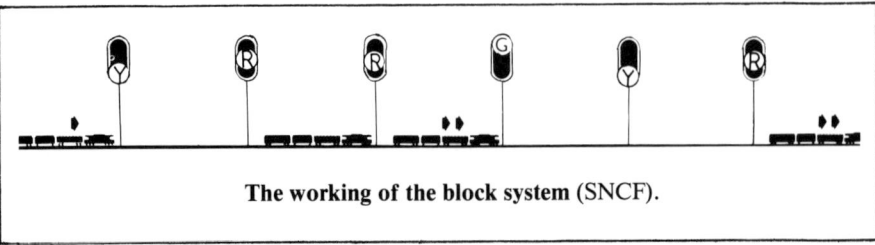

The working of the block system (SNCF).

signalman will send the Train Entering Section bellcode and restore his signals to Danger behind the train. The receiving signalman changes the block instrument indication to Train on Line, and then, usually, in the case of a through train, will send his own 'Is line clear?' message to the next following signal-box.

A block section is regarded as stretching from the most advanced stop signal of one station to just past the rearmost stop signal of the next. The margin beyond the latter signal, typically a quarter-mile, is known usually as the clearing distance and is intended to provide a safety zone in case a train should overrun the signal through defective or tardily applied brakes. Usually then, there is a stretch of line between two block sections, which can be defined as the area falling within 'station limits'. In this station area, trains may move without reference to the adjoining signal-boxes.

Generally, the 'closed-block', rather than the 'open block', is used on lines with non-automatic signalling. That is, the stop signals controlling entry to the next block are kept at Danger until a train is accepted. In the 'open block' system (which was widespread in 19th century Britain until a series of accidents made it unpopular) signals are normally held at Line Clear and go to danger only so long as a train remains in the block whose entry they control.

There is an important distinction between 'permissive' and 'absolute' block systems. Whereas in the latter only one train at a time is allowed in a block, permissive working admits second and perhaps subsequent trains, after they have been slowed down or momentarily halted at the entry to the block. They are required to proceed slowly, prepared to stop at sight of the preceding train. Permissive block is used very occasionally in Britain, usually on busy freight-only lines or at passenger stations to permit one train to draw up behind another. It is somewhat more common in France, and is general in North America. On single-track lines in North America, the block system may be regarded as a supplement to, not a replacement for, the train order system, and as such is an extra measure of safety.

Locking and interlocking The idea of interlocking signal and point levers, so that clear indications could not be given for two conflicting routes at the same time, seems to have originated in England in the 1850s. At first achieved by heavy mechanical installations, it became more compact when electric control of signals was introduced. In the 20th century, route-interlocking became feasible and was widely adopted at busy junctions. Several patented systems were, and are, involved in this, but in essence it consists of apparatus whereby the operator can, by actuating an entry and an exit switch, set up an entire route between the entry and exit points, with all signals and points being automatically set and fully interlocked so as to prevent conflict with other movements. In the power signal-boxes, or interlocking towers, which house these installations a 'panel' replaces levers and the old-style track diagrams.

This panel shows all the routes controlled by the installation, with illuminated lights showing the position of trains and the aspects of signals and points.

Lock and block Known usually as 'controlled manual block' in North America, the first practicable installation of this description was introduced by Sykes in England. In this, the signals separating the blocks are electrically connected in such a way that the co-operation of the signalmen in the two block-posts is required in order to operate them. Moreover, the second signalman (whose electrical release of the signal controlling entry to his section is required to clear the entry signal), cannot give that release until certain safety precautions have been taken.

Train detection and track circuiting Devices enabling a train to signal its presence, and hence its movements, to operators, take several forms – the track circuit is the best known. Where track circuiting is ruled out because of expense, axle-counters are sometimes used. These are treadle-operated machines which electrically record the passage over them of each axle. Typically, one is provided at the entry and a second at the exit of a section, and until the second has recorded the passage of an identical number of axles as passed the first, the signals permitting the entry of another train remain locked. A predecessor of the axle-counter is the simple treadle. This is a metal strip fixed inside the rail which is depressed by the flanges of passing wheels and thereby opens a switch to cause an indication to be received in the signal-box. As this does not count axles it cannot guarantee that a train recorded as leaving the section has not, perhaps by a coupling failure, left some of its vehicles on the track behind it.

The track circuit was invented in America by William Robinson in 1872. It is now a very complex piece of equipment, but basically it consists of a low-voltage power source at one end of the circuit and an electrical relay at the other. The circuit itself is the pair of rails, which are insulated at each end from the rails adjoining the circuit. Current passes down one rail, energises the relay and then passes down the other rail back to the source. When a train appears on these rails its wheels and axles short-circuit the system so the relay loses its power supply and releases a pivoted armature which in turn can operate an array of contacts. Thus the track circuit can be used not only to inform operators of the presence of a train, but to lock signals protecting that train. From this it is a very short step to automatic signals, operated by the trains themselves.

Automatic block signals With these, a train entering a block actuates a track circuit beside the signal, causing the latter to move to danger behind it. When it enters the next block another track circuit will release the first signal and close the second. With automatic block, it is usual for the 'open block' to be used, the signals presenting a green aspect except when following blocks are occupied. Among other things, this system makes it easier to shorten block sections to the maximum braking distance of the trains in operation, an important contribution to line capacity. In traditional block signalling, the shortening of block sections (that is, increasing their number) entails a corresponding addition of signal-boxes and signalmen. On lines with multiple-aspect signalling, the capacity is further increased because an advance warning signal to supplement the warning (or distant) signal preceding the stop signal becomes possible. This means that trains with a longer braking distance (by virtue of speed or weight) can be accommodated while not allowing excessive braking distances for smaller or slower trains.

Panel control on British Rail: the London Bridge installation which controls the South East London suburban network (BR).

Centralised train control (CTC) From automatic block signalling it was only a short step to CTC, which developed fast in North America between the wars and is now extensively used throughout the world; outside the USA the first application of CTC came in New Zealand where, in 1938, a first section of the single-track Main Trunk (Wellington–Auckland) was equipped. There are several variants, often under different names, but the common, fundamental, feature is that one despatching centre directly controls (by signals) all train movements over a very long length of line (measured in hundreds of miles in the USA, usually less in Europe). The control decks are small, desk-like machines and are furnished with a panel which gives a complete indication of the trains, signals and points on the section under CTC.

A predecessor of CTC was the 'absolute permissive block' (APB) system, widely used in the inter-war USA as a means of increasing the train capacity of single-track lines. Before APB, security on such lines was obtained by maintaining a safety overlap so that trains would be separated by two blocks. This was to avoid a situation in which opposing trains would not be able to brake fast enough to avoid head-on contact, but it had the disadvantage that trains moving in the same direction were also spaced at the same interval, which was inefficient. With APB, the signals were so interlinked that when, say, a westbound train entered the block sections between crossing loops, the clearing of the first, admitting, signal prevented all the signals controlling eastbound trains up to the next crossing loop from being cleared. This included the Absolute Stop signal admitting eastbound trains from that crossing station to the section. At the same time as the westbound train cleared successive sections, the signals behind it cleared for a following train; these signals, apart from the Absolute Stop signal at the beginning of the section, were Permissive Stops.

The great virtue of CTC is that it can plan train-meets on single-track lines with great refinement, so that a train does not have to waste time standing in loops waiting for a delayed opposing train. When the loops are sufficiently long, trains can in fact pass without stopping. This means an enormous increase of train capacity on single-track routes, often allowing increasing traffic to be handled without the expense of laying a second track. Conversely, CTC may permit the reduction of a double-track line to single-track, with worthwhile savings on track maintenance. However, CTC is not at all limited to single-track lines and its British variant, known as 'track circuit block' (TCB) or, loosely, as panel signalling, is used on double-track trunk lines.

Train describers An early form of train describer can still be seen on some of the stations of the London underground railways. In this, the destination of a train is registered, manually, in the equipment at the starting station and, as the train proceeds down the line, its destination is automatically displayed in advance on train describers suspended above the platform. In principle, earlier train describers used as aids to signalmen are similar, but the development of electronics has meant that present-day describers are not only more compact but can perform more functions. It is now possible, for example, for a train's number to be displayed on the illuminated panel that shows its progress through a control area. Programme machines, which carry details of a day's train service and set the route accordingly (being moved forward from train to train by the passage of the trains themselves), are used on several underground railways. On most railways all trains have a number, although in Britain reporting numbers are no longer carried by locomotives.

In Germany a system is used in which trains carry their numbers in a position in which they can be read by a photo-electric scanner. Transferred to a computer, this number indicates the destination and other timetable characteristics of the train, enabling the route to be set automatically. Inside the huge control towers which may be seen outside many big German stations, these numbers appear on the illuminated diagrams which register their passage through the controlled area. The supervisors in these towers only intervene when circumstances prevent trains running to the regular timetable.

The automatic railway A combination of train description and automatic signalling needs little addition to create a railway which requires neither a locomotive driver nor signalmen, apart from a supervising operator. Where trains are similar in size and speed this is most easily achieved, and the Victoria Line of London's underground railway is capable of automatic operation, although semi-automatic, with train-crew in attendance, is preferred for human reasons. Several other specialised railways are equipped for driverless operation.

Automatic warning system (AWS) or automatic train control (ATC) This consists of trackside apparatus to ensure that trains actually respond to signals (see next chapter). It includes cab-signalling by means of coded impulses. Experimental systems include those in which long trackside conductor loops transmit messages about signals, gradients and speed limits to the train; this is enough information to enable on-train computers to formulate appropriate instructions for the traction motors and brakes.

Radio systems Radio communication between trains and controllers has not come into general use, partly because other systems perform adequately and partly because there are blind spots on a railway line where radio signals may be blocked by hills and other obstructions. But several railways—especially those having long lines with infrequent but regular trains—have, in recent decades, installed microwave systems, with repeater stations distributed along the route.

One railway, the ore-carrying Hammersley Railway in Western Australia, is a good example of train control by radio. It is about 250 miles (402 km) long, single-track with long crossing loops, and runs about ten trains daily. The single train controller at Dampier can arrange train-meets, take measures in emergencies and arrange, where necessary, gaps between trains to allow track maintenance to be done. In England the minimum-gauge Ravenglass & Eskdale Railway, a tourist line, uses a radio-controlled block system for its trains, with enginemen in continuous communication with a controller who arranges, and orders, the crossing of trains at loops. BR is experimenting with radio control on its Highland line in Scotland.

Transponders These are an advanced form of track-to-train communication and are in experimental use between London and Birmingham. They are electronic devices fixed between the rails in a light casing every mile or so. They derive power from the inductive energy created by the passage of the train above them and, with this energy, transmit a message to receivers on the train. Each has its own coded emission, so a train passing overhead receives a set signal, perhaps a request for a certain speed, as well as the precise location of the train. Transponders are capable, by providing a series of instructions, of controlling the speed of a train and therefore, within limits, of providing an automatic train-driving system.

Electric token instruments The first of these devices for single-track operation was patented in Britain by Edward Tyer in 1878. It overcame the disadvantage of the train staff systems insofar as it permitted more than one symbol to be withdrawn from the same machine, while preventing more than one being in use at the same time. The symbol in this case was a tablet, but successive machines of this type use the metal, so-called 'electric' staff, or keys, all being carefully inscribed and designed so as to be easily recognisable as belonging to one, and one only, section of track.

In these systems there is a token instrument at both of the stations or signal-boxes, marking the end of a section or block. These machines are electrically linked, so that neither can issue another token or staff until the one first issued has been returned to one or other of the instruments. It thereby becomes possible for one token station to issue a succession of tokens, provided each one is promptly returned to the token instrument at the other end of the section. Tokens are usually attached to a wire hoop, so that they become easier to pick up and deliver while the train is moving. Some railways introduced mechanical tablet-exchange apparatus with an arm on the locomotive engaging with another arm on the ground; such apparatus has now been removed from British Rail locomotives.

Other single-track control systems To eliminate the delays occasioned by token working, an interlocking block instrument (interlocked with the signals at both ends of a section so as to prevent conflicting movements) found limited application in Britain and elsewhere. A more recent method has used direction levers. These are fitted in the signal-boxes at both ends of a section and, when both are set for the same direction of travel, it becomes possible to clear the stop signal admitting a train going in that direction. So long as the train remains in the section, all the other signals are locked.

Tokenless block instruments, dispensing with track circuits, have been revived in Britain in recent years. They make use of a modified type of indicator instrument. On the line between Salisbury and Exeter, formerly double-track, the system dispenses with bell codes and the accepting signalman need not, in fact, be present in his box to receive a train because he is free to leave his instrument at the Train Accepted position. Most movements are according to timetable and, for irregular movements, arrangements are made by telephone.

Light railway regulations In Britain, light traffic lines may be granted 'light railway orders'. These stipulate certain conditions, notably severe speed limits, in return for which normal safety precautions, including signalling, may be partially or entirely relaxed.

Chapter 8

Signals

Signals are the essential element in the control of train movements, being the link between the controllers and the train crews. As might be expected, they have developed from the hand signals of the early days of railways through increasingly complicated mechanisms to ultra-modern electronic forms whose presence is invisible to the outside observer. But since signalling equipment tends to be both longlasting and expensive, old signals tend to survive long after they have been outmoded. They are replaced not because they are worn out but because new equipment is sometimes required to deal with increasing traffic flows, or because it is more economical in use, largely through saving labour.

Knowledge of the signals likely to be encountered is one of the most important skills expected of train crews, and is not as simple as is sometimes thought, given the range of signal types still in service, as well as the local peculiarities of their use. The employees' operating instructions of almost all the world's railways detail, for example, the use of that most early and primitive form of signalling, the red flag, which is still sometimes resorted to. This chapter can only mention some of the signal types in use, for not only is there a very long time-span to be covered but there is the complicating fact that different railway companies, or different countries, have their own variations.

A signal *indication* is the message conveyed, whereas a signal *aspect* is what the signal shows; this is a fine distinction which is often blurred. In Britain a signal is said to be 'on' when indicating Stop and is 'pulled off' to show Line Clear. Signal arms are often referred to as 'boards'.

A useful, but sometimes over-emphasised, distinction may be made between 'speed signalling' and 'route signalling'. The latter is favoured in British-style systems, and implies that signal indications before junctions and stations inform enginemen of the route their train is to take and it is their responsibility to reduce speed to the limit for that route.

With speed signalling, as practised in North America and most of Europe, signals indicate where speed has to be reduced rather than the route to be taken. But in speed signalling the train crew can usually guess which route they are to take by the presence or absence of the speed restricting signal. Where there might be confusion, route indicators are often provided; for example, in France white lights are shown, the number of lights indicating the route to be followed while, in Germany, route indicators, showing a capital letter, are frequently attached above colourlight heads. In these countries speed restrictions to levels above the standard 30 or 30–40 km/h (19–25 mph) implied by the signals are indicated by board displays. In most countries temporary speed restrictions, typically occasioned by track work, are indicated by three boards or light signals; one in advance of the location, showing the speed, one to mark the beginning of the speed-restricted sector and a third to show where the limit ends.

Hand signals were found to be inadequate in the first decade of the railway age and various mechanical models were introduced, most having the disadvantage that they provided only one indication; for example, if the signal was visible the train had to stop but if it was invisible the train could proceed. Because in practice there is no difference in not seeing and not noticing, this could cause accidents. However, the Great Western Railway's disc and crossbar design, presenting a horizontal bar to a train which had to stop, and rotating 90 degrees to present a disc to signify Line Clear, eliminated this fault. Moreover, the GWR mounted such signals on tall posts so that locomotive men could see them well in advance.

By 1850 the semaphore signal, basically a movable arm mounted on a lineside post, had proved its superiority; its first use appears to have been on the London & Croydon Railway in 1841 and it remained dominant until the introduction of colourlight signals. It took many forms. Originally it gave three indications; Line Clear was shown by the arm hanging vertically (and hence invisibly) inside a slot in the post, Caution by an inclination of the arm 45 degrees downward and Stop by the horizontal position of the arm.

At night, a white light indicated Line Clear, green was Caution, and red meant Stop. The use of white for Line Clear was one of several potentially dangerous practices which in course of time were corrected; not only did that colour risk confusion with other lights in town areas, but the accidental breakage of the red lampglass could result in a white light showing when the signal was at danger. The modern green for Line Clear, yellow or amber for Caution, and Red for Stop was standardised in Britain from 1893, and in the USA more gradually in the second decade of this century. As will be seen, many railways do use white lights, but only for purposes where confusion with off-line lights is neither likely nor dangerous. Often these are 'lunar white', a white from which all trace of yellow has been filtered out.

In 1876 the Abbots Ripton accident in England, when snow and ice held down a signal arm to indicate a false Line Clear aspect, led to abolition of the three-aspect signal. It was replaced by a two-position arm pivoted in such a way that, in the event of mechanical failure, it would return to the Stop position. Such two-aspect signals used a horizontal position of the arm to indicate Stop and a downward inclination of about 45 degrees to signify Line Clear. A variant, found especially on the Great Northern and Taff Vale railways, was the 'somersault' signal. In this the arm and the spectacle were separate, with the arm falling clean away from the post to signify Line Clear.

In Britain, the American-style three-position semaphore found a small-scale application around 1920, but this development was soon curtailed when the influential professional body, the Institution of Railway Signal Engineers, recommended against its adoption in 1924. The three-position type uses a horizontal arm to indicate Stop, a vertical (upward) position to give Line Clear and an inclined arm upwards at 45 degrees to indicate Caution. The rejection of this idea left the way clear in Britain for the two-position 'upper-quadrant' signal in which a 45 degree upward inclination indicated Line Clear. With the exception of the Great Western Railway, which stayed with the existing 'lower quadrant' type, the British railways began to change over to the upper-quadrant style. In the USA, upper-quadrant signals were recommended for standardisation in 1908. Since upper-quadrant signals in the USA are three-aspect, only one arm per post is necessary for block signalling.

The way was open for colourlight to replace semaphore signals as soon as the technology had evolved to the point where lenses could transmit low-consumption (5 watts or less) electric light clearly up to a distance of one mile; this situation had been reached by the end of the First World War. However, the expense of replacing all semaphores has meant that most of the world's railways still employ colourlights on only their busiest sections. There are two basic types of colourlight signal. In the searchlight type, there is a single lamp and lens, with a movable three-colour spectacle glass changing the aspects. Then there is the multi-lens type (often referred to in North America simply as a colourlight) in which the head contains as many bulbs and lenses as the number of colours required. It is usual practice for green to be the upper light and red the lower, an opposite arrangement to highway traffic signals.

In general, the searchlight signal provides a longer sighting distance, but is more expensive. It has a very narrow beam, which means that it has to be aligned with great care, and that line curvature or obstructions may nullify its greater range. Where modern signalling systems require one signal to show more than one colour simultaneously, two-, three-, or four-light heads have to be provided.

Just as semaphore signals could differ in their details from country to country and from company to company, so did the control installations which actuated them. The signal-box concept was characteristic of British-type signalling, and could vary from the ground frame to high, two-floor glass-fronted buildings dominating the approach tracks of big junctions like Crewe and Rugby. The ground frame is a small array of levers controlling points which are used only occasionally and do not justify continuous manning. Often unprotected from the elements, such an installation consists essentially of a footwalk alongside the levers. Next in size comes the signal-box between two stations where the distance and the traffic justifies the division of the section into two or more block sections. Such a signal-box, controlling the entry and exit to the adjacent blocks, may have only one stop signal in each direction, each with their corresponding distant signals. But even though there may be only four levers, all the essentials of a signal-box are there; the block instruments, the train register, the red and green flags and a rudimentary interlocking of stop and distant signals.

In larger boxes, the ground floor of the cabin is filled with the rods, levers and frames of the interlocking equipment. In Britain, switches may be connected to the signal-box levers by rodding; this is quite heavy to move, even with a lever, so 350 ft (107 m) is regarded as about the maximum possible distance between the box and its points. In turn, this necessitated, until electric or electro-pneumatic point mechanisms could be introduced, more than one signal-box at certain stations. In the USA, where one-inch piping was usually used for the same purpose, 1,000 ft (305 m) was regarded as the maximum practicable distance for fully manual operation.

Such lengths of rodding are considerably affected by expansion and contraction, but this problem is easily solved by the insertion, half-way down the length, of an expansion compensator, of which the pivoted lever is the most common type. With signal wires, such an easy solution is unavailable, so British signalmen are required to tighten or relax their wires according to the season and, often, according to the daily temperature. Despite this, there have been occasional cases of wires which had been tightened for a hot day, cooling sufficiently at night to pull a signal off; other safety devices, however, prevented these occurrences causing a disaster.

In continental Europe and elsewhere (including some British Empire railways) this problem was avoided by the use of the double-wire system. Instead of the single wire, pulled and released by a man-sized lever, there is a double wire which passes round a cam at the base of the signal post, actuating the arm and, at the signal-box, passes round a drum which is turned by a small handle, the extent of the turn being determined by the slackness of the wire.

Power operation, by gas, compressed air, electricity or by air and electricity (electro-pneumatically), made its fastest strides in the USA, especially after 1900. In the early days of electric signalling, each piece of equipment needed to be connected to the signal-box or interlocking tower by its own electric wires and the expense of this was a limiting factor. In modern equipment, the actuating motors of signals and points can be controlled by coded impulses, all of which can pass down a single cable. Similar impulses travel by a second wire in the opposite direction, informing the controllers of the position of the points and signals.

In Britain the traditional signal-box with its multi-coloured levels (red for stop signals, yellow for distant, black for points, blue for facing point locks) is by no means extinct, even though on main lines the introduction of automatic block signalling has meant the closure of many small boxes, and panel control on a few routes has meant the closure of all intermediate boxes. In the USA, where the train order system required no signal-boxes except at interlocked junctions, the equivalent installation, the morse-connected operator's office, has also been reduced in numbers by automatic block signalling. In continental Europe, where it was traditional for the stationmaster rather than a specialised signalman to regulate train movements at the smaller stations, the signalling apparatus was placed in the station building, often inside the ticket office. This arrangement still survives, although the equipment is now modernised and typically includes an illuminated track diagram and push-button controls. Except when the installation is switched out, when the far-distant train despatcher acts alone, the stationmaster controls the signals within his station limits.

Visible lineside signals are not the only form of communication between trains and operators. Acoustic signals are typified by the detonator, known as a torpedo in North America. This is a small container of explosive which is fixed to the rail surface, and explodes noisily on being run over. Such audible signals are used by train crews protecting their train in the case of an unexpected and lengthy stop between signals. Also, especially in England, they are used as fog signals, being placed either by hand or by a signal-box controlled machine, at distant signals showing the Caution indication.

Communication from the locomotive crew to the operators has traditionally been less developed. On busy lines a telephone is often provided at stop signals to provide a link with the signalman or operator. Two-way radio, which can link the locomotive crew not only with controllers but also with other members of the train crew, is also in use. Only on a very few railways, with a simple operating pattern, has a radio block system been instituted. On-train radio can facilitate one-man operation (omo) of trains which is perhaps why its introduction has not everywhere been received enthusiastically.

The locomotive whistle was one way for a locomotive crew to make signals. In Britain, the advent of modernisation has attenuated this practice, although the warning blast is still utilised. In steam days the latter was one long blast, and was used both as a warning and as a means of attracting attention; a characteristic use was by a locomotive held at a stop signal and wishing to draw the signalman's attention to the situation. Where visibility or other circumstances make accidents to men working on the line a possibility, or in other situations of potential danger, there is a permanent requirement for approaching trains to whistle. In most countries a lineside sign, typically bearing the initial letter of the local word for whistle or sound whistle (in England 'W' or 'SW', 'S' in France, and so on) is placed at these locations. With steam traction, in Britain, a short blast served to acknowledge a signal (as, for example, when a signal holding a train was cleared) and also, in trains without continuous brake, to request the guard to release the brakevan brakes. To apply the latter, three short blasts were sounded. Dangers or emergencies were signalled by a series of short blasts. In the USA, whistle codes are more complex and more firmly established. The following are the most common:

US railroads' standard whistle codes

One short	Apply brakes
Two short	Acknowledgement of signal
Three short	Stopping at next station; or (when train already stopped) about to back
Four short	Signal required
Four long	Approaching stations, junctions, level (grade) crossings
One long two short	Second section of train is following
One long three short	Flagman to protect rear of train
Two long	Brakes to be released and train to proceed
Four long or five long	Flagman to return to train
Series of short	Warning to people on track ahead

These are to be distinguished from the bellcord signals from the conductor of a US passenger train to the locomotive crew, of which the most used code is two short, which signifies Proceed when the train is standing and Stop when it is moving.

British-style signal indications

Because of the dominant role of the British in railway building in the 19th century, the British style of semaphore signals was, and in some cases remains, the standard in many countries. Such countries included not only territories of the British Empire, but other nations with large railway networks, Belgium and the Argentine being conspicuous examples. There were local variations in the design of signals, and indeed different railway administrations inside Britain as well as in other countries introduced different styles; a railway might be recognised by the 'cut' of its signals. But there were certain fundamentals, one of which was the colour used for the facing surface of the signal arm. Another was the adoption of the concept of the 'distant' or Caution signal.

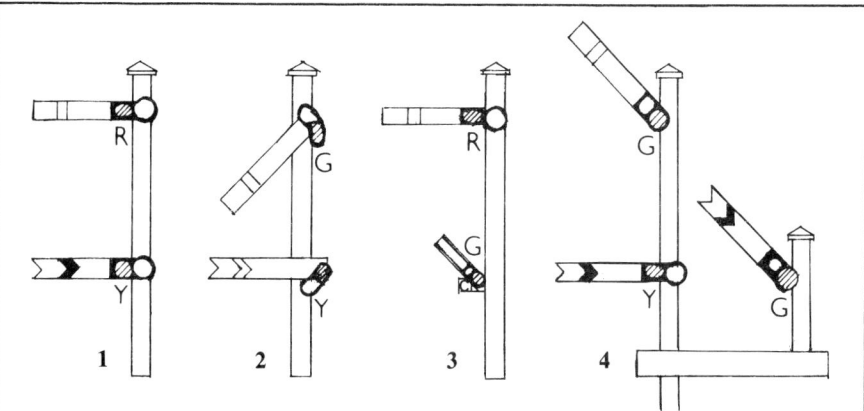

British semaphore signals. 1 *Upper-quadrant home and distant signals, both at danger.* **2** *Lower-quadrant home (clear) and distant (danger) signals, the indication being Line Clear but only up to the end of the block section.* **3** *Upper-quadrant home signal at danger, with small calling-on signal cleared.* **4** *A bracket signal carrying 'splitting distants' beneath a home signal. The indication of this upper-quadrant array is Line Clear, with the right-hand diverging line clear at the following junction.*

Whereas the Stop signal was red, with a white band on its facing surface (and usually white and black on its rear face), the distant signal was yellow and black on its facing surface, and showed a yellow or green light at night. Originally such signals were red and white, with red and green spectacles, and they were distinguished by a fishtail (V-notched) outer end. This notched end was retained after the yellow and black colouring was adopted. The purpose of a distant signal is to give advance notice of the Stop signal which controls entry to the following block section. In other words, it usually repeats the aspect of the next Stop signal. Faster and heavier trains made this development necessary, because drivers could no longer sight the stop signal sufficiently far away to bring their train to a halt without overrunning it. In foggy countries like Britain, this was especially important. The essential message of the distant signal, when in the 'on' (danger) position, is that the train must be ready to halt at the next Stop signal. Since this implies a speed reduction, the 'fixed distant' signal also came into use. This had an unpivoted arm, which was therefore always at danger, and served to give notice of permanent speed reduction, as in the approach to a terminus.

Where a line divides, the signals protecting the junction provide separate arms for each route, the arms for the main route being placed on the highest post, and the arms for the diverging route being placed lower down and to the appropriate side of the main line arms. Signal arrangements of this type are known as bracket or 'splitting' signals. Occasionally 'splitting signals' are dispensed with; a route indicator, with changing letter codes to indicate the route which has been cleared, is used instead. Very occasionally, the arms of a junction signal are mounted not side by side, but one above the other, the topmost set relating to the main line.

Stop signals in Britain are described as starters when they control the entry to

the next block section, and as home signals when they control the approach to the starter. A small signal-box, which merely controls the end of a block section and has no local complications like crossovers and sidings, may have simply one starter and its distant signal for each direction, but more complex signal-boxes may have outer and inner home signals, and an advanced starter supplementing the starter. This enables more than one train to be held on the line, and for localised train movements to take place.

It is standard practice to maintain a safety margin, or clearing distance, of about 400 metres (1,300 ft) beyond a home signal, in case an approaching train should overrun the latter; the provision of an outer home preserves this safety margin while enabling, for example, a shunting movement to take place on the section protected by the inner home. Naturally, a distant signal may only give a clear indication when the corresponding starter (or advanced starter if provided) is clear, irrespective of the indication of the home signals.

Signals for movements within station limits, typically shunting signals, cannot resemble the main signal types because this could mislead the crews of approaching through trains. Hence an array of different ground or dwarf signals has been evolved, together with some modifications to main signals which so change their shape as to avoid confusion. Taking the latter first, a red semaphore signal with a large white 'S' fixed close to its tip signifies Shunt Ahead; when in the off position this enabled a train or locomotive to draw forward beyond the stop signal in order to move back in a shunting movement. Nowadays a small semaphore, painted longitudinally with a central white stripe, sandwiched between upper and lower red bands is used for Shunt Ahead (in which case a small letter 'S' is shown), or for Calling On (with a small letter 'C'). Calling-on is used when it is desired to allow a train to draw up immediately behind another so that, for example, two trains can stand at one platform face.

Left *Thornton Junction, Scotland, with a bracket signal indicating Line Clear for the next two blocks over the principal (non-divergent) route.*

Right *A dwarf shunting disc in the 'off' position, as a locomotive runs round its train on a Southern Region branch of BR in the 1960s* (M. Deane).

For controlling movements over crossovers or across running lines to gain access to yards and sidings, several British companies favoured dwarf semaphore arms, mounted close to the ground. Some of these are still in use, but a modern version now predominates. This is a white rotating disc on which is pointed a representation of a red semaphore arm. In a complex location, several may be needed to cover each diverging route; where possible they are then placed side by side, but often limited space means that they are placed one above the other, reading downwards from left to right so that, for example, the bottom disc refers to the extreme right-hand route. Shunting discs which are painted black with a yellow 'arm' may be passed at danger by a train which is merely moving to a siding or head-shunt. Only when the train is about to move so as to obstruct the running line must this signal be cleared before the train passes it.

Repeater signals are extra arms which enable locomotive crews to obtain a better view of the signal indication. A common example is the provision of an extra-tall post on which one set of arms is mounted at a great height so as to be visible from a distance, while another set of arms, moving in unison with the upper arms, may be seen conveniently from a close distance. A modern variant is the banner signal, a pivoted black arm, mounted in a glass-fronted circular box. Usually this is placed some way to the rear of the signal it is repeating. In a few cases, usually in stations, these banner signals take the place of conventional stop signals.

British colourlight signals are of the multi-lens type usually, and equip about half of the British Rail mileage. For many signals just two aspects are required, corresponding to the Stop and Clear or the Caution and Clear indications of semaphore signals. On lines where there is a heavy traffic and trains, because of speed or weight, may have very different braking distances, four-aspect signals are used. Colourlights which provide three or more aspects are usually known as

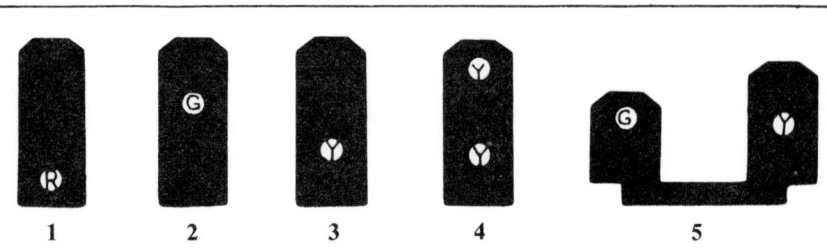

British colourlight signals. *4-aspect signals indicating* **1** *Stop.* **2** *Line Clear.* **3** *Caution.* **4** *Advance Caution. 3-aspect signals are similar but lack the double yellow Advance Caution.* **5** *The colourlight equivalent of the splitting distant. The indication is Line Clear for a left-hand divergence at the following junction.*

multi-aspect, within a multi-aspect system, abbreviated to 'mas' in Britain. The indications are as follows:

Red	Stop
Single yellow	The next signal is red
Double yellow	The next signal is single yellow
Green	Line clear at least for next two blocks

On routes with a regular High Speed Train service, a new variant, the flashing yellow, may be occasionally seen. This is placed before diverging junctions where a speed restriction is in force over only one of the two possible routes; the double yellow aspect in the approach to the junction is ambiguous, but since both interpretations lead to a conventional train slowing down this is not important. But an HST driver might slow down in good time for one interpretation (a single yellow at the junction followed by the next signal at red along the higher speed route), but not in time for the second (a divergence to the slower speed route, which would not be made clear until the route indicator at the junction signal became visible).

Route indicators often replace the indications provided by the positioning of semaphore signals at stations and junctions. There are two main types. The 'theatre' type is a screen fitted to the signal post on which an appropriate letter is illuminated to indicate the route to be taken. This is more suitable for lines where speeds are not high. For fast-moving trains the easier-to-read directional type is better suited. This consists of one or more rows of white lights placed above the colourlight head. These lights point to the right or left, whichever is appropriate, and are inclined at 45 degrees, (also at 90 and 135 degrees if there is more than one diverging line). These indicators remain unilluminated if the route is set for the main line.

In colourlight areas the ground signals may include miniature colourlight types (two lenses, showing red or white) and also position-light signals. Equivalent to the old-pattern shunting disc is a three-light installation showing red and white lights, horizontally placed, in the 'on' position and two whites, diagonally, for 'off'. The yellow shunting disc is replaced by a similar signal, having a yellow instead of red light. A miniature yellow light exhibited below a colour-light head permits movement into a loop or siding outside the block

Signals

system. A calling-on indication may be provided by a rotating disc bearing the letter 'C' and floodlit at night, or a dwarf position-light with a letter 'C' displayed; both these may be fixed to a signal post beneath the colourlight head.

The signal post in Britain may carry additional information provided by fixed plates. One plate normally carries the signal's identification number. The preceding letters of this may indicate the district or, if an A, may indicate that the signal is automatic. A lozenge-shaped plate, both in semaphore and colourlight territory, indicates that the line is track-circuited, or the presence of the train is otherwise obvious to the signalmen and the crew of a train halted by that signal are freed from the rule (Rule K3) that they must report their presence to the signal-box after two minutes. A rectangular plate with one end rounded and containing a circle indicates that there is a telephone or plunger connected with the signal-box for the purpose of Rule K3. A rectangular white plate with a horizontal black central band indicates a semi-automatic signal, but a similar plate, fixed vertically, shows that the signal is an intermediate block signal.

The underground lines in London use a system generally similar to that of the main line railways, although there are local variations. Two-lens heads are usual, with red and green for the stop signals and yellow and green for the

Below left *British Rail AWS ramp.*

Below right *A British Rail bracket signal. The main heads are 3-aspect, and dwarf shunting signals, usually at ground level, have been mounted alongside. A 'theatre' type route indicator is above the right-hand colourhead.*

distant, or 'repeater' signals. Sometimes both are mounted in one installation with four lenses; among other things, this means that a double green is commonly shown.

Locomotive cab-signalling was pioneered by the Great Western Railway, contributing to that company's fine safety record. The GWR system, however, was abandoned by British Rail. The BR system, derived from an inductive apparatus developed but little-used by the LMS Railway, is operated by a small magnetic installation placed between the rails. When the distant signal is 'on' the permanent magnet causes the locomotive siren and brake to act, but in a Line Clear situation a second (electro) magnet cancels the action of the permanent magnet to give the appropriate bell signal in the cab. There is also a visual presentation, which changes to black on passing a caution signal and to yellow and black when the driver presses the resetting button to silence the siren and cancel the brake application.

Two books giving more detail on British signalling are O. S. Nock's *British Railway Signalling* (1965) and *British Railway Signalling* (1978) by G. M. Kitchenside and A. Williams.

France

In France, the formation of French National Railways in the 1930s coincided with a standardisation of signalling, hitherto subject to the variations imposed by the different companies. What was decided then, in connection with mechanical signals, also determined the manner of use of the subsequent colourlight signals.

French mechanical signals. The signals for both approaching tracks are cleared. The three signals controlling the nearest track are, from left to right: lozenge board (yellow with black and white border, single yellow or single green light at night), indicating that the following stop signal is cleared; semaphore signal (Permissive Stop), showing Line Clear; red and white Absolute Stop chequerboard, likewise showing Line Clear, being turned edge-on towards the approaching train.

Signals

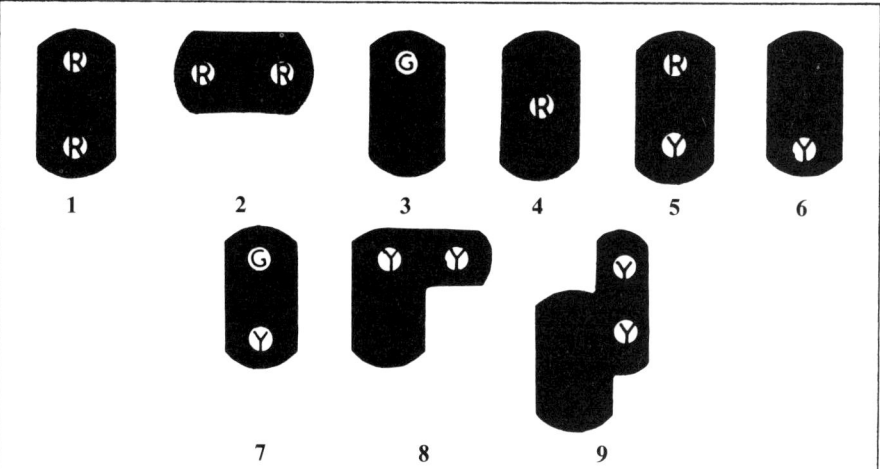

French running signals. 1 *and* **2** *Absolute Stop.* **3** *Clear.* **4** *Permissive Stop (corresponding to semaphore).* **5** *Proceed Slowly, prepare to stop at signal box controlling this signal (corresponding to red disc mechanical signal).* **6** *Next Stop signal (Permissive or Absolute) is at Danger.* **7** *Advance Warning (that is, the following signal is showing yellow).* **8** *Speed restriction over deviating line.* **9** *Speed restriction reminder (located just ahead of switch set for diverging route). These last two signals show a single green when the direct, non-diverging, route is set.*

In brief, on French lines still not equipped with colourlights, there are several forms of stop signal. Red lower-quadrant semaphore arms protect the entry to block sections. These, in certain circumstances, can be cautiously passed when at danger. At night they show conventional red and green lights. For the so-called Absolute Stop, used when a collison might ensue if passed at danger (as, for example, where lines beyond the signal intersect) a board signal is used. This is a square red-and-white chequerboard which faces the oncoming train when at Stop and is pivoted to present its virtually invisible edge to show Line Clear. At night it shows two red lights or a single green. A third Stop signal is the so-called Deferred Stop. This is a rotating circular board, painted red, which at night shows a yellow and red light side by side, or a single green. When showing the Stop aspect (that is, the board facing the oncoming train) it requires the driver to proceed cautiously up to the signal-box which controls the signal. There are two types of Caution signal, the warning (or distant) signal which is a lozenge-shaped yellow board pivoting in the same way as the Absolute Stop board, and showing a yellow or green light. Then there is the speed restriction signal, placed before a junction or crossover where a speed restriction to 30 km/h (19 mph) is required. This is a yellow triangular board, which is pivoted to present just its edge to trains proceeding along the main line and not subject to the speed restriction. This board, which is bordered in black, is apex-down, and is situated just before the junction. However, it has a warning signal, placed well before the junction, which is a similar triangle placed apex-upwards. The latter shows two yellow lights side by side, or a single green, whereas the former shows two yellow lights one above the other. When there is more than one mechanical signal on a post, the most important one is placed lower. 30 kph is the standard speed for negotiating a diverging line; where the junction permits a higher speed, speed restriction boards (TIV) are used. With these the warning board is lozenge-shaped with a black number on a white background while that at the start of the speed restricted-sector is square with white figures on a black background. In France, signals controlling movements within station limits (which in Britain are effected by dwarf and ground signals) are made by square pivoting boards, painted violet with a thin white border; at night these show a violet light for Stop and a lunar white light for Line Clear.

With colourlight signals, the French indications are the same as the night aspects of the mechanical signals. The advance warning signal, not provided by the older regulations, and corresponding to the British double-yellow, is given by a green-over-yellow aspect, requiring a speed reduction to be achieved before reaching the following distant signal, and a single green for Clear. Since two lights side by side are required in some situations, the shape of the French colourlight heads may be that of an inverted 'L'. But a quite common installation is the four-aspect head, with the lights in a vertical arrangement and with the top light being a small red, which shows together with the main red to indicate Absolute Stop; this configuration cannot show the double yellow aspects, for which a different design is required.

On the French high-speed TGV line, with three sections regarded as the standard stopping distance, a system of conventional colourlight signals was rejected, not because the high speed would have made them less visible, but because the train driver would have had to remember too many indications in too short a time; conventional signals, after all, have to be memorised because once passed they cannot be looked at again. Cab signalling was therefore

Left *SNCF colourlight signals at the Gare de Lyon, Paris. The Z boards indicate the beginning of a speed-restricted zone (the end of such a zone is marked by an R board). See text for explanation of NF boards.*

Right *The French 'crocodile' AWS ramp.*

adopted for this line. There are no lineside signals, although square blue boards with yellow triangles mark the divisions between block sections.

A small white light to be seen below the main indicators of French signals has an important qualifying role. On signals carrying an Nf plate, one red light is taken as Absolute Stop if the white light is extinguished, and as Permissive Stop if the white light is showing. With signals carrying an 'F' plate, the single red is Permissive Stop; that is, the 'F' shows that the colourlight is equivalent to a semaphore rather than to a chequerboard signal.

The French railways were somewhat retarded in their application of advance warning systems. They did have a system resembling the Great Western Railway's device, but this did not produce an automatic application of the brakes, should the locomotive crew ignore the cab whistle which signalled a distant signal at danger. However, even before the end of steam traction, electric and diesel locomotives were equipped with this automatic braking facility, opening the way to a relatively modern system after steam locomotives had been withdrawn. In this system the old method of actuation is still used. It consists of a ramp placed between the rails at distant signals; this is known to railway workers as the 'crocodile', thanks to its distinctive shape. A plunger beneath the locomotive brushes this ramp, and picks up the latter's electrical indication. For many decades French locomotives have been fitted with the 'Flaman' permanent speed recorder; this traces speeds continuously on a moving paper roll, which is examined after each trip to ensure, among other things, that speed limits have not been exceeded. With modern versions of this machine a mark is made on the trace when the locomotive driver pulls a lever to signify his notice of a distant signal at caution. This mark should precede the mark which is automatically inscribed on the trace through the 'crocodile' placed at the distant signal itself.

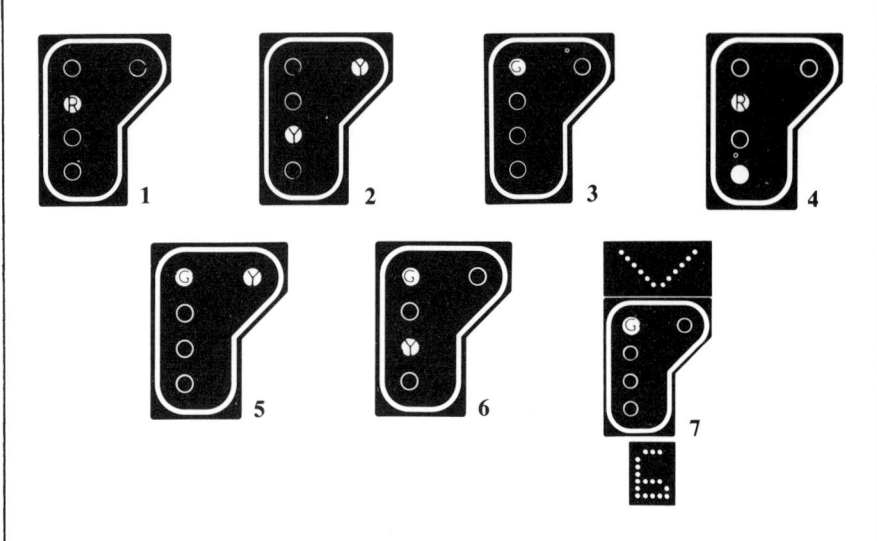

Belgian running signals. 1 *Stop.* **2** *Caution.* **3** *Line Clear (following signal also clear).* **4** *(Red over white): Proceed slowly and prepare to stop at sight of preceding train.* **5** *The following signal is clear but requires a speed restriction.* **6** *The following signal is clear but a third signal closely following the latter is at Danger.* **7** *Here the illuminated chevron indicates that signals are in operation for wrong-line working (in which case they stand on the 'wrong' side of the track and the colour lights are of the flashing type); the lower panel indicates a speed restriction of 60 km/h* (SNCB).

Germany and central Europe

In Germany and central Europe there is a signalling system whose distinctiveness is said to reflect the German character. The Stop semaphore signal has a red arm which widens into a disc at the outer end. This is horizontal for 'on', raised 45 degrees for Clear, and shows a conventional red or green light. This signal, when placed before any point where a speed restriction may be necessary, has a second, lower, arm which hangs vertically, with no light, in the Clear position but is raised parallel to the upper arm and shows a yellow light when a speed restriction is required; the standard speed restriction is 40 km/h (25 mph).

Distant signals are amber discs with narrow black and white borders, which face the train when in the 'on' position and are raised and laid flat to give the Clear indication. Two diagonally-set green or amber lights provide the night indications. Most distant signals have a yellow pivoted pointer below the disc; this repeats the aspect of the lower arm of the following stop signal. When, therefore, the stop signal indicates Proceed at Reduced Speed the distant signal presents the yellow disc in the 'on' position with the pointer swung outwards diagonally. Distant signals are often provided with 'countdown' warning boards at 50, 150 and 250 metres in advance; these are white rectangles with diagonal black stripes.

The German equivalent of the British shunt signal, intended to control move-

Signals

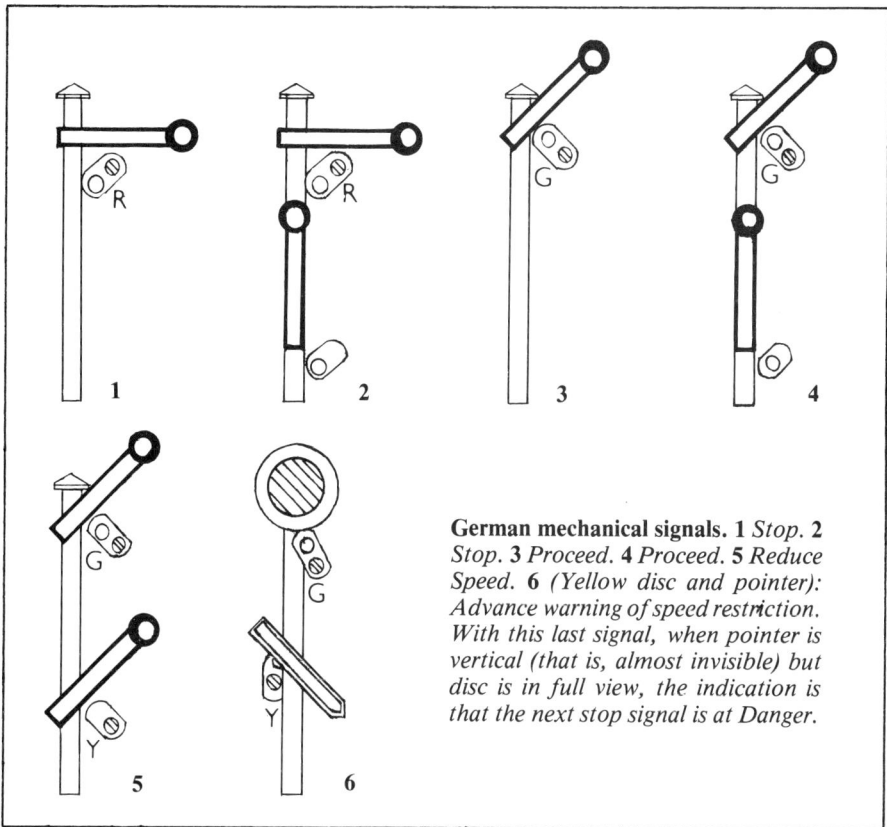

German mechanical signals. 1 *Stop.* **2** *Stop.* **3** *Proceed.* **4** *Proceed.* **5** *Reduce Speed.* **6** *(Yellow disc and pointer): Advance warning of speed restriction. With this last signal, when pointer is vertical (that is, almost invisible) but disc is in full view, the indication is that the next stop signal is at Danger.*

ments in yard or station limits, is a white disc with a black strip; the latter is normally horizontal and rotates to a diagonal position to indicate that the line is clear for a shunting movement.

Colourlight signals match the colour indications of the mechanical signals. To match the diagonal presentation of the distant signal lights, distant colourlight heads are mounted diagonally on the posts. Four-lens colourlight signals have, at the top left-hand indication, a red emergency light. This is normally out of use, being illuminated when the normal red light has failed for some reason. A special head is used for the Stop-Shunting Prohibited indication, which is shown by two red lights side by side. When shunting is allowed, this changes to one red and two diagonally set white lights, and the Proceed indication is given by a green or a green and amber combination. Route indications are presented by illuminated letters (often the initial letter of the main town served by the route in question). At stations the Right-Away signal, if provided, is a circle of green lights.

The German speed restriction indicator is a triangular board with a white digit on a black background; the required speed is the digit multiplied by ten. The modern version has the number portrayed by white lights.

The German railways employ several kinds of dwarf or ground signal, of which one is common throughout central Europe. This is the points and crossover signal, a black and white rectangular and rotating box, with a light inside.

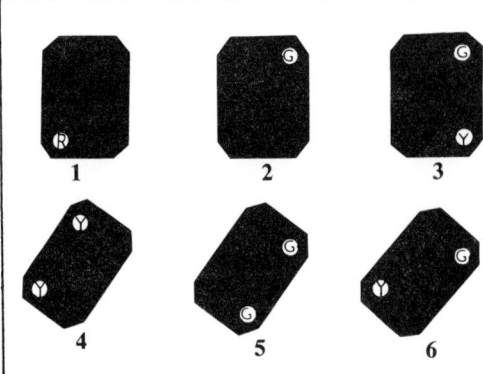

German colourlight signals. 1 *Stop.* **2** *Proceed.* **3** *Reduce Speed.* **4** *Prepare to stop at next signal.* **5** *Following signal is clear.* **6** *Next signal indicates speed restriction. On German rapid transit routes two-colourhead signals may be used, permitting different permutations of these indications.*

Below *German semaphore signals in operation. Such signals are still widely used in both West and East Germany, although heavy steam freight locomotives like the one shown here are now to be seen only in East Germany.*

A diagonal white arrow faces a train to indicate that the switch is set for a diverging movement; in this position the rear of the indicator shows a white circle. When the switch is set for the through routing a white rectangle shows at both front and rear. These signals are much more widely used in Germany than the corresponding disc signals in Britain; in particular, they are used within German freightyards at each set of switches, not just for the points giving access to the yard from the running lines.

The German AWS (cab-signalling) system is known as the Indusi system and is an inductive method. The fixed installation consists of two magnets under one cover and is placed on the sleepers outside the rails. Apart from this location, it is very similar to the British inductive equipment.

North America

Since the first decade of this century, the Association of American Railroads has been making efforts towards the standardisation of signalling rules and practices between the various American railways. However, complete success has not been achieved, and in fact was not expected. The following information refers to what is generally the situation in the USA; each railroad's employees' rulebook specifies its own interpretations and regulations, which sometimes may differ from the majority of railroads.

North American railways use both searchlight and multi-lens colourlight signals. With the latter, a vertical arrangement with green on top and red at the bottom is usual. However, the New York Central Railroad (now part of Conrail) used a triangular arrangement, while the Chicago & North Western and Reading railroads favoured a horizontal configuration. Another constituent of Conrail, the Pennsylvania Railroad, had a preference for the 'position-light' signal. This does not use colours; its circular head has eight lights around its edge, with a ninth in the centre. In use, this signal can present indications consisting of a line of three lights, whose positions conform to the positions of semaphore arms; since both upper- and lower-quadrant inclinations can be used, four aspects are possible. Additionally, the PRR on its electrified sections used a circle of lights (that is, all lights except the central one) to warn locomotive crews to lower their pantographs. There was also an X-shaped indication which signified Take Siding. An additional bar of three lights was sometimes placed beneath the head to provide the supplementary indications needed in interlocked territory.

The advantages of this type were that a single bulb failure did not incapacitate the signals, and the single colour could be yellow, which was best for fog penetration. Other eastern lines, notably the Norfolk & Western and the Lehigh Valley, also favoured this type of signal. A variant, used on the Baltimore & Ohio Railroad, had an eight-light main head, a supplementary marker light both above and below, and a coloured light alongside the upper marker.

Apart from differences between companies, North America signals are also distinguished by the fact that the same aspects may give different indications according to the type of train control in force on a given stretch of line. In particular, where signals and switches are interlocked by an interlocking tower (signal-box or control tower) the signals are different from ordinary block signals in their interpretation and are quite complex.

On train-order lines there are semaphore signals which do not, however,

US three-position upper-quadrant signals. One of the arms has presented all three positions during the time-exposure used to make this picture (Association of American Railroads).

directly convey any right to occupy a track. These are provided at the operators' offices which are usually located at stations. They are three-position upper-quadrant semaphores, with one post usually carrying the arms for both directions of traffic. When the relevant arm is vertical (showing a green light at night), approaching enginemen know that there is no train order to be picked up at this point and can proceed at normal speed. When the arm is at 45 degrees (yellow) a Form 19 train order has to be picked up. Form 19 is for orders whose non-observance would not lead to an accident and they do not, therefore, have to be signed for. The train may therefore proceed, picking up the order without stopping ('on the fly'). Form 31 train orders, which typically restrict the normal rights of the train to which they are addressed, have to be signed for. The train must therefore stop and the semaphore conveys this by a horizontal position of the arm and a red light.

Surviving semaphore signals in manual block territory are mainly of the three-aspect semaphore type. In these, stop signals are usually red with a black band. When vertical they show a green light and signify Line Clear. At 45 degrees, with a yellow light, they convey that the block ahead is occupied but, so long as freight trains only are involved, the train may proceed into the block, prepared to stop when the preceding train is sighted. In a horizontal position, showing red, the indication is that the next block is occupied but the train may, after stopping at the signal, proceed into the block under the protection of a flagman. The corresponding distant signal is usually yellow and shows a green light when vertical and a yellow light when it is repeating the 45 degrees of its stop signal. It is also at 45 degrees when the stop signal is horizontal.

In automatic block territory the same signals serve both as stop and distant indications; being three-position they can be used in the same way as three-aspect colourlight signals (in the few surviving cases where two-aspect lower-quadrant semaphores are still in use, a separate distant arm is carried beneath the stop signal). A vertical arm (green light) shows that the next and the following blocks are clear, a 45 degree arm (yellow) signifies that the next block is unoccupied but the train must be prepared to stop at the next signal, protecting entry to the following block, which is occupied. The latter signal, until such time as the preceding train leaves it, will be horizontal and red, signifying that the approaching train must stop and wait; it may then proceed slowly, under flag protection. Thus there is no real Absolute Stop under this system. Moreover, where gradients are steep, or loads heavy, trains may be permitted to pass the Stop signal without halting, providing speed is adequately reduced. Most railroads fit a circular plate on the signal post with a letter 'G' or 'P' to indicate where this concession operates.

Block signals generally have only the Permissive Stop, whereas the signals employed in an interlocked area include the Absolute Stop. Since the same signals are used, Permissive Stop signals are usually differentiated by providing arms with pointed blades, and marker lights in a diagonal configuration lower down on the post. Where semaphores are used in interlocked territory, they are typically mounted with three arms to the post, corresponding to the three-light colourlight signals. In either case each of the three arms or three lights is used as part of each message. The signals, which are designed to show the required speed for the chosen route, rather than to indicate the route itself, can show a wide range of indications. With position-light signals, the required number of aspects is obtained by the addition of secondary lights below the main head, and sometimes additionally by a triangular metal plate in yellow or silver. Lunar white marker lights above or below the main head serve the same purpose where two-aspect colourlights are in use.

Dwarf, or ground, signals are often encountered in interlocked territory. When employed as calling-on signals (corresponding to red over red over yellow), they present two white or lunar white diagonal lights. For the Slow Clear indication (two white lights arranged vertically), dwarf signals are probably more often used than high signals.

Locomotive cab signalling (Advance Warning System) in the USA is similar in principle to that of other countries, with an automatic application of brakes should the locomotive crew ignore the visual and audible signals provided in the cab. The inductive system is used with the track equipment consisting of an inductor bolted to the cross-ties outside the rail. The locomotive's receiver is usually mounted on a journal box, so as to pass over the inductor with a clearance of 1–2 in (25–50 mm). Inside the cab, a visual indication is presented either by miniature colourlights or by three-bulb position lights. A locomotive with increasing mileage is now fitted with continuous coded inductive cab-signalling, in which the signal received, picked up from the rails, is continually displayed and shows the condition (that is, the appropriate speed) for the block in which the train is moving. However, in unsignalled territory, the indication relates to the block immediately ahead of the train.

Chapter 9

The measurement of locomotives

The purpose of the locomotive designer is to create machines which will haul trains of a prescribed weight at prescribed speeds, while not exceeding the limitations of locomotive weight and size imposed by the lines on which they are to run. The compromise by which these conflicting requirements are satisfied should not ideally impose heavier costs; that is, the locomotive should not be unduly expensive to build, nor should it consume an excessive value of energy nor demand excessive maintenance. To a certain extent, and especially in the steam age, the selection of an appropriate wheel arrangement could ease this problem of meeting conflicting demands, but in the past decade or so it is technological progress which has enabled successively more demanding specifications to be met. Nevertheless it is capacity and size which remain the key statistics of a locomotive design, and it is measures of these which always figure prominently in tabulated descriptions of locomotives.

Measures of capacity

There are two measures of a locomotive's haulage capacity. Tractive effort is a measure of the load that can be pulled, while horsepower measures the amount of effort, or work, the locomotive can achieve.

Tractive effort The American term *drawbar pull* gives perhaps a better idea of what tractive effort means. It is the strain, measured in pounds, exerted on the coupling of the leading vehicle behind the locomotive. It tends to decrease as speeds increase, but the tractive effort/speed curve is of different shape for steam and non-steam locomotives. The steam locomotive cannot exert its maximum tractive effort at speeds over about 7 mph (10 km/h). The tractive effort figure given as part of a steam locomotive's specification is its maximum effort. Since maximum effort is required when starting a train, this figure does in fact determine the weight of train that a given locomotive may handle. It may be measured by formula or by taking actual measurements in road tests.

It might be noted that the formula ignores the effect of the weight of the locomotive itself, calculating the tractive effort at the wheel rim rather than at the coupling, which means that it is slightly in excess of the latter value, the drawbar pull. However, this discrepancy is masked by the lack of precision which the formula provides in any case, due to the impossibility of knowing exactly the loss in steam pressure which takes place between the boiler and the cylinder. To allow for this drop it is usual to use not the full boiler pressure, but 85 per cent

The measurement of locomotives

of the pressure, when calculating the tractive effort (75 per cent when the locomotive is not superheated). The formula is this:

$$\text{Tractive effort (lb)} = \frac{D^2 \times S \times P \times N}{2W}$$

where D is the cylinder diameter in inches; S is the stroke of the cylinder in inches; P is 85 or 75 per cent of the boiler pressure in pounds per square inch; N is the number of cylinders; and W is the diameter of the driving wheels in inches.

Electric locomotives are more limited than the steam locomotive in that they cannot exert their maximum tractive effort at slow speeds for long periods because their traction motors overheat in these conditions. Their tractive effort at different speeds may be obtained by a rearrangement of the formula given below for determining horsepower; this formula can also be used to determine the tractive effort of steam locomotives, but with some difficulty because of the problems of arriving at a steam locomotive's horsepower.

Horsepower This is the best general measure of maximum performance as it takes into account both tractive effort and speed. The formula for horsepower exerted at the wheel tread is as follows:

$$\text{Horsepower} = \frac{TE \times V}{375}$$

where TE is the tractive effort (lb) and V is the speed in mph.

With diesel and electric locomotives, it is possible to obtain the theoretical horsepower using engine, motor and transmission data, without recourse to tractive effort. The figures thus arrived at may be termed the *rated horsepower*. With steam locomotives, where so much is dependent on the amount and condition of the steam reaching the cylinders, the taking of actual measurements during tests is really needed. Momentary achievement of very high horsepower can, of course, be registered by a steam locomotive, but what is important is the sustained horsepower output; that is, the horsepower which can be produced without exceeding the boiler's steam-raising capacity. Similarly, with electric locomotives, a distinction has to be made between short-term and long-term outputs.

It is conventional to provide an *hourly rating* and a *continuous rating*. The former is the horsepower which can be exerted for one hour without a dangerous heating of the traction motors, whereas the latter is the work which can be performed without the heat produced in the traction motors ever outpacing the cooling provided by the ventilation. Diesel-electric locomotives produce little-changing horsepower over a wide speed range, the HP finally dropping at speeds above about 50 mph (80 km/h). In this they differ from steam locomotives, whose HP is low at slow speeds but will then rise in accordance with the speed and the size of driving wheel; the bigger the wheel the higher the speed at which HP begins to fall.

The term *brake horsepower* (BHP), sometimes encountered in reference to diesel engines, describes the engine performance at the output flange itself and exceeds the *indicated horsepower* (IHP) of the engine by the amount of power required to drive the engine's injection and water pumps and overcome certain frictions. It should be noted that neither the BHP nor the IHP indicate the power of the locomotive in which the engine is installed. In the case of the diesel-electric locomotive, there are generator losses to be absorbed and moreover by no means all the generator output is available for traction purposes. There is the locomotive's own auxilliary equipment to be powered and, in the case of passenger trains, lighting and heating systems to be provided for. Generator efficiency is about 95 per cent, and traction motor efficiency 86 per cent (both figures covering the appropriate cable losses too).

The official horsepower rating of British diesel locomotives is the diesel engine output, whereas the American rating is the horsepower available to the generator for traction use. This means that an American 2,000 hp diesel locomotive has an engine of about 2,250 hp, but a British 2,000 hp unit has a 2,000 hp engine.

A low speed with high tractive effort, and a high speed with low tractive effort, represent the same horsepower. High speed and high tractive effort together require a high horsepower. It is possible to determine a locomotive's tractive horsepower output (*drawbar horsepower*) from its performance over a given length of route, but great care has to be taken in determining the main ingredient of such a calculation, the *tractive resistance*. This resistance is a combination of train weight, gradient and speed with the less easily-measured values for wind resistance and the *rolling resistance* appropriate to the particular design of rolling stock being hauled. As a matter of interest, a following wind represents a 'free gift' of substantial horsepower while a head wind represents the opposite. Side winds increase train resistance by driving the wheel flanges against the rail edges, so the worst kind of wind is one which is obliquely opposed. Obviously wind strength is hard to measure, and a good deal of knowledge is required to arrive at rolling resistance. Some useful hints for the amateur are to be found in *Railway World* (August 1973) and *Modern Railways* (July 1977).

With electric locomotives, it is common for power output to be expressed in hourly and continuous *kilowatts*. Kilowatts are convertible to horsepower by multiplying by the factor 1.341 (or 1.3597 to obtain metric HP).

Whereas the maximum horsepower of a diesel locomotive can be closely calculated, being limited by the horsepower of the diesel engine, the maximum horsepower of a steam locomotive varies according to circumstances. However, the size of the *grate area* is a useful guide to steam-raising capacity, as it determines the rate at which fuel can be converted into energy. Total heating surface is another indication of boiler capacity. It includes those walls of the firebox in contact with water, and the heating surfaces provided by the tubes. Unlike the grate area, it does not determine the combustion rate. In the case of line-service locomotives, the superheater surface, or the designed temperature of the superheated steam, provides an indication of how effectively the steam will be used. Electric locomotives are less predictable than is sometimes thought, for they depend on an external power source; voltage drops in the conductor wire can occur, especially when hardworkng locomotives are in close proximity, and the efficiency of the pantograph in collecting the current may drop at high speeds.

Adhesion This is the grip of the rails upon the rail surface, preventing wheel slippage when power is applied. In practice there is minuscule slipping (creep) whenever there is tractive effort, but it is the perceptible slipping which causes concern. Not only does it prevent the realisation of the locomotive's nominal tractive effort, but it can also inflict wear and tear on rails and wheels. The condition of the rail surface is crucial, the adhesion of a wet or greasy rail being much less than that of a dry rail, while an accumulation of wet leaves has been known to bring trains to a standstill. In India trains have been brought to a halt and robbed by means of grease applied to the rails on gradients.

The measurement of locomotives

The *adhesion factor*, which indicates a locomotive's resistance to slipping, is calculated by dividing the tractive effort into the weight carried on the driving wheels. However, the smoothness of the impulses transmitted through the driving wheel is important. A 2-cylinder steam locomotive has a particularly variable thrust because the leverage exerted by the connecting rods varies as the wheel (more precisely, the crank) changes position, and this is not smoothed out as it is in the case of 3- or 4-cylinder locomotives. The suspension also plays a role and it is often the case that a locomotive designed for smooth riding at high speed will experience a transfer of weight from the driving wheels to the carrying wheels when exerting its maximum tractive effort; this is why the British Pacific passenger locomotives seemed so prone to slipping, when compared to the Great Western Railway's corresponding locomotives, which had a wheel arrangement which excluded a carrying axle at the rear end. Another reason for GWR superiority in this respect was the provision of a regulator which was less stiff, and hence more finely adjustable to match tractive effort with the rail conditions.

Weight transfer is also experienced with electric and diesel locomotives, a common result being wheelslip in the rear driving wheels but not in the forward wheels. Traditionally locomotives are provided with rail sanding gear to improve adhesion temporarily. But this is no longer a favoured solution, given the deleterious effect of sand; as an alternative or supplement, various types of wheelslip detectors are used. A simple device relied on the detection of differences in voltages across the traction motors but, recently, electronic devices have been introduced which, typically, count gear wheel teeth and instantly check whether the gear wheel rotation speed thus arrived at is the same for each axle, and whether the axles are accelerating at an unnatural rate. Action taken when wheelslip is indicated can be a driver's readjustment of power (ideally a cut in power followed by an edging upwards) or an automatic reduction in tractive effort exerted by just the axles which are slipping.

A short-wheelbase locomotive, designed for shunting on the tightly-curved lines of Swansea docks.

With steam locomotives, designers aimed at an adhesion factor of about 4.0 for a 2-cylinder locomotive and 3.5 for 3- or 4-cylinder. Freight locomotives were expected to have slightly higher factors. Before the introduction of thyristor control, which provides exceptionally smooth turning motion (torque), electric and diesel locomotives were expected to have a factor of 3–3.5

Locomotive testing Locomotive testing is designed to arrive at a practical assessment of what a locomotive can do, as opposed to its theoretical performance. Ideally, too, testing procedures can vary one factor while holding the others constant, thereby obtaining insight into the behaviour of the varied factor. Varying inputs, while maintaining a constant power output, is a basic approach. Testing may be done on the line, or in stationary testing plants. Both kinds of testing were pioneered in Russia, but it was an American, Professor Goss, who built the first (1891) full-size locomotive testing plant. In England, the GWR built a plant at Swindon, and a much larger one was later opened at Rugby by British Railways in 1948. A French plant was opened at Vitry in 1934 and notable American plants were installed at the University of Illinois and by the Pennsylvannia Railroad at Altoona. The principle of these plants is that the locomotive driving wheels rotate on rollers which enable the locomotive to remain stationary while providing variable resistance as loading.

With line-testing, it is customary to place a *dynamometer car* behind the locomotive. This measures, among other things, tractive effort. It is also possible to measure the actual steam pressure on the pistons by means of a small instrument which produces a tracing known as the *indicator diagram*. In such tests the technicians riding at the front of the locomotive may be provided with a temporary structure known as the *indicator shelter*.

Characteristically, testing has been very much involved with steaming rates and boiler efficiency, but not exclusively so. At the close of the steam era, testing by the Western Region of British Railways was concerned largely with draughting and exhaust arangements, and revealed that large economies of coal consumption, with increased horsepowers, could be obtained with a redesign of the front ends of many British steam locomotives.

Measures of size

Locomotive weights are usually given as *weight in working order*. With a steam locomotive this can be significantly greater than the empty weight. It is customary to include the tender in the total weight. Diesel locomotives also carry fuel and water and are similarly, though to a lesser degree, affected. From the point of view of the civil engineer, the total weight of a locomotive is crucial, in particular, when it crosses bridges whose spans are of greater length than the locomotive; the full weight is then borne by the span and produces a deflection which must be kept within determined limits.

However, *axle weight* is regarded as more limiting than total weight. It is the share of the total weight which falls on the most heavily loaded axle, although in practice designers strive at least to equalise the weights carried by the driving axles. It is axle weight, above all, which determines the stress inflicted on the rails, and it is not without its significance for bridgework. In practice, railway administrations classify their routes according to the weights they can bear, with many secondary routes barred to the heavier types of locomotive. In the steam age, British locomotives were limited to a maximum of about 22 tons of axle weight and such locomotives were confined to the main lines. Continental limits were similar but, in America, some lines could take 30-ton axle loads. Civil engineers took a more generous view of 3- and 4-cylinder steam locomotives because these imposed lower *hammerblow* values on the track; hammerblow can be generally described as the successive downward thrusts as the reciprocating masses (connecting rods, piston assemblies) hit the limits of their travel.

Locomotive balancing, which sought to compensate for the surges caused by rotating and reciprocating masses by putting one against the other and by fitting counterbalancing masses (usually to the driving wheels), made great advances in the 20th century but could only palliate an unavoidable phenomenon. It was thought that diesel and electric locomotives, without reciprocating parts, would be easier on the track than steam locomotives, but in fact the stresses imparted by traction motors suspended (that is, unsprung) or partly suspended on the axles was more deleterious than had been anticipated. With modern traction and high speeds, unsprung weight, axleweight and speed are all important. Because powerful locomotives are heavy, the horsepower required by high-speed trains is best provided by multiple-unit, rather than by locomotive-hauled formations. Finally, it is worth remarking that actual weights have often been different from design weights, due to the accumulation of small errors in design or construction.

Because of overhang on curved track, the length of a locomotive to some extent may determine the permissible width. Width limitation, preventing the use of very large cylinders, was one of the restrictions hampering locomotive designers in the final decades of steam traction. The length of a locomotive is sometimes given as the extreme length, usually termed *length over buffers* or *length over couplers*, and sometimes as *length of wheelbase* or *length of rigid wheelbase*. The extreme length is important in relation to fixed structures, especially the need to ensure that a locomotive is not too long to be handled in workshops and in locomotive depots.

The length of the wheelbase, which measures the distance between the centres of the leading and trailing wheels, is important in determining the minimum radius of curve which can be passed, while the rigid wheelbase, measuring the distance between wheel centres of coupled wheels in a steam engine unit or in a power truck of a diesel or electric locomotive, gives an indication of how much rail grinding will occur on a curve and is another index of the locomotive's ability to take curved track. Locomotives intended for dockyard work usually have exceptionally short rigid wheelbases to suit the tortuous tracks on which they operate.

The riding of a locomotive, especially around curves, and the stresses, especially lateral stresses, which it imposes on the track, are influenced by the wheel arrangement. The provision of carrying wheels, able to move sideways or to pivot, before the driving wheels on a steam locomotive, helped to ease the passage of the latter. The 0-6-0 type of locomotive, so popular in Britain, which lacked these carrying wheels, was notably unkind to the track; the 3-axle power trucks of some modern electric and diesel locomotives are, in this respect, little improvement.

Measures of efficiency

Total efficiency is a combination of several factors which produce a certain total cost per unit of transport work performed. Utilisation of locomotives, the time they spend under repair, their first cost, their labour costs, as well as their fuel consumption per ton-mile, are all involved in this and a locomotive which burns above-average amounts of fuel may be more efficient than others overall. However, in locomotive design, and in the choice between diesel, electric and steam traction, the index of *thermal efficiency* is regarded as crucial. This index is the ratio of the heat which the fuel is capable of producing to the heat equivalent of the work actually done. It can be expressed as a formula:

$$\frac{\text{IHP expressed in British Thermal Units (BTU)}}{\text{Fuel consumed (in BTU) per drawbar horsepower hour}} \times 100$$

With a steam locomotive, this index is a function of three components, the *boiler efficiency* (which can be quite high, as much as 75 per cent), the *cylinder efficiency* (rather low because of steam cooling and the relatively low steam pressure, about 5 to 12 per cent) and the *mechanical efficiency* (quite high, because frictional losses are relatively small). In diesel-electric locomotives the main factors are *engine efficiency, generator efficiency* and *traction motor efficiency*. Electric locomotive thermal efficiency is a less precise measure than is sometimes believed, as it is a combination of the locomotive's own efficiency with that of the power station and of the distribution network. Power station efficiency varies greatly according to the peak load value.

The overall, or thermal, efficiency of a steam locomotive is from 3 to 10 per cent, and that of diesel and electric locomotives over 20 per cent.

Wheel arrangement notation

The wheel arrangement of a locomotive was initially indicated simply by description, so Stephenson's *Rocket* was said to be carried on one pair of driving wheels with a pair of carrying wheels forward. As locomotives became bigger, and brevity in communication more valued, several notation systems were devised. In the English-speaking world that proposed by the American engineer, Frederic Whyte, and adopted by American railroads in 1901, has been generally accepted. In this there are three numbers, separated by dashes; the first number gives the total of leading carrying wheels, the second the number of driving wheels and the last the number of rear carrying wheels (tenders are excluded).

In France, Spain and some other countries, the same principle was used, except that axles rather than wheels were counted. On German-style railways yet another variation was used, in which the axles were counted, with the carrying

An exceptionally (and excessively) long rigid wheelbase sealed the fate of this 4-14-4 locomotive built for Soviet Railways in the 1930s.

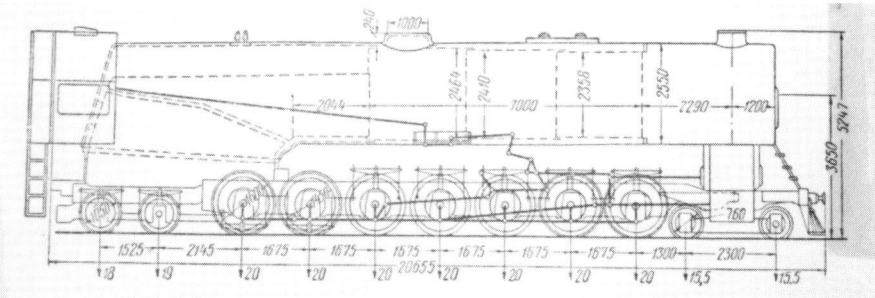

axles given as numerals but the driving axles as letters, A being one driving axle, B two and so on.

Meanwhile, in America, the practice of having a distinctive name for each wheel arrangement continued alongside the Whyte system. Such names were often connected with the railroad which first used that wheel arrangement. Many such names, like Pacific and Mogul, were also used in other countries. In the following table, which shows some of the more common wheel arrangements, a * indicates those names which have little or no currency outside American railroading.

Wheels (front of locomotive at left)	Whyte system	French	German	Name
o O	2-2-0	110	1A	Planet
O O	0-4-0	020	B	Four-wheel switcher*
o o O O	4-4-0	220	2B	American*
o O O o	2-4-2	121	1B1	Columbia*
o o O O o	4-4-2	221	2B1	Atlantic
o O O	2-4-0	120	1B	
O O o	0-4-2	021	B1	
O O O	0-6-0	030	C	Six-wheel switcher*
o O O O	2-6-0	130	1C	Mogul
o o O O O	4-6-0	230	2C	Ten-wheeler*
o O O O o	2-6-2	131	1C1	Prairie
o o O O O o	4-6-2	231	2C1	Pacific
o o O O O o o	4-6-4	232	2C2	Hudson*
O O O O	0-8-0	040	D	Eight-wheel switcher*
o O O O O	2-8-0	140	1D	Consolidation
o o O O O O	4-8-0	240	2D	Mastodon*
o O O O O o	2-8-2	141	1D1	Mikado
o o O O O O o	4-8-2	241	2D1	Mountain*
o O O O O o o	2-8-4	142	1D2	Berkshire*
o o O O O O o o	4-8-4	242	2D2	Northern*
O O O O O	0-10-0	050	E	Decapod (in Europe)
o O O O O O	2-10-0	150	1E	Decapod*
o O O O O O o	2-10-2	151	1E1	Santa Fe*
o O O O O O o o	2-10-4	152	1E2	Texas*

Articulated locomotives have the two wheelsets given individually, joined by a plus sign. With Mallet (but not Garratt) types it is common to omit zeros. Some authors use a dash in place of the plus sign; this is misleading because such a form should be reserved for the (admittedly few) locomotives whose drive has been split between two sets of driving wheels which are not coupled together but form a rigid wheelbase. Thus, a Mallet articulated locomotive consisting of a pair of 2-8-0 engine units should ideally be expressed as 2-8-0 + 2-8-0 but it may be encountered as 2-8-8-2. Tank locomotives have the suffix T.

When electric and diesel locomotives appeared, attempts were made to continue with the Whyte notation, but eventually a system more akin to that of the German one was used. In this, a modification was made so that those locomotives (the majority at that time) which had individually driven axles (that is, a traction motor for each set of driving wheels) had the suffix 'o' placed after the driving wheel denominator. Thus some of the more common wheel and motor arrangements in the inter-war period were written as follows:

```
o O O O O o         1-Do-1
o o O O O O o o     2-Do-2
O O O               C (when wheels coupled)
O O O               Co (when all axles individually powered)
```

At this period the driving wheels were larger than the carrying wheels, usually being of steam locomotive type. The appearance of electric and diesel locomotives riding on power trucks, with uniform and rather small wheels, was accommodated by the system with little difficulty. When the two (or more) trucks were joined together by an articulated drawbar, a plus sign was inserted between the notations for the trucks; when they were not (that is, when the tractive force was transmitted through the body of the locomotive) a dash was used instead. Thus a locomotive riding on two four-wheel trucks would be notated as follows: two 4-wheel trucks, with the axles of each truck coupled, B-B; two 4-wheel trucks individually driven but not connected, Bo-Bo; and two 4-wheel trucks with drawbar connection and individual axle motors, Bo + Bo.

Similarly, an electric locomotive on three-axle trucks is C-C if the wheels of each truck are coupled and Co-Co if the axles are individually powered. It might be noted that the coupling of wheels on electric or diesel engines is inconspicuous, only a few types having coupling rods. The refinements of this system are falling out of use, and it is common to describe, for example, any locomotive with two 4-wheel trucks simply as B-B or even BB.

Chapter 10

The anatomy of the steam locomotive

The steam locomotive has two fundamental components, the thermal (or steam-raising) and the mechanical (converting steam to power and motion). Sometimes, and especially in the past, the term *engine* is restricted to the mechanical part of the locomotive. The following pages describe the main parts of the steam locomotive and their functions; a quite agreeable follow-up, for those readers who wish to pursue the subject in more detail, is B. Hollingsworth's *How to Drive a Steam Locomotive* (1979).

The floor of the *cab* is known as the *footplate*. The forward wall consists largely of the *backplate* of the firebox and among its levers and gauges are the glass *water gauge*, showing the water level inside the boiler. This gauge is under the constant scrutiny of the firemen, for there is a minimum safe level of water, below which the firebox crown may become uncovered and, even if the resultant burn-out is limited by the safety plugs, the consequences can be perilous. Water may be impelled into the boiler by the *injector*, which is typically situated beneath the cab. Injectors are notoriously unreliable, so it is the practice for locomotives to carry two of them.

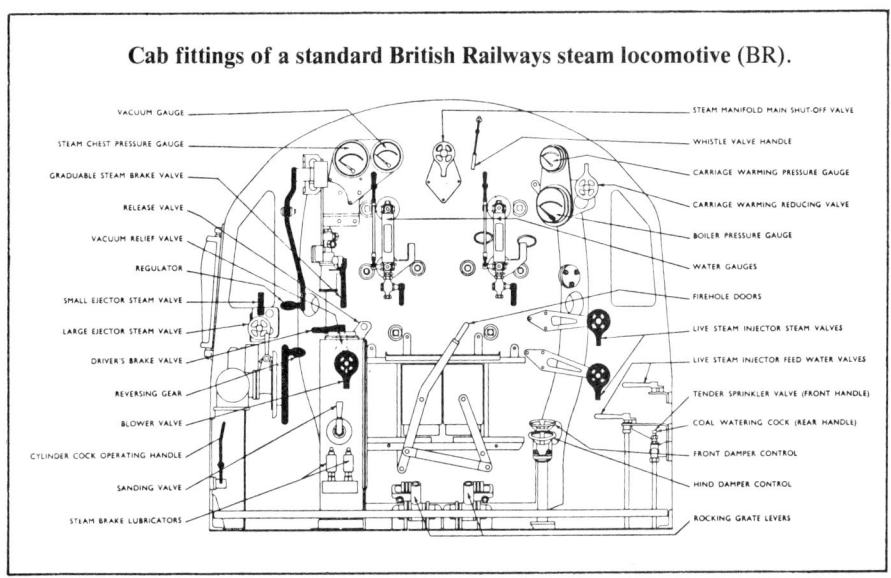

Cab fittings of a standard British Railways steam locomotive (BR).

Also in the cab is the *pressure gauge*, showing the steam pressure in the boiler. The *regulator handle*, controlling the admission of the steam to the cylinders, is usually a long lever fitted in the centre of the front wall. The *reverser*, which adjusts the valve gear to determine at what point of the piston's stroke the steam is cut off (allowing the remainder of the stroke to be accomplished by expansion of the steam already in the cylinder) might take the form of a lever or a wheel. Since it controls which end of the cylinder the steam enters first, it acts also as a reversing mechanism. Also prominent is the *brake handle*. The *firehole*, when open, dominates the cab with bright light and intense heat. However, except when coal is being fed to the firebox by the fireman's shovel, it is kept closed.

The *firebox*, immediately in front of the cab, is part of the boiler and contains the grate on which the fuel burns. There is an inner firebox, sometimes of

Below *Basic components of a British (LMS) mixed-traffic 2-6-0 locomotive.* **1** *Coupling rod.* **2** *Sandbox.* **3** *Mechanical lubricator.* **4** *Balance weight.* **5** *Cylinder.* **6** *Steamchest.* **7** *Pony truck wheel.* **8** *Buffer beam.* **9** *Vacuum brake pipe.* **10** *Frame plate (one of two).* **11** *Smokebox door.* **12** *Smokebox.* **13** *Boiler barrel.* **14** *Steam dome.* **15** *Safety valves.* **16** *Belpaire firebox.*

Bottom *Features of the North American (Canadian National) steam locomotive.* **1** *Headlight.* **2** *Marker light (one of two).* **3** *Feedwater heater.* **4** *Sand dome.* **5** *Bell (off-centre because of height restriction).* **6** *Vanderbilt tender.* **7** *Pilot ('cowcatcher').* **8** *Air brake reservoir.* **9** *Buckeye coupler. Also to be seen are the disc driving wheels, and the air brake compressor suspended alongside the rear coupled wheels.*

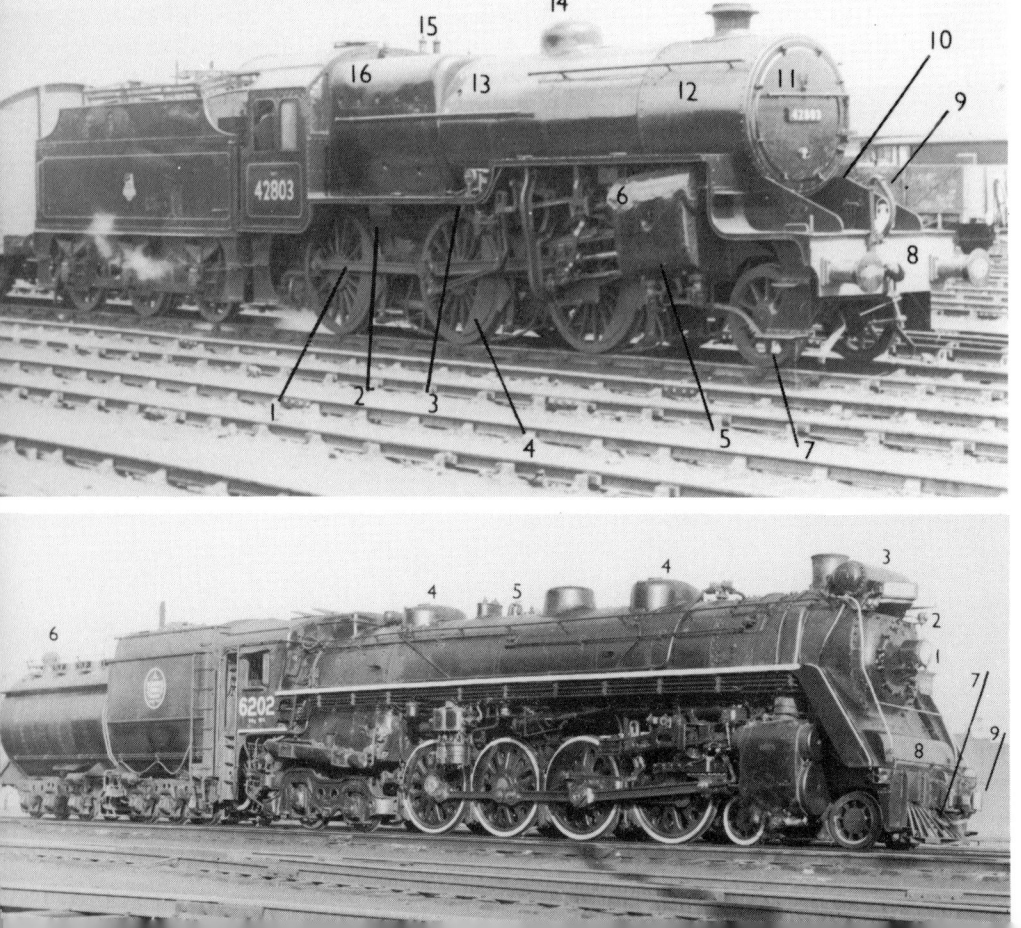

The anatomy of the steam locomotive 93

A compound locomotive. This is a Mallet-type articulated design; use of the compound principle is revealed by the different diameters of the rear (high-pressure) and leading (low-pressure) cylinders.

copper and sometimes of steel, and an outer firebox, with water circulating between the walls and the two roofs. Fireboxes may be either *roundtop* or square (*Belpaire*). The latter are more expensive and heavier, but the interior staying between the two walls is simpler, and they provide a slightly improved heating surface. Beneath the grate bars is the *ashpan*, while the front wall is formed by the *tubeplate*. The water around the firebox is heated directly, but the gases from the fire retain considerable heat. These gases rise over the fire, are deflected by the *brick arch* inside the firebox, and then pass down the *tubes* which run from the tubeplate, through the main part of the boiler (the *boiler barrel*), to the smokebox. As they pass down the tubes they give some of their heat to the surrounding water.

Efficiency improves with higher steam pressure, but the problems and expense associated with high-pressure boilers mean that 300 lb per sq in (22 kg per sq cm) is about the maximum feasible pressure and the great majority of boilers are of 180 to 250 psi (13–18 kg). *Safety valves* are fitted to ensure that these limits are not passed. To reduce the amount of water spray carried into the cylinders, it is desirable to situate the regulator valve as high as possible in the boiler, and a *steam dome* is fitted to most boilers to accommodate the valve. A *tapered boiler*, with the diameter at the firebox end greater than at the forward end, can achieve the same effect, or add to the effectiveness of the dome.

The regulator valve, sometimes called the throttle, controls the amount of steam passing through the internal steampipes to the cylinders. En route, in most line-service (as opposed to yard) locomotives, it passes through the superheater, which is a steamtube of several bends running up and down boiler flue tubes (rather wider than the other boiler tubes, being typically 5 in (127 mm) diameter as against 2 in (51 mm). The *saturated* steam entering this extra heating process becomes *dry steam*, less liable to condense in the cylinders, and therefore enhancing cylinder efficiency.

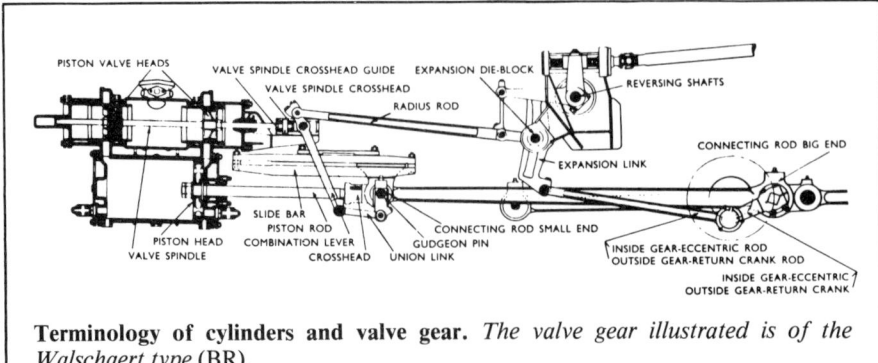

Terminology of cylinders and valve gear. *The valve gear illustrated is of the Walschaert type* (BR).

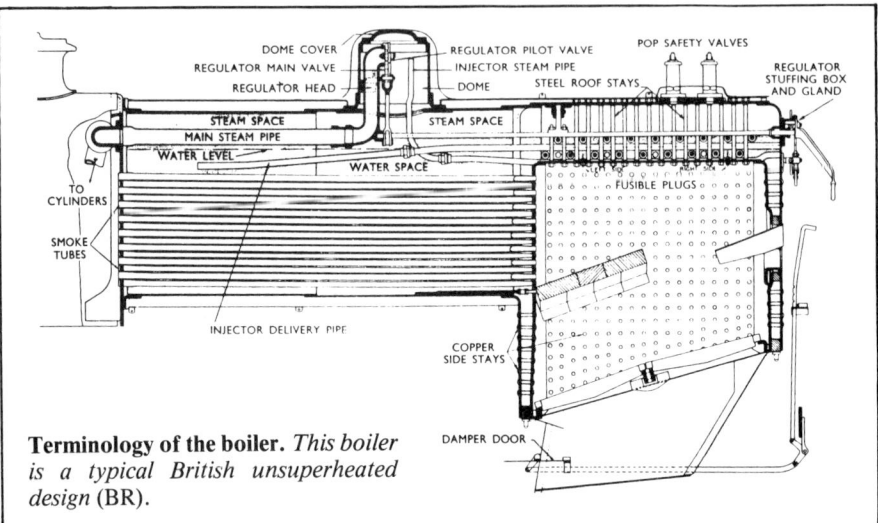

Terminology of the boiler. *This boiler is a typical British unsuperheated design* (BR).

The *steamchests* may be regarded as antechambers. The steam arrives in them and awaits admission to the cylinders. This admission is controlled by the covering and uncovering of apertures, or *ports*. The steam admitted to the cylinder moves the pistonhead, which in turn moves the piston rod to which it is attached. At some point in the travel (*stroke*) of the piston, the steam entry port will be closed, enabling the energy contained in the steam's pressure to be released by expansion of the steam; the longer the *cut-off*, the more steam is admitted before this point; long cut-offs make poorer use of the steam's energy, but produce greater power; they should therefore be used only when the locomotive really needs to work hard. On many railways it was believed that a long cut-off, combined with a reduced regulator opening, was equally efficient, but this is fallacious.

One method to increase cylinder efficiency is to use the steam twice, once in a high-pressure and then in a low-pressure cylinder. This is called *compounding*. So as to impart equal thrust, the low-pressure cylinders have to be larger than the high-pressure ones, and there are several permutations. In continental Europe the 2-cylinder compound, with one cylinder visibly larger than the other, was once quite popular even though in practice it was impossible to equalise the work done by the two cylinders. In Britain the three-cylinder compound (one high-pressure and two large low-pressure cylinders) enjoyed some success on Midland Railway passenger locomotives, but the London & North Western Railway's large-scale move towards compounding was unsuccessful. In France, compounding was found worthwhile for many large passenger locomotives and a few main line freight types, but for other duties its extra expense, in terms of maintenance, was not thought worthwhile.

In America, compounding had little vogue, except for an interlude when the *Vauclain compound* was used by some companies. This was a 4-cylinder compound in which all cylinders were outside, with a low-pressure and a high-pressure cylinder lying one above the other. A number of Mallet-type articulated locomotives also worked on the conventional 4-cylinder compound system in the USA. A rare form was the *tandem-compound,* in which a low- and high-pressure cylinder were placed directly in line on each side of the locomotive, with each pair having a common piston rod.

The to-and-fro movement of the piston rod is converted to rotary motion at the wheel by a crank arrangement, the transmission being effected by a *connecting rod*. At its forward end this acquires the necessary swivelling up-and-down freedom by its pivotal connection to the *crosshead*. The latter is attached to the piston rod and is kept in alignment with the latter by means of the *guide bars* along which its runs. The rear end of the connecting rod is attached to a crankpin on the *driving wheel*, when the cylinder is outside the frames. The crankpin is offset from the wheel centre, thus permitting the rod to exert leverage around the centre and thereby apply rotating force. When the cylinder is inside the frames, the axle of the driving wheels is cranked and the connecting rod drives on that crank. Building up crank axles strong enough to withstand continuous pounding of the connecting rod thrusts is expensive, and this is one of the reasons why outside cylinders are usually preferred. However, two inside

Outside frames and sharply-tapered boiler of a GWR turn-of-the-century design.

A side-tank locomotive of the LMS. This was the commonest configuration for tank locomotives.

A saddletank locomotive (MR), a layout favoured for small industrial-type shunting designs.

cylinders was a favoured layout on British railways; it does have some advantages, among other things causing less oscillation of the locomotive. Inside cylinders are also used when two cylinders are insufficient for the required power.

Usually, outside-cylinder locomotives have their valve gear outside the wheels while inside-cylinder locomotives have theirs inside the frames. Conventional valve gear, although it looks complicated, is in fact a very simple way of providing a means whereby the timing of steam admission, cut-off and exhaust may be varied, the movements of the small pistons or slides which cover and uncover the ports being imparted, through the gear, by the rotating wheels or by the connecting rod. Although simple, such valve gears are not conspicuously efficient, different types of gear being most efficient at different settings of cut-off. The fact that the steam exhaust ports are actuated by the same gear as the admission ports is a fundamental disadvantage, for it would be more efficient if they worked independently to provide the most ample exit for the steam (to avoid back-pressure, when the returning piston runs into steam still in the cylinder from the previous stroke).

There are very many variants of valve gear, but the Walschaert design has been the most favoured in the 20th century, although the older Stephenson gear retained its adherents, notably on Britain's Great Western Railway. Attempts to

A pannier tank locomotive, an arrangement favoured by the GWR.

A well-tank locomotive (LSWR), carrying most of its water in a tank between the frames.

move away from conventional gears included several attempts at poppet valves, similar to those used in automobiles. These attempts were not unsuccessful, but it was not until steam traction was in decline that really promising poppet valves were designed. Had steam traction continued for another decade or so, the enhanced efficiency of poppet valves would probably have led to their general adoption.

The connecting rod is attached at its rear end to the crankpin of the *driving wheel*. The latter transfers some of the tractive force thus imparted to neighbouring wheels through a *coupling rod*. Strictly speaking, the wheels so connected are known as *coupled wheels*, but in practice all the wheels transmitting tractive force are called driving wheels. Obviously, they have to be of the same diameter; unequal wear of the tyres may occasionally result in discrepancies, and this puts an undesirable strain on the coupling rods.

The conventional driving wheel is spoked and carries segmental weights to assist in balancing. A few of the more recent locomotive designs, especially in the USA, had spokeless *disc* wheels, sometimes known as *'Boxpok'*. In these a plate, suitably perforated to reduce weight, replaces the spokes. Depending on duties, and especially on the locomotive's susceptibility to wheelslip, the outer part of the wheel, or *tyre* has to be periodically re-profiled or replaced. Reprofiling is done by a special machine, while re-tyring is accomplished by using heat to expand the new tyre, slipping it on the wheel and allowing it to shrink tight. Retaining pins prevent it slipping on the wheel while in service.

With a steam locomotive, driving wheel size is crucial in determining the type of duty performed; there is no gear change. The larger the wheel, the slower the movement of the pistons and other mechanisms at any given speed. Particularly in the pre-1914 period, when lubrication, balancing and metallurgy were relatively unsophisticated, the high speed of moving components was undesirable. Hence the use of 8 ft (2,438 mm) driving wheels for fast passenger locomotives by some 19th century British railways. On the other hand, a smaller driving wheel enables a greater tractive effort to be exerted. This was why some American freight locomotives had driving wheels of only 3 ft 6 in (1,070 mm) in the mid-19th century. The running of such locomotives at high speeds was forbidden, being harmful both for the locomotives and for the track, which would have been subject to a hammerblow pounding as the balance weights rotated at unaccustomed speed. The Borki accident in Russia, when the imperial train left the rails and Tsar Alexander III found himself holding up the roof of his dining car, was caused by a rail broken by the two freight locomotives hauling that excessively fast train.

In the early 20th century the 'mixed traffic' locomotive, which was becoming so popular and useful, was reckoned to need driving wheels of from 5 ft 3 in (1,600 mm) to 6 ft 3 in (1,905 mm), fast passenger locomotives from 6 ft 3 in to 7 ft (2,135mm) and freight locomotives from 4 ft 3 in (1,295 mm) to 5 ft 3 in. By mid-century, however, better lubrication and balancing had meant that it was possible to obtain higher speeds from the smaller wheels and there were cases of locomotives with 5 ft driving wheels hauling fast trains with success. Later fast passenger locomotives sometimes had wheels smaller than the generally accepted standard; these included the British 'Merchant Navy' type (6 ft 2 in or 1,880 mm) and the Norfolk and Western RR's 4-8-4 (5 ft 9 in or 1,752 mm), both of which could run at very high speeds.

Carrying wheels, in the form of a *truck* or *bogie*, have no tractive value and are intended to spread the weight (that is, to reduce the axle weight) and to help guide the locomotive. They are of two and four wheels, although in America a 6-wheel carrying truck was not unknown. The two-wheel truck at the front of some locomotives is sometimes called a *pony truck*; in America the leading truck is sometimes termed the *engine truck* and a rear truck a *trailing truck*. Trucks are of various designs, but in general they can move sideways either by a swing link, a radial movement, or by a sliding action controlled by swing links, springs or weight applied by inclined planes.

The driving wheel axles are held in axleboxes which can rise or fall within the *hornblocks*, the latter being rigidly attached to the *frame*. Frames are to the locomotive what a keel is to a ship, being the foundation of all else, and carrying the other components. They are two vertical plates, about 4 ft apart, running lengthwise. Sometimes, especially in American locomotives, they are built up from bars and described as *bar frames*; otherwise they are plate frames, cut from solid steel plates of about 1.5 in (40 mm) thickness. Plate frames are somewhat more expensive but are lighter than bar frames. A number of very big locomotives were built with *cast steel bed frames*, in which a single casting included the whole frame and its spacing and stretching bars, the cylinders and smokebox saddle. With bar frames, the placing of the springs for suspending the axleboxes is usually simpler.

The anatomy of the steam locomotive

Some or all of the driving wheels are flanked by pipes leading from the sandboxes and delivering sand by means of a steam jet to the rail surface beneath the wheel. In American-style locomotives, the sand is carried in a container, or dome, on top of the boiler. British-style locomotives usually carry their sandboxes lower down, typically on or under the *running board* (sometimes called the *footplating*) which is the steel platform around the side and front of the locomotive. Also associated with the driving wheels is the brake gear; it is not usual to fit brake gear to the carrying wheels.

Exhaust steam from the cylinders passes upwards into a cylindrical chamber which forms the foremost part of the boiler and is known as the *smokebox*. The rear wall of this is the *forward tubeplate*, and the firetubes convey hot gases, soot and ash from the fire to the smokebox. The exhaust steam passes, via the *blastpipe*, up the chimney and, in doing so, drags, or entrains, the firebox gases with it. This creates a draught for the fire. In the 20th century much thought was given to arranging the blastpipe so as to provide the most powerful and steady

A British locomotive depot towards the end of the steam era. British engineers, both at home and overseas, favoured the 'straight-road' layout, in which locomotives were kept on parallel tracks in a rectangular building. In this depot, which is a main depot, there is a four-road shed (with inspection pits) and also, adjacent, a workshop capable of handling intermediate repairs (for capital repairs a visit to a locomotive works was required). Incoming locomotives went first to the ashpits to clean their grates and smokeboxes, then to the coaling and watering facilities before proceeding, via the turntable, to the storage tracks of the main shed. Inside the latter, minor repairs and the periodic boiler washout could be performed. The cramped layout of this depot will be noted; there is no space for the more efficient 'through-road' arrangement, in which locomotives enter one end of the shed and eventually leave by the other. In the early days of railways the roundhouse layout was favoured, in which a circular building encloses a central turntable from which radiate storage tracks (stalls) extending to the roundhouse wall. A later variant of this is a rectangular shed with a similar indoor turntable, as can still be seen at York Railway Museum, a converted depot.

draught; fluctuations tend to pull unburnt or partially burned coal from the fire. The form of blastpipe *nozzle* was found to be crucial, and multiple nozzle forms, like the *Kylchap* and the later *Giesl* arrangements were found to be very effective. The *double chimney* (with two orifices) is associated with a Kylchap arrangement, an elongated chimney denotes a Giesl exhaust, while the *Lemaître* multi-jet exhaust is accompanied by a large diameter chimney. Access to the smokebox, necessary for removing deposited ash and soot, is through the *smokebox door* at the front, which is tightly secured to prevent any air leakage, which would disturb the partial vacuum effect on which the draughting arrangement depends.

Behind the locomotive is the tender, whose leading floor forms part of the footplate. The bulk of the tender is devoted to water storage, while the upper and forward section, sloping downwards, is for coal. The *Vanderbilt tender*, especially popular in America, has a cylindrical rather than a rectangular water-tank. The *corridor tender*, used on certain British (LNER) locomotives gave access to the train and thereby allowed enginemen to change shift on non-stop trains.

Tank locomotives are without tenders, carrying their coal in a bunker behind the cab and the water in tanks, which are usually beneath the bunker and alongside the boiler. They have the advantage that they are equally suitable for running in either direction and so do not need to go to a turntable between runs.

Steam locomotives can burn a variety of fuels and wood-burning locomotives, once so widespread in America and Scandinavia, are still not quite extinct. Coal, however, is by far the most usual fuel. In some circumstances of price and availability, oil ('mazout') is used, the fuel being carried in a tank on the tender. Oil fuel requires a pump and a special nozzle in the firebox and somewhat different skills on the part of the fireman. It reduces the problems associated with ash, soot and sparks. In Britain, oil-burning locomotives have not been used except when governments anticipated coal crises (which in the event did not occur).

Locomotive working

The basis of locomotive working is the locomotive shed, or depot. This is not only the place for day-to-day maintenance and minor repair, but is also a signing-on point for locomotive crews.

The steam locomotive had a limited radius of action. Usually this radius was determined by the coal supply, for locomotives were coaled at locomotive depots except in a few cases (as in North America, where coaling stages spanned main line tracks to enable locomotives to take coal without being uncoupled from their trains). In general, routes were divided into traction sections, locomotives being changed at the divisional points between sections; these points, for convenience, were usually placed at or near a main centre, where many trains would originate or terminate. Locomotive depots were provided at these points (sometimes a so-called sub-depot, with limited facilities, was provided instead). Locomotives attached to a given depot were collectively known as the latter's allocation and, in principle, worked to and from that depot ('out and home'). In many countries, especially in Europe, where the rail network was intensive, a locomotive might not take the first return working back to its depot but work a pattern of services (its 'diagram') which would eventually bring it

The anatomy of the steam locomotive

In North America and continental Europe the open roundhouse was favoured, in which the central turntable is uncovered, and is partially or entirely surrounded by a circular or segmental building in which tracks radiating from the turntable terminate as covered locomotive stalls. With the end of steam, old locomotive depots have usually been adapted for electric or diesel units pending the construction of purpose-built facilities. Modern locomotives demand a clean environment, and their repair requires, among other things, very good lighting.

back home. With non-steam motive power, traction sections are longer, with many depots being closed or reduced to signing-on points. Complex ('cyclic') diagrams are common, so as to maximise locomotive mileage.

With steam locomotives, an ideal manning arrangement was to have one crew for each locomotive, in the justified expectation that this crew would look carefully after its own machine. However, as crew working hours are limited by legislation, such a system limits a locomotive's daily mileage. A compromise was double-manning, in which two crews shared one locomotive. Pooling, or common-user, manning implied that any crew might be given any suitable locomotive for their shift; it increased locomotive utilisation but this gain was partly balanced by a deterioration in the condition of locomotives.

In Russia the Moscow-Ryazan Railway pooled its crews for the busiest season, reverting to one crew for each locomotive for the rest of the year. With modern traction it is usual for several crews to successively take over a given locomotive during the latter's diagram. Crew changes were not unknown in the steam era, when it could happen that the radius of action of a crew-shift did not coincide with the optimum locomotive run. In post-war Britain a change of enginemen half-way through a locomotive's run was often made so that the crew could return home during their shift, rather than stay overnight in lodgings or a railway hostel; so-called 'lodging turns' were very unpopular.

Traditionally, locomotive drivers at British locomotive depots have been grouped into 'links', each link comprising men of similar seniority and, usually, with locomotives being pooled within each link. The most experienced drivers, handling the most important trains, became known as the 'top link'.

Chapter 11

Steam locomotive trends and trend-setters

Richard Trevithick built the first steam railway locomotive in 1804 but the age of steam may be reckoned to have lasted from 1830 to about 1960. Over the decades there was a steady increase in the size of locomotives until, in the 1950s, several railway administrations gave as their reason for abandoning steam the virtual impossibility of increasing the size, hence the power, of conventional locomotives. Insofar as total cylinder diameter is an important element in determining power, this explanation was valid, because cylinder dimensions were limited by width limitations. With the increase in size there was, of necessity, the creation of new wheel arrangements to accommodate the larger number of axles. In the beginning, wheel arrangements could be patented; the adoption of a new arrangement always presented technical problems.

George Stephenson's son, Robert, designed and built his *Rocket* for tests on the new Liverpool & Manchester Railway in 1829, incorporating several improvements over previous machines. To create a freer-running unit he omitted the coupling rods, the *Rocket* being a 2-2-0 rather than a 0-4-0. It carried a multi-tubular boiler; whereas previous locomotives had a single wide flue carrying the hot gases from the fire through the boiler to the chimney, the *Rocket* had 25 smaller tubes, giving a bigger heating surface.

At the Rainhill Trials the *Rocket* triumphed, but Timothy Hackworth's failure at these trials was ill-deserved, for it was Hackworth who had developed the blastpipe, that vital ingredient of the advanced locomotive. By carrying the exhaust steam through the chimney, the blastpipe created a draught for the fire, and that draught automatically corresponded in strength to the amount of work the locomotive was doing. After *Rocket* came *Planet*, built by Stephenson for the Liverpool & Manchester Railway and having its cylinders between the frames under the boiler. His later *Patentee* was similar, but had an extra carrying axle, making it a 2-2-2. Finally, Stephenson popularised the 0-6-0 wheel arrangement, which became a great favourite among British railway engineers, almost up to the end of steam traction.

Meanwhile, other engineers were making their own contribution to locomotive technology. Edward Bury in 1830 built the first engine with horizontal cylinders and then took charge of the locomotive department of the London & Birmingham Railway. His locomotives had bar frames and those exported to the USA led to the general adoption of bar frames in that country. In 1847 he built the first locomotive designed specifically for yard work. Thomas Crampton introduced locomotives with one pair of huge driving wheels placed

Steam locomotive trends and trend-setters

behind the firebox. They were not well received in Britain, but many were used abroad, being exceptionally speedy. This speed was probably due less to the layout than to Crampton's appreciation that wide internal steam pipes were essential for fast free-running locomotives. On the Great Western Railway's broad gauge, Daniel Gooch was building large high-performance machines with 100 lb/sq in (7 kg per sq cm) boiler pressure. A little later David Joy designed the celebrated 2-2-2 *Jenny Lind*, which had a 120 lb (8.5 kg) pressure and a suitably large firebox to produce it. Joy also invented his own valve gear, which later became quite popular in Russia and central Europe. However, the valve gear invented, independently and simultaneously, by the Belgian, Egide Walschaert, and the Prussian, Edmund Heusinger, in the 1840s, proved superior in the long run.

One of the most prolific innovators was John Ramsbottom of the London & North Western Railway. He vastly improved a number of important details: his sight-feed lubricator (enabling enginemen to see how the oil was running), his split piston rings (which, for the first time, provided a long-lasting steam-tight fit between piston and cylinder wall) and his Ramsbottom Valve (a safety valve consisting of two vertical outlets with a coiled spring between them to hold them down), were all inventions which became standard equipment. He also devised water troughs, long open pans of water between the rails, enabling locomotives (whose tenders were fitted with a retractable scoop) to refill their tanks without stopping. These troughs were widely used in Britain until the end of steam; a few lines in France and the USA also had them (in America they were called track pans).

Alfred Belpaire, a Belgian who became an international railway personality, invented the Belpaire firebox in the 1860s. This design originated from experiments he made with a wide grate suitable for burning low-grade coal. By this time Britain had lost its near-monopoly of locomotive innovation; in fact

The American 4-4-0. This example has a prominent spark arrestor, a necessity for wood-burning locomotives working in dry forest or prairie regions.

American engineers had begun to work out their own technical solutions soon after the first Stephenson and Bury locomotives had arrived in the USA. John Jervis, of the Mohawk & Hudson Railroad, built the *Experiment*, whose swivelling 4-wheel truck, designed to ease its passage over curves, earned him the credit for inventing what British engineers termed the bogie. Joseph Harrison's equalizing beam, which was an improved suspension for the coupled wheels of locomotives, made the 4-4-0 wheel arrangement a practicable proposition for the bumpy tracks of the American railways.

Until the end of the century, the 4-4-0 was the classic and most numerous American type, both for freight and passenger work. However, rivalry between American locomotive builders, at first between Baldwin and the Norris brothers, and then involving later entrants like Harrison and Winans, meant that not only was there a spate of patented innovations, often valueless, but also a steady progression involving bigger locomotives and new wheel arrangements. Winan built his so-called 'Centipede' in 1855; this was a 4-8-0, a wheel arrangement which was somewhat ahead of his time. Winans was also the originator of the 'camelback' type of locomotive (see chapter 15). Even earlier, he had built 0-8-0 freight locomotives. Later in the century, the USA was still, and would remain, the world leader in locomotive size and new wheel arrangements. In 1883 A. J. Stevens built his *El Gobernador*, a huge 4-10-0, for the Central Pacific RR and, three years later, the first true Pacific (4-6-2) locomotive was designed by George Strong for the Lehigh Valley RR.

In Europe, locomotives were smaller. For freight work the 0-6-0 was the most popular, although the 0-8-0 appeared towards the end of the century. The 2-6-0, which had become widespread in the USA as a medium freight locomotive, was rare elsewhere. For passenger work the 2-4-0 and 2-4-2 were well-established. The latter type was represented among the most successful designs of V. Forquenot, the chief locomotive engineer of the French PO Railway from 1860 to 1885, who was among the first in France to take seriously the idea of locomotive standardisation.

Towards the end of the century, the 4-4-0 became the favourite wheel arrangement for new passenger designs. In Britain, where the 0-6-0 was well-established for freight work, the so-called 'single', a locomotive with only one pair of driving wheels, had an exceptionally long life as a fast passenger locomotive, first as a 2-2-0, and progressing to 2-2-2 and 4-2-2. Various 4-2-2 designs (by men like Gooch of the GWR and Patrick Stirling of the Great Northern Railway) won reputations for fast running and easy riding, with their large driving wheels—up to 8 ft (2.4 m) diameter—and freedom from the stresses produced by the up-and-down motion of coupling rods. When, towards the end of the century, steam-assisted sanding equipment became available, the great weakness of the single, low adhesion, was partly compensated, and the type made a comeback with S. W. Johnson's 'Midland Single', the last of which was built in 1901. However, the 2-4-0 and then the 4-4-0 were the basic passenger locomotives of the late 19th century.

Johnson was also the designer of the 'Midland compounds', the most successful of the few experiments with compounding undertaken in Britain. Earlier, Francis Webb of the LNWR had made a persistent and expensive effort to develop the compound, but his designs, though built in large numbers, were unsuccessful. The Midland compounds, on the other hand, continued to be built into the 1920s. It was the French who really developed successful com-

One of the 'Midland compounds', the only really successful class of compound locomotive in Britain.

pounding; one of the objections to this concept, which could certainly improve economy and performance of locomotives working hard over long periods, was the extra complexity, but this was compensated in France by the superior technical training of French enginemen. Whereas in Britain a locomotive driver would learn his job by spending decades as first a cleaner and then a fireman, French locomotive men began their career with something of the status of apprentices.

The Midland compounds worked on the arrangement pioneered by the Frenchman, Edouard Sauvage of the Nord Railway, in which the high-pressure steam entered first a single cylinder between the frames and was then led to two outside low-pressure cylinders. A. Henry, of the French PLM Railway, at about the same time (1888–92) was building 4-cylinder compounds in which there were two high-pressure cylinders between the frames. But it was the partnership of Gaston du Bousquet and Alfred de Glehn, an Englishman employed by the French *Alsacienne* locomotive company, which produced the most successful

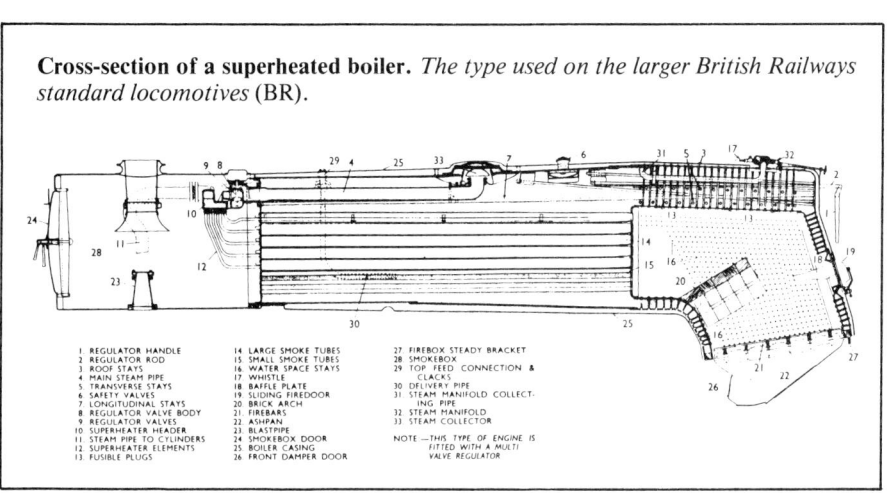

Cross-section of a superheated boiler. *The type used on the larger British Railways standard locomotives* (BR).

French compounds. Their machines had four cylinders, high-pressure outside and low-pressure inside. A new by-pass arrangement, with separate sets of valve gear for each cylinder, enabled the engines to be worked as compounds or as 4-cylinder and 2-cylinder simples (non-compound). This concept took full advantage of the French enginemens' skill and initiative and, by 1915, about a third of French locomotives were of this system. A handful were tried on Britain's Great Western Railway but, as the corresponding locomotives of the latter had superior steam passage design, the compounds did not seem to be markedly superior, while being more expensive to build and maintain. In central Europe, the most widespread compounds were of August von Borries' Prussian 2-cylinder type, despite its unbalanced piston thrusts.

One reason for the only partial acceptance of the compound concept was the development of the superheater, which tackled the same problem (inefficient use of the steam inside the cylinder) from another angle. The idea of passing steam, on its way to the cylinders, up and down wide flues carrying hot gases from the firebox was not new when Wilhelm Schmidt of the Royal Prussian State Railways evolved this system at the end of the century; the theoretical foundation for raising the steam to a higher temperature was already established. Schmidt's achievement was in finding a practical arrangement for applying it and, by the time he died in 1924, about 75,000 of the world's locomotives were fitted with his device.

Another problem towards the end of the century was that, as locomotives became bigger, they were less acceptable on curved track. Increased tractive effort needed greater weight on the driving wheels to provide wheel-rail adhesion and, since axle loads were restricted, a larger number of driving wheels was desirable. This in turn meant a longer rigid wheelbase, which was unsuited to curved track. The problem had first become evident on narrow-gauge lines, and a number of solutions had been adopted. One of these was Robert Fairlie's articulated locomotive, which had two power bogies (independent sets of cylinders and wheels) and two boilers back to back with the cab in the middle, with the power bogies pivoted to ease passage over curves. A weakness of this Fairlie locomotive was that there had to be a flexible steam pipe connection, which tended to leak.

Then there was the articulated concept of J. Meyer, favoured by many

A Meyer-type locomotive at work on an East German narrow-gauge line.

Steam locomotive trends and trend-setters

A Mallet-type locomotive.

German narrow-gauge lines. In this there was a single boiler, beneath which were two pivoted power bogies with the cylinders of each set beneath the centre of the boiler. Meyer locomotives survive in the German Democratic Republic, and there are two Fairlie locomotives on the Ffestiniog Railway, but these two concepts had a limited appeal. Much more important was the Mallet articulated locomotive, not least because it was adopted by several American companies (but not by any British).

Jules Anatole Mallet, a Genevan, devised his first articulated locomotive as a vehicle for a compound system which he wished to demonstrate. In his system, there were two engine units beneath a long boiler. The rear unit was rigidly attached to the locomotive boiler, but the forward unit pivoted. Steam went first to the rear cylinders, no flexible pipe being necessary. Then, as low-pressure steam (and therefore less likely to leak through the flexible steampipe joint), it was led to the larger, low-pressure, cylinders of the leading power unit. At first intended for European, and especially narrow-gauge and mountainous, lines, the Mallet locomotive was widely welcomed in America as a means to increase the number of coupled wheels while retaining the flexibility on curves of smaller locomotives. One US railroad even acquired a 'triplex' locomotive, a Mallet with three power bogies. The world's largest-ever steam locomotive type, the 'Big Boys' of the Union Pacific Railroad, were of Mallet type. As Mallet locomotives grew in size, powering North America's heaviest freight trains, it was found that clearances were insufficient to permit larger low-pressure cylinders, so simple expansion replaced compounding on most of those built between the wars.

An alternative to the Mallet was the Beyer-Garratt locomotive, patented by the Englishman, Herbert Garratt, before the First World War. This had two pivoting engine units, with the boiler swung between them. There were several advantages; the weight of the locomotive was spread over two wheelsets which were some way apart (thereby reducing stress on bridgespans); fuel and water was carried not in a separate tender but over the engine units, contributing significant (but variable) adhesion weight, the suspension of the boiler high above the rails gave really good air access for the grate; either-way running was possible, saving time and dispensing with turntables. The Garratt locomotive was widely used in the British Commonwealth and in a few other countries, but never in the USA.

The decade preceding the First World War was also notable for the innovations of George Churchward on the Great Western Railway. Churchward combined traditional GWR methods with American practice, and with what had been learned from the trials with French de Glehn compound locomotives, to produce a range of standard, efficient and distinctive locomotives. His initial 2-cylinder 4-6-0, progenitor of the famous 'Saint' Class, was a landmark in British locomotive history. From America he took the outside-cylinder layout, hitherto untraditional in Britain, the method of casting one cylinder with one half of the smokebox saddle, and the tapered, or coned, boiler (known in America as the 'wagon-top' boiler). From the continent Churchward took the Belpaire firebox, improving it with wider water-space. Above all, he arranged his cylinder valves to be actuated by pistons whose travel was far greater than in previous locomotives. The significance of this latter innovation was not immediately apparent to outside observers, but it permitted much larger steam ports to be used, thereby ensuring that at high speeds the steam was not throttled as it entered the cylinders. The prompt exit of the steam from the cylinders also determined the characteristic short and sharp exhaust from GWR chimneys. The success of No 98 set the pattern for a range of standard designs, including the 'Star' type 4-cylinder 4-6-0 which Churchward's successor, Charles Collett, developed into the famous 'Castle' and 'King' series.

Churchward's engines were not only distinctive in engineering, but in appearance too. Despite traditional GWR embellishments like copper-capped chimneys, brass domes and nameplates, and a pleasant Brunswick green paintwork, the gaunt aspect of these locomotives was not well received. The sharply tapered boiler, without dome, the very exposed driving wheels and the angular outside cylinders, all made the modern GWR locomotive something quite distinctive.

Among Churchward's designs had been a 2-6-0 which could be used for most passenger and freight duties. This idea of a 'mixed traffic' locomotive was taken further by the four British companies which emerged from the Railway Amalgamation of 1923. Other features of the British scene were the quest for high passenger train speeds, sometimes associated with streamlining, and the emergence of the 2-8-0 as the wheel arrangement for most heavy freight locomotives. On the larger of the new companies, the LMS, the locomotive situation was unsatisfactory until the appointment of William Stanier, a GWR man, as chief mechanical engineer in 1932. His new designs incorporated Churchward features, sometimes improved, and included the 'Class 5' mixed traffic 4-6-0, built in hundreds of units, and the 'Duchess' series of Pacifics. Some of the latter were streamlined, while *Duchess of Abercorn* in 1939 produced 3,300 indicated horsepower on test, a creditable output for a locomotive of that size. His 2-8-0, owing something to Churchward's 2-8-0, became a wartime standard locomotive, serving on several railways in Britain and overseas, just as J. G. Robinson's Great Central Railway 2-8-0 (the 'ROD') had served the Railway Operating Division in the previous conflict.

On the London & North Eastern Railway, locomotive policy was in the hands of the innovative Nigel Gresley, who had already designed a 3-cylinder Pacific for his previous employer, the Great Northern. One of the first of this series was

Above *A Beyer-Garratt 2-8-0+ 0-8-2 locomotive built for banking (pusher) service on a heavily graded LNER line.*

Right *One of the celebrated 4-cylinder 'King' class of 4-6-0s of the GWR.*

Below *The 'Class 5', the most numerous of the British mixed-traffic 4-6-0 locomotives. Several of these LMS units are operated as preserved locomotives.*

the celebrated *Flying Scotsman*. In this, Gresley followed the policy of his two GNR predecessors, Stirling and Ivatt, in favouring a 'big-boiler' policy. From these Pacifics was developed the streamlined A4 Class, which included the record-breaking *Mallard*. For mixed-traffic work, Gresley at first favoured the 2-6-0, before introducing his novel *Green Arrow* 2-6-2 for this. It was left to his successor, Edward Thompson, to design a good mixed traffic 4-6-0, the B1. Thompson undid much of Gresley's work; there was partial justification for this in that Gresley's valve gear arrangement for his favoured 3-cylinder configuration did cause severe maintenance problems.

The Great Western continued in the Churchward tradition, while not hesitating to build new units of older and sometimes antique-looking designs which still seemed satisfactory. Prominent among the latter were the 0-6-0 pannier tanks, a GWR speciality built in hundreds of units. The Southern Railway was unique in that electrification meant that steam traction had smaller

Left *One of the Gresley A4 streamlined Pacifics, of the same design as the record-breaking* Mallard.

Below *A late development of the 4-4-0 wheel arrangement: a three-cylinder 'Schools' Class locomotive of the SR.*

A 'Merchant Navy' Class Pacific, designed by Oliver Bulleid for the Southern Railway.

chance of development. Its first chief mechanical engineer, Richard Maunsell, built efficient 2-6-0 locomotives for mixed traffic, and the 2-cylinder 'King Arthurs' and 4-cylinder 'Lord Nelsons' for passenger work, as well as the powerful 'Schools' 4-4-0. This railway had no heavy freight and so did not require 2-8-0 locomotives. Maunsell's successor was the highly original Oliver Bulleid, whose 'Merchant Navy' and 'West Country' Pacifics were unusual both in appearance and design. They had such un-British features as disc driving wheels and electric lights to enable the firemen to see how the injectors were working at night. Their boilers, tapered at the bottom, and their chain-driven valve gear working in an oil bath, were among other unusual features. They performed magnificently, but presented maintenance problems and were rebuilt on somewhat more conventional lines by Bulleid's successors after nationalisation.

During the war the British railways received 2-8-0 locomotives of Stanier and Riddles (Ministry of Supply) design. Increased attention was paid in the mid-1940s to labour-saving innovations like rocking gates and smokebox-cleaning devices. The standard designs built by the nationalised British Railways owed much to LMS practice; the most interesting type was the 2-10-0. Balancing, lubrication and other techniques had so improved by this time that these 2-10-0s, designed for heavy freight, could also work fast passenger trains. It was one of these units, *Evening Star*, which in 1960 was the last steam locomotive to be constructed by British Railways. That this happened only eight years before the end of regular steam working is frequently, and justifiably, taken as evidence of mismanagement.

In America the inter-war period was essentially the era of the so-called 'superpower' locomotive evolved by William Woodard of the Lima Locomotive Works. Higher speeds and heavier loads were required to compete with highway transport and Woodard's designs of 2-8-4 and 2-10-4 supplied the required power. The four-wheeled truck enabled a much bigger firebox to be carried, thereby increasing the available horsepower. Woodard also used a novel form of articulated connecting rod so as to redistribute the stresses and make fractures less likely, despite the higher horsepower. To prevent crews 'thrashing'

their machines, he incorporated 'limited cut-off'; this meant that steam admission to the cylinders was automatically stopped after 60 per cent of the piston stroke, instead of the 90 per cent usual with American locomotives. For the heaviest trains and stiffest gradients, however, many railroads preferred to buy large Mallet locomotives.

With the advent of the streamline fashion in the 1930s, several passenger locomotives were streamlined and a few high-speed locomotives were specially built for the crack trains; prominent among these were the streamlined *Hiawatha* units. These were of the 4-4-2 wheel arrangement, a configuration which had been popular in America and Europe before 1910, but had soon given place to the Pacific. Most American railroads dieselised in the decade after the war, the last of the large companies to do so being the coal-carrying Norfolk and Western which ended steam traction in 1959. In Canada, the Canadian Pacific, which had built its locomotives at its own Montreal workshops, and possessed some distinctive types (including a fast 4-4-4, the 'Royal Hudson' 4-6-4, and the 'Selkirk' 2-10-4 used in the Rockies), ran its final steam trains in 1960, as did the Canadian National.

In France the locomotive scene was dominated by André Chapelon, often regarded as the world's greatest locomotive designer of this century. Working from theoretical principles, Chapelon rebuilt a conventional Pacific in 1929 to increase its horsepower from 2,000 to 3,000, with reduced fuel and water consumption per unit of horsepower. This he achieved by improving the draughting arrangements with his wide 'Kylchap' exhaust, widening and smoothing the internal steam passages, increasing the superheater temperature and providing a feedwater heater. When the magnitude of this step forward was realised, many French designs were 'Chapelonised'. Chapelon's No 242 A-1, a 4-8-4, was finished after the decision to abandon steam had been taken, but its performance was superior to those of contemporary electric locomotives. This unit was a compound on the Sauvage system; most other French designers had abandoned the compound system in the inter-war period.

In Germany, Richard Wagner took over the locomotive department of the newly unified German railways and carried on the Prussian tradition. This tradition was exemplified in the work of Richard Garbe, who designed well-known Prussian standard types like the 0-8-0 and 0-10-0, as well as the P38 4-6-0, the world's most numerous passenger locomotive. This tradition preferred reliability and ease of construction and maintenance above all else. So compounding was not favoured and locomotives were rather underpowered for their size, but liked by those who had to drive, fire and maintain them. Wagner designed a range of standard locomotives, and also achieved fame with a series of very high-speed steam locomotives of which one, a 4-6-4, reached 124 mph on level track. His best-known locomotive was his type 50 2-10-0, for this became the basis of the wartime *Kreigslok*, thousands of which were used all over Europe both during and after the war.

Like the French, unlike the British, the German railways handled the change-over from steam traction quite wisely, keeping steam units in service until most

Top left *Chapelon's 4-8-4 of 1946 being prepared for exhibition.*
Centre left *A Prussian P38 type locomotive, still at work in Romania.*
Left *A German* Kriegslok *war-service 2-10-0. Many still survive in central Europe.*

main lines had been electrified, thereby reducing the need for diesel locomotives. In western Europe, the most precipitate end of steam traction occurred on the Netherlands Railways, but this was due to the extent of wartime damage which made rapid electrification a better alternative than rehabilitation of the steam locomotive establishment.

In 1982, with the demise through landslide of the Austrian Garsten-Klaus line, regular steam traction came to an end in western Europe outside steam preservation schemes. In Eastern Germany, Poland, Roumania, Hungary and Yugoslavia it persisted, with quite large steam operations continuing in China, India, Turkey and parts of South Africa, Indonesia and South America.

The work of locomotive designers can be examined in more detail with J. N. Westwood's *Locomotive Designers in the Age of Steam* (1977).

Chapter 12

Electrification

Electric railways were a practicable proposition by the end of the 19th century and had a great appeal both to engineers, who appreciated their superior traction capabilities, and to the general public, who associated electric railways with speed, cleanliness and a proper use of the gifts of progress. That railway electrification proceeded so slowly was due to economic rather than technical reasons. This, however, might be qualified with the remark that in retrospect it was advantageous to delay electrification, for the technology was advancing so fast that an electrification system of one decade could be outmoded in the next; this is why so many railways have accepted the inconvenience of using more than one electrification system.

In general, electrification systems differ in the type of current they use and in the means whereby the current is transmitted to and from the locomotive. The main systems are summarised below.

Low-voltage direct current with conductor rail This is one of the earliest systems and is still widely used, being superior for commuter services. Direct-current (dc) traction motors were usual for electric locomotives and trains, so the use of this current in transmission meant that rectifiers associated with alternating current (ac) transmission were not needed, with a consequent saving of weight and expense. The low voltage permitted the use of conductor rails. Typically, the conductor rail is laid outside the running rails, as with the British Rail's Southern Region, but some systems employ a fourth rail to make current return more secure; on the underground lines of London Transport this fourth rail lies between the running rails. Typical voltages for this system lie between 600 and 750 volts. The Long Island RR is 650 V and British Rail Southern Region is 750 V.

With this system, current collection is usually by a metal contact shoe running over the top edge of the conductor rail, even though this risks a break in electrical continuity when ice forms on the rail. The big advantage of the system is that the third rail, thanks to its large cross-section, carries a powerful current, so that close-running trains can draw the great power needed for their numerous accelerations from stops. However, with a low voltage, the lineside sub-stations, which convert the high voltage ac current received from the power station into low voltage dc and feed the latter into the conductor rails, need to be quite close together (about 5 miles or 8 km, although with an intensive train service this distance might need to be reduced). With third-rail systems, the return current passes through the running rails, which are electrically bonded but of lower

Fourth-rail electrification. A London Passenger Transport Board train, running from Baker Street to the outer commuter areas of Buckinghamshire. These trains used to be hauled by electric locomotives of the former Metropolitan Railway, as shown here (M. Deane).

conductivity than the soft conductor rails and therefore entail rather more transmission loss than the latter. There is a tendency for voltages to rise slowly. Thus the London & South Western Railway's electrification out of London was at 600 V, but the Southern Railway system based on the LSWR scheme was 660V, and more recently lines of the successor organisation, the Southern Region of British Rail, have been changed to 750 V.

Medium-voltage direct current with overhead conductors Over long distances with trains at relatively wide intervals, the low-voltage conductor rail system becomes uneconomic. A higher voltage permits sub-stations to be further apart (4–10 miles or 7–16 km, depending on traffic), but needs to be conducted well clear of the ground. Hence the use of overhead wire conductors with the current collected by gear attached to the locomotive or train roof. Usually a pantograph is used for current collection, but tramway-style trolley poles are not unknown. When long-distance railway electrification really got under way in continental Europe between the wars, it was this system which was frequently chosen. France, the Netherlands and the USSR were among those countries which chose the 1,500 V (1.5 kV) standard; Italy chose the more advanced 3,000 V and the USSR and Spain subsequently changed their dc lines to this voltage.

Higher-voltage alternating current with overhead conductors The two main systems are what might be called the American Westinghouse system (11,000 V ac at 25 cycles) and the Central European system (15,000 V ac at 16⅔ cycles). Both of these use single-phase current. The Westinghouse system was adopted for the inter-war electrification of the Pennsylvania and New Haven railroads. The somewhat similar European system was adopted in Scandinavia, Germany, Austria and Switzerland (which means, now that the main lines of these countries are electrified, that central and northern Europe are linked by lines of the same system). These two systems enjoyed the advantage of higher voltage ac transmission; that is, greater distances between substations, lower losses in transmission and conductor wires of smaller cross-sections, enabling the whole overhead structure to be cheaper and lighter. On the other hand, ac traction motors are more complex than dc, and in addition the locomotives had to carry heavy transformers.

Three-phase alternating current with overhead conductors Devised by the Hungarian, Kando, this system exploited the transmission advantages of alternating current, making use of a novel traction motor which worked on three-phase ac. A disadvantage of this motor was that it had only four fixed speeds. So, although the system was adopted in Northern Italy and Hungary, it was later abandoned by those countries. It could be recognised by the use of two conducting wires with a corresponding split pantograph.

High-voltage alternating current with overhead conductors With the development of cheap and lightweight rectifiers to convert ac to dc, the high-voltage industrial frequency alternating current became more attractive. This was in the 1950s and the French were the leaders in this development. The advantages were so great that several railways, which were already partially electrified, decided that it would be better to suffer the inconvenience of two systems than to forego the advantage of using the high-voltage system for future schemes. France itself was among the countries which made this choice, and so was Britain, although the central and northern European block decided to retain the well-developed 15,000 V (15 kV) rather than make the relatively small jump to 25,000 V 50 cycles of the new system.

In general, the advantages of the new standard were the small cross-section of the conductor wires (reducing the demand for expensive copper), the greater distance (about 20 miles or 32 km) between sub-stations, the ease of drawing the electricity from national electric grids, and the high-power but low weight of the locomotives. A disadvantage was that the high voltage increased the risk of flash-overs, so structures like bridges had to be raised to provide a greater clearance above the wires. On some of the earlier British lines electrified on this system, the voltage was intitially stepped down to 6.25 kV in urban sections where structures came close to the catenary. The current also tended to generate electrical disturbances which could affect electric signalling and communication systems.

Further advances beyond 25,000 V (25 kV) have already been embarked upon with specialised railways. In South Africa the ore-carrying Sishen-Saldanha line uses 50 kV, as does the coal-carrying Black Mesa and Powell Lake Railroad in the USA.

Electricity transmission

Especially in Europe, many of the first main line electrifications were in regions where coal was scarce but hydro-electricity abundant. But whatever the electricity source, the transmission network is similar. From the power station directly, or through the national electricity grid, the current is passed to the railway's sub-stations at a high voltage as alternating current; in central Europe, for example, its transmission voltage is 110 kV, and in Britain 136 kV. The sub-station reduces the voltage and may rectify (convert to dc) the current, according to the system in use. The current is then passed into the conductors.

Outwardly the design of catenary and its supports differs markedly from place to place and from system to system. Supports for the catenary may vary from plain timber poles through various concrete types to modern steel lattice and plain steel designs. The supports for the lower voltage systems are markedly more substantial than those designed to carry the lighter catenary of the modern 25 kV system. With the latter, the catenary has separate masts for each track of double-track line and, even with four-track lines, two poles are sufficient, with a strong head-span wire and two cross-span wires straddling the tracks to support the conductor and contact wires.

The British 25 kV lines, which are typical, use what is known as the simple catenary, with the copper contact wire suspended by stainless steel vertical wires, called droppers, from a single aluminium and steel conductor wire. The length of a span (that is, the space between supports) varies, but 250 ft (76 m) is about the maximum desirable. Because the conductor wire is pushed upwards by the locomotive pantograph a greater distance in the centre of the span, it is customary to allow for a specific sag, reaching 3–4 in (75–100 mm) midway between supports. To prevent the contact wire wearing a groove in the metallic carbon contact strip of the pantograph, it is staggered, on straight track being typically 9 in (225 mm) off-centre at one support and another 9 in the other side of the centre line at the next. The conductor of the return current is carried at the top of the supporting masts, as far away as possible from telecommunication wires (usually buried) with which its electromagnetic emanations might interfere. Correct tension in the wire is obtained by tension weights at each end of the wire lengths; these lengths, 'tension lengths', are up to about one mile (5,350 m) long.

Midway between feeder stations, and usually also at the feeder station itself, there is a neutral section to break the electrical continuity. The neutral, or dead, section of contact wire is 15 ft (46 m) in length in British practice and is situated between insulators which are of only slightly greater cross-section than the wire. This permits a pantograph to slide over the section without complications. As the locomotive approaches a neutral section, track magnets actuate its circuit-breaker so that when it enters that section it is not drawing any current (which otherwise could arc over into the neutral section). A similar automatic process closes the circuit-breaker as the new, energised, section is reached.

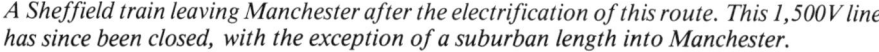

A Sheffield train leaving Manchester after the electrification of this route. This 1,500V line has since been closed, with the exception of a suburban length into Manchester.

The course of electrification
Werner von Siemens demonstrated a small electric locomotive at a Berlin exhibition in 1879. What may claim to be the world's first public electric railway is the still-functioning Volk's Railway at Brighton in England, which carried its first passengers in 1883. In the 1890s, electric locomotives made a hesitant appearance on some of London's underground lines. Meanwhile, in America, successful experiments were made, with van der Poele using overhead wire for power transmission and Frank Sprague devising a multiple-unit form of control in which several powered vehicles of a train could be controlled from one driving cab.

In the beginning, electrification was resorted to where special circumstances made steam traction undesirable: operations in long tunnels, intensive commuter services, and heavily-graded lines where the superior tractive power of electric locomotives could eliminate the double-heading of steam locomotives. It was only later that the superior performance of electric power and its higher thermal efficiency, together with a public demand for something modern, persuaded railway administrations to study long-distance electrification of main routes. Conversion was an expensive undertaking, for a whole infrastructure of power generation, transmission and conduction was required apart from the locomotives. Hence intensity of traffic was a prime consideration; only heavy traffic, over which the high cost of electrification could be spread, seemed likely to justify an electrification scheme. The price of coal was another important determinant. Low traffic density on most American railroads, and abundance of cheap coal in Britain, explain why those two countries lagged behind in electrification.

Switzerland, Austria and Scandinavia Swiss engineers have made many contributions to the technology of electric traction and today Swiss railways are the most electrified of all, possessing a bare handful of diesel locomotives. Mountainous terrain, heavy traffic, lack of coal, abundant hydro-electric resources account for this pre-eminence. Switzerland's neighbour, Austria, has these characteristics too, but to a lesser degree, and moreover coal is not so short in that country. It was only after 1945 that the Austrian main line electrifications were completed. Interestingly, the first line to be electrified was of narrow gauge; it was a mountain line from St Polten and is still open, with some of the original 1911 equipment in service.

In Scandinavia, Sweden was the leader. Her ore-carrying Lapland Railway was electrified in 1923, followed by the Stockholm–Göteborg main line. After Switzerland, she was the most electrified of the world's nations by 1945, in terms of proportion of mileage converted. Norway, although beginning electrification in 1906, was rather slower, but now has about a third of the network electrified. Denmark, a flat country with moderate traffic, has hardly entered the electrification field, but Finland has begun to convert her main lines out of Helsinki, and is the sole export market for Soviet electric locomotives. Finland uses the 25 kV system, whereas Sweden, Norway, Switzerland and Austria opted for the 15 kV German standard.

Italy Italy, in the inter-war period, was a leader in the rate of electrification. Italian scientists had played a great role in the discovery and utilisation of electricity, so there was a national tradition to provide enthusiasm. Coal was absent and there was hydro-electricity in the Italian Alps. And there was Mussolini.

Moving to the 3,000 V dc system, away from the ingenious 3-phase Kando

Electric traction on the DB in the Bavarian Alps. In continental Europe the availability of hydro-electricity has made mountainous areas an attractive proposition for electrification.

system which had been used for the earlier conversions, Italy began to electrify very fast, spurred by Mussolini's quest for renown and economic independence. By 1939, fast electric trains, luxuriously appointed, could run from Milan to Naples at average speeds of around 70 mph (113 km/h). In the post-Mussolini period the process continued, although perhaps with less emphasis on luxury trains.

Germany With a strong steam engine tradition, and abundant coal, the German railways were slow to electrify, despite the advanced technology of the domestic electrical engineering industry. However, in 1911, the Prussian Royal State Railways began the conversion of the line through the mountains of Silesia. This was finished, at 15 kV, in 1928, only to be dismantled by the Russians in 1945. Elsewhere by 1945 there were electrified commuter routes around Hamburg and Berlin, and a few other electric lines, principally in the mountainous areas of Bavaria and in Württemburg, but including the Magdeburg–Leipzig trunk route. Post-war electrification has embraced all the main lines of the German Federal Republic and several secondary routes as well. In the German Democratic Republic, progress has been slower, although the main east-west line between Dresden and Karl Marx Stadt has been converted.

The Low Countries The Netherlands, because of war damage, embarked on a rapid electrification programme, utilising the 1,500 V dc system which had been used for the small electrified pre-war mileage. Like Switzerland, the Netherlands now possesses very few diesel locomotives. Belgian electrification, at 3,000 V, proceeded more slowly, and in fact is still under way, although the principal main lines are now electric.

France There were some technically interesting electrifications in France before the First World War and the biggest venture was that of the PO Railway which, from 1900, was electrifying its main line out of Paris at 1,500 V. Orleans was reached in 1926 and by 1939 the electrified line stretched to Bordeaux, Toulouse and the Pyrénées. In addition, the Ouest Region of the SNCF had finished its Paris–Le Mans electrification by 1939. When the war ended, electrification of the trunk line from Paris to Marseilles was begun, still on the 1,500 V

Electric traction in France. On the left is an elderly 'box cab' locomotive, now relegated to shunting, while a TGV high-speed electric multiple-unit stands on the right.

system. In the 1950s the electrification, at 25 kV, was undertaken from Metz to Thionville, in the industrial east of the country. This system was soon adopted for all future schemes, except for extensions of lines already on the older system. The next main line conversion was of the old Nord Railway main line from Paris to Lille and the Belgian frontier. Since then, electrification has proceeded steadily, culminating in the new Paris–South East high-speed route, built from the start as an electrified line.

Britain Some of the British railway companies showed considerable enterprise before the First World War, quite apart from the London underground railways. Several systems were used. In 1904 the Lancashire & Yorkshire Railway began its 37-mile Liverpool–Southport conversion with a third-rail 600 V system. This system was also used the same year when the North Eastern Railway began its Newcastle area project. Technically more adventurous, both using 600 V 25 cycles ac current, were the Midland Railway's 10-mile Lancaster–Heysham and the London Brighton & South Coast's South London schemes.

During the First World War the London & North Western Railway was converting, on the four-rail 630 V system, its London suburban lines; the L & Y was building on experience with its 1,200 V dc third rail Manchester–Bury project, and the LSWR was electrifying from London to Wimbledon at 650 V with third rail conduction. Moreover, the North Eastern Railway was finishing a freight-only electrification from Newport to Shildon; unlike other British schemes, which used electric self-propelled passenger trains, this latter scheme used electric locomotives.

After the railway amalgamation of 1923, the NER's scheme for electrifying its York–Newcastle main line was abandoned by its successor company, even though a first locomotive had actually been built for this line. However, the LSWR's electrification out of London (Waterloo) became the nucleus of the Southern Railway's really large-scale third-rail electrification of, first, its suburban and, later, its outer-suburban services. By 1939 this scheme had reached Brighton and Portsmouth, the electric trains were generating vastly increased passenger traffic, and the Southern's electrified mileage was about 700 miles (1,125 km). After the war, the Southern Region of BR continued with this conversion, extending main line electrification to Dover, Southampton and Bournemouth.

Although several detailed studies showed that high returns on capital might be achieved by electrification, the investment capital itself was not willingly forthcoming in the inter-war period. Nine miles of suburban track, jointly owned by the LNER and LMS companies, from Manchester to Altrincham, were electrified at 1,500 V in 1931, and the LNER did embark on the electrification of its steeply graded line between Manchester and Sheffield through the Woodhead Tunnel and of its commuter line from London (Liverpool Street) to Shenfield. The war interrupted both these projects but they were finished in 1954 and 1949 respectively. However, the Woodhead electrification, apart from its commuter extremity, came to an end with the closing of the route in 1982, while the Shenfield scheme, an immediate success, was extended to Southend but converted to the 25 kV system in 1960 from its original 1,500 V dc.

In 1956, after the adoption of the 1955 Modernisation Plan which envisaged further electrification, British Railways decided that future electrification, apart from that on the Southern Region, would be on the 25 kV system. Some preliminary trials with the new high voltage system had been started in 1953 on the Lancaster–Heysham line. The first big main line project was from Liverpool to Crewe, rather a strange choice which, however, justified itself when the London (Euston) to Crewe conversion was achieved in 1965. The consequent vastly improved service between London, Manchester and Liverpool (Birmingham was included a year later) produced enough new passenger traffic to return the invested capital sooner than had been anticipated. In 1973–74 this scheme was extended to cover the whole West Coast Route, right up to Glasgow. In the meantime Glasgow suburban and outer suburban lines had been electrified.

Other suburban electrifications were in the London area, from Fenchurch Street to Shoeburyness in 1962, with further services out of Liverpool Street

Suburban electrification in Scotland. An electric multiple-unit train at Glasgow Central, on BR's 25,000V Glasgow network (BR).

Electrification

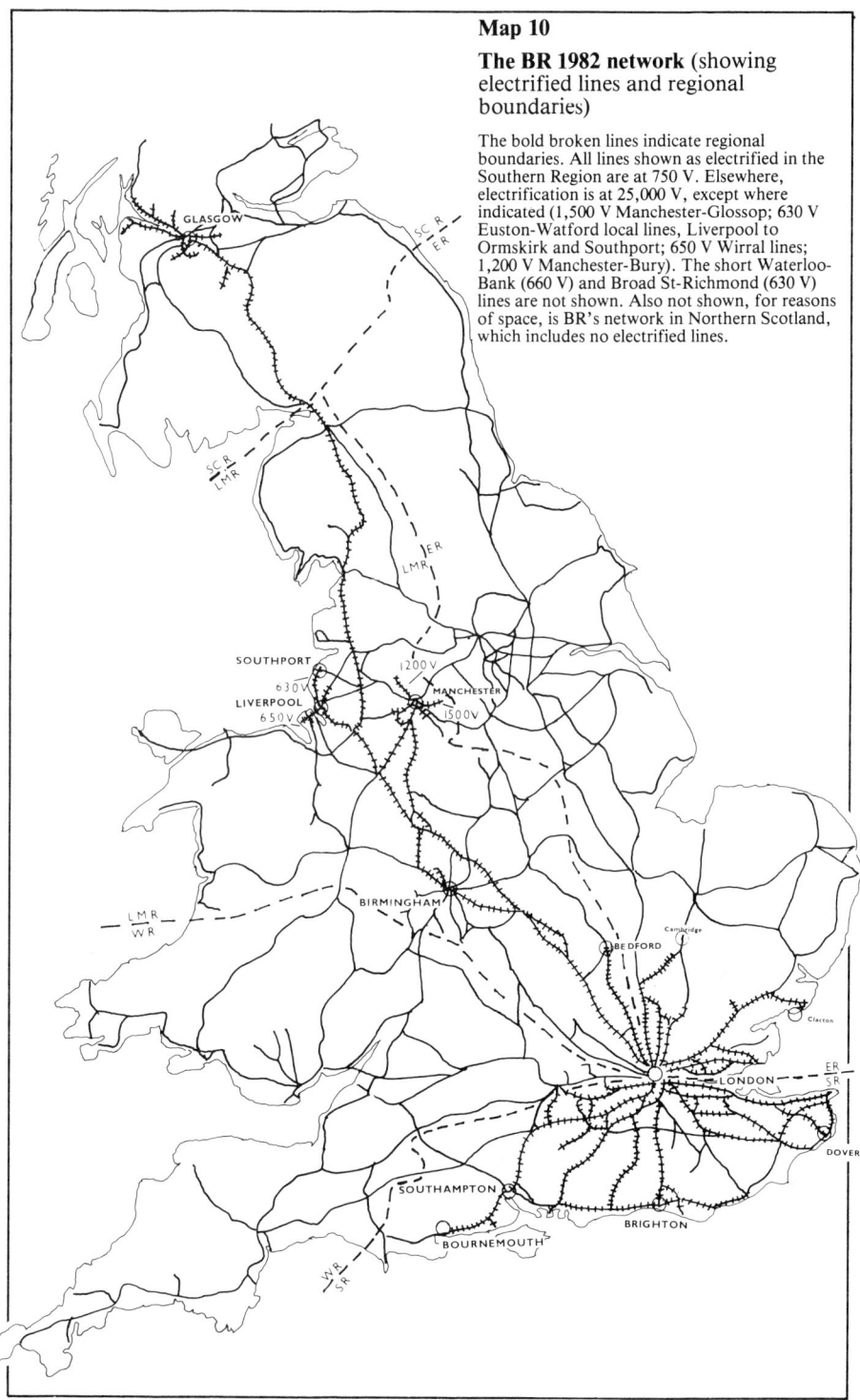

Map 10

The BR 1982 network (showing electrified lines and regional boundaries)

The bold broken lines indicate regional boundaries. All lines shown as electrified in the Southern Region are at 750 V. Elsewhere, electrification is at 25,000 V, except where indicated (1,500 V Manchester-Glossop; 630 V Euston-Watford local lines, Liverpool to Ormskirk and Southport; 650 V Wirral lines; 1,200 V Manchester-Bury). The short Waterloo-Bank (660 V) and Broad St-Richmond (630 V) lines are not shown. Also not shown, for reasons of space, is BR's network in Northern Scotland, which includes no electrified lines.

converted as well as the outer-suburban route from London (Kings Cross) to Royston. This latter scheme, finished in 1977, was known as the Great Northern scheme. Finally, electrification work began on the old Midland Railway's line out of St Pancras, London, the completion as far as Bedford being achieved in 1982.

North America This continent is remarkable, not only for the low proportion of its mileage which is electrified, but also for the long lengths of line which, after some years of technically successful electric operation, have been 'de-electrified'. The first electrification schemes were undertaken for environmental reasons. The Baltimore & Ohio Railroad, as early as 1888, decided to build a new route across Baltimore as an underground electrified line. This was finished in 1895, using the 600 V dc system with overhead third-rail pick-up. In 1903 the New York legislature obliged New York Central RR to electrify (for reasons of pollution) its line into Grand Central Terminal. This was accomplished with a third-rail system operating at 600 V.

In 1918 the Canadian Northern Railway decided to electrify its new line northwards out of Montreal, since the first 3 miles (4.5 km) were in tunnel. Meanwhile, the Norfolk & Western RR electrified the line through its Elkhorn Tunnel, which was a single-track tunnel on a heavy grade interposed between two double-track sections. To speed the traffic through this bottleneck, the railroad had previously powered its coal trains with three Mallet-type locomotives, which produced enough smoke to half-suffocate, and potentially to suffocate completely, the enginemen. A novel system was used, with an 11 kV single-phase current, picked up by the locomotives and converted to three-phase; the Westinghouse designers at this time thought the three-phase traction motor was the motor of the future. The conversion was successful; it was opened in 1915, grew to 70 miles (112 km), but was abandoned after the Second World War when a line diversion eliminated the troublesome tunnel and enabled steam locomotives to return.

Not far away, another coal-hauling line, the Virginian Railroad, electrified 134 miles (215 km) of its heavily-graded route from Mullens to Roanoke in the 1920s but later this line was de-electrified in favour of diesels. Meanwhile, the Milwaukee RR, from 1914 to 1927, electrified 656 miles (1,055 km) of its trans-continental line from Montana to the Pacific. This project was not for environmental reasons, but for economic advantage; moreover it enabled the Railroad's publicity department to produce a rich harvest of self-congratulatory advertising. Hydro-electricity was available, and this was fed to locomotives by overhead wire as 3,000 V dc.

The Milwaukee RR's competitor, the Great Northern, after a brief experiment with three-phase power, electrified some of its mountainous tunnel sections at 11,000 V ac. Despite the use of very large bi-polar locomotives, this electrification, like that of the Milwaukee RR, came to an end in the 1950s. Electric traction was not sufficiently superior to diesels, it was thought, to justify a railroad maintaining both forms of motive power. The oldest of the main line schemes is that of the New Haven RR from New York to New Haven, achieved by 1914 and totalling 72 miles (116 km) of route. It was the New Haven's successful exploitation of the 11 kV ac system which helped persuade the Pennsylvania RR to adopt that system for its own project, which was the most successful of the US main line schemes. The route was from New York to Washington and Harrisburg, carrying a heavy freight as well as passenger

Electrification

The major American electrification was that of the Pennsylvania RR. This picture shows one of the latter's Washington–New York trains, headed by a distinctive GG-1 type locomotive.

service. The conversion was undertaken in the 1930s and was an immediate success in terms of economics, operating, and public esteem.

Like other railroads, the successor of PRR, Conrail, has been studying the possibility of further electrification in view of the increased price of diesel fuel. So far, largely because the cost of electricity generation has risen by almost as much, further electrification still seems uncertain. But the chief deterrent is still the low traffic density of US railroads, even after line closures and mergers. Over the past decades the only new electrifications have been short lines owned by electric-power companies. Of these, the coal-hauling Muskingum Electric RR of 1968 is technically interesting, as it uses 25 kV current at, unusually, 60 cycles. The common-carrier lines no longer haul freight trains with electric locomotives, although Amtrak is a user of passenger electric units. The electrification at 25 kV of the New Haven to Boston line, the section of the North East Corridor still unelectrified, awaits federal funding.

Other countries The USSR stands out as the biggest operator of electrified railway, using both 3,000 V dc and the more modern 25 kV ac. Electrification began in the 1920s but the big spurt came in the 1960s. It is now possible to travel by electric train from Murmansk to the Persian frontier, and from the Polish frontier to Vladivostok, with one small break in Siberia. Elsewhere, most railway administrations have embarked on electrification projects, or at least are studying the possibilities. The first Irish electrification is to be from Dublin to Howth and Bray, at 1,500 V.

Chapter 13

The electric locomotive

Up to the 1940s, electric locomotives followed two opposing patterns. For a long time they were characterised by steam locomotive-type driving wheels, and often by coupling rods. But the locomotive on motored trucks provided a better riding locomotive and, nowadays, the rigid wheelbase locomotive is built only for yard and slow-speed work.

Soon after the acceptance of the powered-truck concept, the electric locomotive began to benefit from the post-war advances in technology. Westinghouse introduced an improved mercury rectifier, incorporating *ignitrons*, in 1950 and, although this was a great improvement, it was the introduction of solid-state rectifiers that really made on-board conversion of ac to dc more practicable. Then came a succession of electronic advances which transformed the performance characteristics of electric traction. The latest of these is the thyristor, but there seems little doubt that other advances will follow. These improvements have made the inter-war electric locomotives obsolete and most of these are being withdrawn from service because of this obsolescence rather than because of longevity; even better than the steam locomotive, the electric locomotive can be kept in service for a half-century or more.

The main features of the electric locomotive are as follows:

Cab The double-ended arrangement is now usual; that is, a cab is provided at each end to dispense with the use of turntables. Single-ended locomotives are still sometimes built, while the so called *steeple-cab* layout is by no means extinct. In the latter there is a single central cab with the pantograph mounted on its roof, and the body usually slopes down towards its extremities to provide a good field of view.

Chopper control This replaces the resistance bank in a dc locomotive and is a modern innovation which appeared in the Netherlands and Belgium in 1967, was widely adopted for new French and Italian locomotives in the 1970s, and has also been used in other countries. The equipment is essentially a set of electronic switches, which switch the current on and off so rapidly that what reaches the traction motors is a series of short pulses. By increasing the length of pulse, the driver increases the voltage reaching the motors, thus effecting a smooth acceleration, as opposed to the stepped acceleration provided by resistances.

If a locomotive uses rheostatic brakes, which need resistances in any case, the *shunt chopper* can be applied instead. The resistance bank is retained, but each resistance has an associated chopper which smoothly diverts current away from

An early German 'steeple-cab' electric locomotive, of a pre-1914 design, and still part of the DB locomotive stock in the 1980s.

it until it is totally short-circuited. In this way the number of resistances in use changes, the change being not in steps but in a smooth progression.

Circuit-breaker This is situated close to the pantograph or collector shoe and is typically operated by air-blast. Its function is to cut off the supply of current while the pantograph or shoe is still in connection with the power supply; in effect, to shut off current while the locomotive is still moving. Its most frequent use is when the locomotive passes over the neutral section dividing the territories of adjacent feeder stations, but its original function of protecting against overload or short circuits is still important.

Collector shoe This is the part, usually of cast iron, which slides over the conductor rail to collect current. It is usually on the side of the power truck.

Current invertor This is another example of modern technology and is significant for both electric and diesel traction. It has its origins in British experimental work, brought to commercial fruition by German industry in 1971. Its effect is to enable three-phase ac traction motors to be used. These motors run at a constant speed for any given frequency. The solid-state current invertor converts dc and may be regarded as three sets of electronic switches, each of which emits the current in pulses. With the three switches carefully adjusted, the combined output resembles three-phase current whose frequency can be varied. This enables the hitherto inflexible ac three-phase motor to operate over the full range of speeds. Such a motor, among other advantages, has fewer components subject to wear. A small class of three-phase invertor locomotives (type 120) has been on trial on German Federal Railways.

Gearing Except for yard locomotives, a geared transmission is now general. In this, the pinion of the traction motor is kept in mesh with a gear wheel on the axle. There are many variations, each designed to overcome the problem of maintaining constant mesh, with the two main components being in up-and-down spring-controlled movement. The *gear ratio*, determined by the number of cogs on the gearwheel, affects the traction characteristics; the higher the ratio the greater the tractive effort and the lower the maximum speed. Sometimes otherwise identical locomotives are fitted with different ratio gears, according to the duties for which they are intended.

High tension conductor This wire, which is usually clearly visible on the roof of pantograph-fitted locomotives, carries the current into the interior of the locomotive, to the transformer.

Pantograph The original trolley-pole method of current collection is still seen on a few electrified industrial railways where speeds are low, but most electrified railways use the conventional rectangular, or diamond, pantograph which folds upwards and downwards as necessary. It is usual, for safety reasons, for it to be raised in contact with the catenary only when the locomotive is moving or about to move. Pantograph design is not as simple as it might appear. In particular, there is always a problem of contact deteriorating at high speed, just when most power is required. The elbow-shaped pantograph, now preferred for many main line locomotives, is known as the Faiveley type, Faiveley being the French company which made a success of it.

A mishap which, though rare, is greatly feared is the involuntary 'de-wiring' of the pantograph when in motion. This not only stops the train and damages the pantograph but, by ravaging the catenary, can bring electric train services to a halt over the section affected. The British main line up the hilly West Coast has experienced this mishap — the swaying of the locomotive and lateral displacement of the wires by high wind being sufficient to pull a too-slack contact wire over the edge of the pantograph. Most locomotives carry two pantographs, although modern British designs have only one. It is usual for one pantograph to be raised, with the other kept as spare, but on heavily graded lines, as in the Alps, both pantographs are often raised so as to maximise current collection.

Rectifier The rectifier converts alternating current to direct current, ac being superior for purposes of transmission with dc, at least until the invention of modern current invertors, being most suitable for powering traction motors. In

Left *An elbow-type (Faiveley) pantograph, fitted to a Belgian locomotive* (SNCB).

Right *A BR locomotive on the West Coast route, showing the single, frame (or 'diamond') type, pantograph* (BR).

dc electrifications the rectifiers are placed in lineside sub-stations whereas with ac schemes the locomotives themselves carry rectifiers (except when ac motors are used). Although Westinghouse was successful in using the old-style and rather heavy ignitron mercury arc rectifiers in locomotives, it was the appearance of solid-state rectification, at first with germanium and later with the superior silicon diodes, that permitted the design of really lightweight on-board rectifiers, thereby encouraging the advance to 25 kV ac electrification schemes.

Regenerative brakes Since an electric motor is basically an electric generator with its functions reversed, there is technically the possibility of braking electric trains, not by means of conventional brake-shoes, but by using the traction motors as dynamos, the energy of the descending train being absorbed by the rotational resistance developed in the motors. The electricity thus generated may be fed back into the catenary to help power other trains, notably those ascending the same gradient. This is called *regenerative* or *recuperative* braking and is used on several heavily-graded electrified routes. However, some administrations have decided that the advantages are not worth the trouble and the extra expense. One difficulty is that the driver of the braking train has to ensure that the current he is feeding back into the system matches that already in the conductor. New technology, however, is simplifying this.

Resistances Resistance banks are the traditional method of applying varying current to dc traction motors. By taking resistances out of the circuit one by one, more power is progressively fed to the motors. The drawback is a certain jerkiness experienced as one step is changed to the next, and this can initiate wheelslip.

Rheostatic brakes In the USA these are often called *dynamic* brakes. They work in the same way as regenerative brakes except that the current generated is not fed back to the catenary but is passed to resistances on board the locomotive where it is converted to heat, which is then dissipated by ventilation.

Rod drive Perhaps because of the lingering steam locomotive tradition, rod drive was favoured by many of the early electric locomotive designers. Typically, the traction motors, mounted in the body, drove a *jackshaft* (which lay athwart the locomotive), whose rotation was transmitted to the locomotive-

style driving wheels by coupling rods. It was convenient, therefore, for the centre of the jackshaft to be in line with the wheel centres, although if it was not there were devices available to yoke it to the coupling rod. Coupling rod drive meant heavy moving weights, which had to be balanced, as in a steam locomotive, but it did avoid the problem of unsprung weight raised by traction motors geared directly to the axles. It is still used, therefore, for yard locomotives in some countries.

Suspension The suspension of the traction motors is a difficult design problem for which many solutions have been proposed. The essential compromise is between the rigidity needed for the close and reliable meshing of the traction motor pinion with the gear driving the axle, and the flexible suspension needed to save track and mechanism from jolting. With *nose suspension*, part of the motor weight is carried by the axle, and is therefore unsprung, while the other part is carried by the framing of the truck, which is itself spring-borne. This is sometimes known as tramcar suspension and is generally used on multiple-unit trains and also most diesel-electric locomotives. It is not so kind to the track as *fully springborne* suspension, but the latter is more difficult and expensive to contrive.

In general, springborne suspension makes use of two devices: (1) a pinion held in constant mesh with the axle's gearing, connected to the motor by a jointed shaft or (2) the *quill*, which is a hollow shaft attached to the locomotive or truck frame (on bearings) and inside which the axle is both held and free to move. Swiss engineers, very prominent in electric locomotive development, did most of the work required to make this a success. They also originated the less widespread but ingenious *Büchli* drive, which uses gears driven by rods.

Tap-changing Control of output on locomotives carrying transformers is traditionally effected by tap-changing, with contacts being moved up and down the windings (usually, nowadays, on the high-voltage side).

Thyristor control The thyristor, which is only now beginning to come into general use, both rectifies and regulates the current. It was Swedish Railways and the Swedish ASEA company which pioneered this device, the first prototype motor coach coming in operation in 1964. The Rc series of locomotives, which include the units built by General Motors for Amtrak, incorporate it. Put simply, the thyristors pass current only during the half-cycle of alternating current. If half the thyristors are active in each half-cycle, what emerges is a direct current. Since the thyristors' current-passing action can be varied in time within the half-cycle, the output can be controlled, thereby dispensing with the tap-changing method of increasing voltage in steps. This smooth, stepless, transition greatly increases the real adhesion, and hence practicable tractive power, of the locomotive.

There also exist *tap-thyristor* locomotives, in which tap-changing is retained but thyristors are applied to increase the voltage between tappings smoothly. In Britain, ASEA thyristor equipment was fitted to the final unit of the type 87 electric locomotives, No 87 101, and to the Advanced Passenger Train.

Traction motors These have steadily improved over the decades. One field of improvement is the method of insulation with the aim of reducing maintenance expense. Another is in ventilation and heat dissipation, permitting a greater output without overheating. Far easier to design, and with better characteristics than ac, are dc motors. They have greatest *torque* (turning effort) at low speeds, like a steam locomotive, so tractive power tends to be greatest when it is most

The electric locomotive

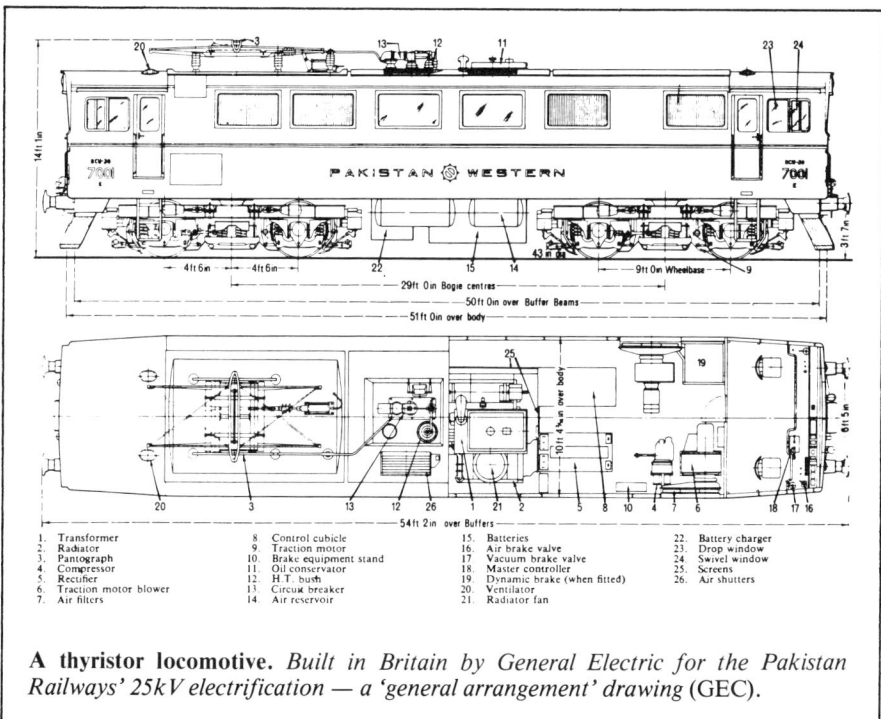

A thyristor locomotive. *Built in Britain by General Electric for the Pakistan Railways' 25kV electrification — a 'general arrangement' drawing* (GEC).

needed. It is usual to connect them on the locomotive so that, at different stages of acceleration, they can be used in parallel, in series-parallel, and in series. At the higher speeds, *field weakening* is used to inhibit the production of opposing current which otherwise would create drag. On the 15 kV system, ac commutator traction motors are used, either series-wound or repulsion/induction.

Transformers These reduce the voltage to a level suitable for use in the traction motors.

Wheel arrangement The practice of having large driving wheel and small carrying wheels is now obsolete. One of the great advantages of the modern electric locomotive is that it is *total-adhesion*, with all the weight being carried on driving wheels. A number of countries, notably the USSR and Italy, favour locomotives which are built in two sections, with a coupling between them to provide articulation. This is one way to provide a multiplicity of axles without the problem of stability and overhang associated with a long rigid locomotive.

Specialised types of electric locomotive
Multi-current locomotives These are locomotives which may work on two or more systems. They are more expensive to build and maintain than conventional types, but eliminate engine-changing at points where one electrification system meets another. They may be used internally within a single country, or on international services. The Belgian National Railways, because of their geographical situation, make great use of *quadricurrent* locomotives, which carry equipment enabling them to work on the Belgian 3,000 V dc, the Dutch 1,500 V dc, the French 25,000 V ac and the German 15,000 V ac systems.

A French-built multi-current locomotive of the Belgian National Railways (SNCB).

Electro-diesel locomotives These are rare, but are used successfully by the Southern Region of British Rail. The BR units are 1,600 hp electric locomotives with a 600 hp diesel engine which, driving a generator, can provide current when the locomotive is on a non-electrified section.

Battery locomotives A few railways have owned these, which are yard units built as electric locomotives but without pantographs and carrying high-capacity batteries. On electrified lines they avoid the need to provide yards and sidings with catenary, but the diesel yard locomotive is now preferred.

Motor coaches Sometimes taking the form of *motor baggage cars*, these are of passenger vehicle shape and dimension, can carry passengers or baggage, but are provided with traction motors sufficient for them to haul several passenger cars. They are popular in Switzerland.

Data, descriptions and pictures of about 140 electric locomotive designs are given in *World Electric Locomotives* by K. Harris (1981).

Chapter 14

The diesel locomotive

As soon as the internal combustion engine became feasible, ideas were put forward for its incorporation in railway locomotives. Since its thermal efficiency was high, and fuel costs were such an important element in a railway's operating costs, this promised to be a very useful step forward. The main problem was (and remains) the transmission of the energy manifested in the fast-revolving crankshaft to the necessarily slow-moving wheels. A system of gears, as in automobiles, was not suited to locomotives because it was found impossible to design a mechanical transmission which could stand up both to the heavier powers and loads required by a locomotive and to the oscillations and jolts to which a railway vehicle is subject. An electric transmission seemed to be one way round this problem; the engine would drive a generator which in turn would supply current to traction motors. In other words, the internal combustion locomotive would be a variety of electric tram, in which the current would be produced on board rather than in a power station.

The first successful application of the new idea was, in fact, on railcars powered by petrol engines driving generators. Such cars, known as gas-electrics in North America, were quite successful on that continent and had a long life there. But the petrol engine, due to its necessarily low compression, is less efficient than the diesel engine and the latter soon superseded the petrol engine in railway use. Diesel-type engines, known as oil engines, had in fact been used to power a handful of yard locomotives built in Yorkshire in the 1890s, even before Rudolf Diesel had developed his own kind of oil engine. The first successful diesel-electric vehicles were some railcars built by the Swedish company ASEA for a Swedish railway in 1912. Also in 1912, Rudolf Diesel, the Prussian Royal State Railways and the engine manufacturer, Sulzer, combined forces to produce the first main line diesel locomotive. This had a 1,200 hp diesel engine but the transmission, or drive, was misbegotten; it had a crankshaft athwart the body driving a jackshaft and coupling rods. Up to 10 mph (6 km/h), compressed air was used to drive it, the intention being to cut in the diesel engine when that speed was reached. This was the weakness on which the locomotive foundered, for the diesel engine customarily refused to fire when it was supposed to, because the air had cooled the cylinders too drastically.

So the first successful main line diesel locomotive had to wait until the 1920s, when the Russian engineer, Lomonosov, encouraged by Lenin and with the cooperation of German locomotive builders, built for the Soviet Railways a 1,200 hp locomotive with electric transmission which, despite its faults, showed that the diesel locomotive was practicable. The Russians and the Germans then wasted a good deal of time, talent and money seeking a non-electric transmission; although the diesel-electric worked, it seemed an unsatisfactory solution to many engineers for it required three major power aggregates (engine, generator and traction motors) to do what, ideally, one engine could do. Nevertheless, a series of diesel-electrics appeared in the USSR. These, like Lomonosov's unit, had a rigid wheelbase and locomotive-type wheel arrangement. They were plagued by mechanical faults and poor maintenance and, in the late 1930s, the USSR abandoned further dieselisation until, at the end of the Second World War, imported US diesel locomotives showed them that their earlier faith in this type of motive power had not been misplaced.

Meanwhile, on a smaller scale, other European countries had built diesel main line locomotives. Among these was a diesel-electric built in Britain by Beardmore for Canadian National Railways, several experimental units for European railways, some novel and successful trains for the Argentine, in which the locomotive was a 'power vehicle', generating electricity to supply traction motors distributed along the axles of the train. But perhaps the most successful was a series of diesel-electric locomotives supplied by the Danish firm of Frichs to the Royal Thailand Railways. The latter, of from 1,000 hp to 1,500 hp, worked satisfactorily for many years.

Meanwhile, in the USA, General Electric built on its experience with gas-electrics to build, first, 400 hp gas-electric locomotives for the Dan Patch Railroad in 1915 and then, in co-operation with the steam locomotive builder, Alco, to market diesel-electric yard locomotives; one of these, No 1000 of the Central of New Jersey Railroad, is now preserved as the first commercially successful diesel-electric locomotive in the USA. The power of these locomotives gradually increased and there was a small but steady market for them.

However, the diesel locomotive faced several handicaps. Although it had much lower fuel costs than steam engines, and had higher availability, being capable of working for days with only short breaks, its first cost was far higher than that of a steam locomotive or of an electric locomotive. A big production run could reduce this cost, but not sufficiently to undercut the competing motive power. To justify this high initial cost, it was essential that the diesel locomotive produced more work, in terms of hours in service or ton-miles produced, than the steam locomotive. A diesel-electric locomotive having this potential appeared in 1939 from General Motors. This US automobile company had the resources to finance a long trial-and-error period and it had the advantage of a new design of engine which was both lightweight and reliable and had powered some streamlined diesel trains in the early 1930s.

Its 1939 prototype, which was demonstrated at GM expense on several railroads, was a freight machine of four units, totalling 5,400 hp. It was immediately accepted by several railroads and, during the ensuing war, GM was the only company allowed to build main line diesel units. This enabled GM to play the leading part in the post-war US dieselisation, completed in the 1950s. The GE-Alco consortium, which on the eve of the war had introduced the revolutionary 'road-switcher' (a diesel-electric locomotive which could be used in passenger, freight or even yard service) did make a post-war comeback, but could not catch up with GM. It is only in recent decades that GE, minus the Alco connection, has become a real competitor of GM.

In Europe the diesel locomotive advanced more slowly. In pre-war Britain the

Road-switchers, which now dominate the US railroad scene, refuel at a depot in Wyoming (Burlington Northern RR).

LMS Railway successfully adopted the six-wheel diesel-electric yard locomotive, the final design of which is perpetuated in BR's numerous Type 08 diesel. The GWR, meanwhile, was having success with its series of diesel-engined railcars. Nationalisation delayed large-scale dieselisation, as it was decided to keep steam in service until electrification was accomplished; a promising dieselisation scheme proposed by the LNER was quietly buried, and main line diesel prototypes ordered by the LMS and Southern railways were put on trial with a marked absence of enthusiasm.

Then, just as the production of a new range of steam locomotives was getting into full swing, BR's 1955 Modernisation Plan committed it to a rapid and total dieselisation. The result was that newly-built steam locomotives were scrapped and that an unnecessary variety of diesel locomotives were acquired from British builders. The more experienced American locomotive builders were not encouraged to participate in this programme, which resulted in the acquisition of a diesel locomotive fleet which could not sustain the promises made for this form of traction. In France and Germany dieselisation was steadier and on a smaller scale. Each of these countries, and Belgium, had its own locomotive industry which produced a number of good designs of which only a handful, after careful trial, were adopted for large-scale acquisition.

Types of diesel locomotive
Diesel-electric This type of locomotive is the most widespread among main line types. Its incorporation of a generator and traction motors makes it heavier and more expensive than a non-electric diesel locomotive, but the reliability and convenience of electric transmission usually is sufficient to outweigh these considerations.

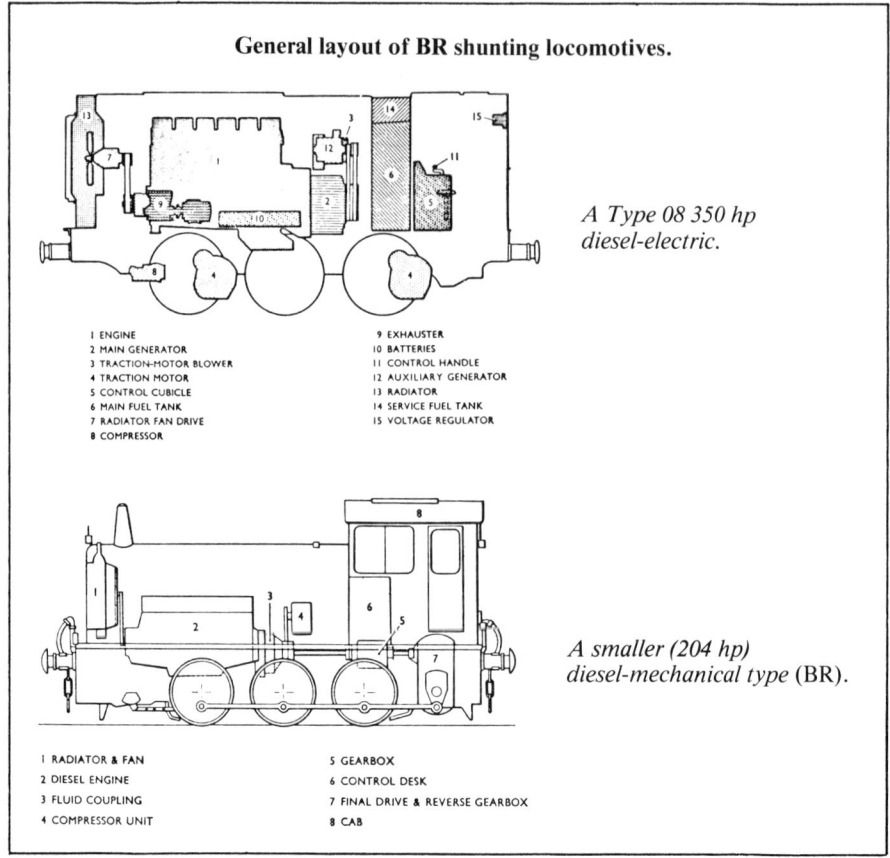

A Type 08 350 hp diesel-electric.

A smaller (204 hp) diesel-mechanical type (BR).

Diesel-mechanical This employs a gearbox transmission, in principle akin to that of an automobile, giving, typically, four speed ranges. It has the advantage of lightness, cheapness and simplicity but, within the space and weight limitations of a railway vehicle, it has not been possible to design such transmissions capable of withstanding the higher power outputs. It is therefore found in low-power yard locomotives and in diesel self-propelled trains.

Diesel-hydraulic These have hydro-mechanical transmission and may be either yard or main line units. German engineers made a success of hydro-mechanical transmission and their Mekydro and Voith systems were used in German Federal Railways (DB) main line diesel locomotives as well as in a range of locomotives built by the Western Region of BR (the 'Warships', 'Westerns' and 'Hymeks'). This transmission was much lighter than the corresponding electric transmissions. However, advances in electric technology, especially those associated with solid-state circuitry, reduced the advantage of hydraulic transmission. The diesel-hydraulic main line locomotives of BR were scrapped after comparatively short lives, while the DB now favours electric transmission. However, the type is still built for certain non-European railways and for yard or low-power duties. A handful of German-built main line examples were acquired by two US transcontinental railroads in the 1950s, but the orders were not repeated.

Major components of the diesel locomotive

Engine Diesel engines work by compression, the upward stroke of the piston so compressing the air that it reaches a temperature sufficient to ignite the oil fuel which is sprayed in at the appropriate moment. Unlike the petrol engine, which cannot tolerate a high pressure, the compression ratio of the diesel engine is high and therefore very efficient in terms of thermal efficiency, but it demands a stronger and therefore heavier cylinder. Engines may work on the two-stroke or four-stroke cycle. In the former there is combustion every second stroke of the piston and it therefore gives more power, other things being equal, than the four-stroke, in which combustion occurs half as frequently. However the four-stroke provides better scope for 'scavenging' (clearance of exhaust elements from the cylinder) and has other advantages which make it somewhat more popular for locomotive use than the 2-stroke. Slow running speeds (up to about 1,250 revolutions of the crankshaft per minute) are accompanied by low maintenance costs while high (2,000 rpm and over) speeds are associated with considerable wear and tear. The latter are used, therefore, where high power and small dimensions and weight have to be reconciled. In Britain and elsewhere it has frequently been found worthwhile to 'de-rate' locomotive engines; that is, reduce their speed below the original specification and accept a somewhat lower maximum power output for the advantage of trouble-free running.

Cylinders may be arranged in V-form or in-line, depending on space available. The triangular arrangement of the cylinders around a central crankshaft was successful in the *Deltic* engine which powered the 'Deltic' locomotives of the Eastern Region of BR, but is uncommon. The non-availability of lightweight engines sufficiently robust to withstand the buffeting endured by a railway vehicle was for long a hindrance to the development of a satisfactory diesel locomotive. Such engines only began to appear in the 1930s. The baseplate of the engine must be very strong; on the early Russian diesel locomotives, and others, it tended to buckle in service.

Since the fuel which can be burned in each cycle is limited by the oxygen

Below left *A Type 08 shunting locomotive of BR. This design is a direct descendant of similar diesel-electric shunters purchased by the LMS in the 1930s.*

Below right *One of the main line diesel-electric locomotives ordered by the Southern Railway just prior to nationalisation* (M. Deane).

available, it is usual to compress the air before admitting it to the cylinder. This is called supercharging, and is usually achieved by a turbo-charger (a compressor powered by a turbine turned by the engine's exhaust gases). Since compressing the air also raises its temperature, with a consequent deterioration of efficiency, it is often cooled in a heat-exchanger; the engine is then described as turbocharged and intercooled.

Generator This is constructed like an electric motor. Its rotating part, the armature, is generally directly coupled to the engine crankshaft, and the end bearing of the latter carries part of its weight. The generator does in fact serve as an electric motor on starting; it is powered by a storage battery for this duty and, as the armature rotates, it 'cranks' the diesel engine in order to start the latter. Development of solid-state rectifiers has now made it possible to substitute an alternator (generating alternating current) instead of the conventional generator. The alternator is both cheaper to buy and to maintain; a rectifier, nowadays cheap and light, converts its output to the dc required by the traction motors. The French 3,600 hp type CC72000 was the first large class of locomotive so equipped. A British prototype of 1968, *Kestrel,* was sold secondhand to the USSR and from the 1970s a number of alternator locomotives have been built, including the Type 56 of BR. Alternators are not used for engine starting, a small auxiliary generator being provided.

Control gear The problem of control long exercised the early diesel locomotive designers. The question concerned both the control of the individual elements (engine, generator, motors) and of the locomotive as a whole. An initial problem was the need to match continuously the output of the generator with that of the engine and with the demand of the traction motors. In some early designs the crew had to match needles assiduously by means of a multiplicity of control wheels and levers. However, in America the Swiss immigrant, Hermann Lemp, created an automatic control system in 1914 and this served as a basis for further development. In brief, this system entails the regulation of the generator field strength by the engine governor. The latter is a simple regulator of the amount of fuel injected, using a long-known centrifugal device which opens up a fuel valve when the engine slows, and closes it when the engine accelerates; in this way the engine goes neither below stalling speed nor above the safe maximum speed. The linkage of this device with the generator meant that a single control lever could control the locomotive's power output.

As locomotive control was electric or electro-pneumatic the way was open for systems of multiple-unit operation, in which the controls of one locomotive could operate other locomotives coupled to it. This concept of multiple-unit operation forms the basis of American and American-style diesel locomotive operation. Instead of building and maintaining a wide range of locomotives of varying power, American railroads build up a locomotive for a given duty from an appropriate number of locomotive units. When a high output is required, two, three or often more of these units are coupled together, connected by jumper cables which convey the control signals to each unit from the leading cab.

The earlier type of American diesel unit, the 'cab' type, originally came in two varieties; 'A' units had a cab, while 'B' units were cabless and designed to be coupled behind an 'A' unit. This is not to be confused with the present-day 'cow-and-calf' locomotive, in which a yard locomotive is coupled to a second unit which is not only cabless but lacks engine and generator. This simply

The diesel locomotive

enables the power output of the leading locomotive to be applied to an additional set of driving axles. In the USA, these auxiliary units are called 'slugs'; variations are called 'road slugs' (with a higher speed limit) and 'mates' (for main line service and serving also as fuel tenders).

Multiple-unit operation is not generally favoured in Europe. In America, units from different manufacturers can be combined to form one multiple-unit locomotive, but this is not usually the case in Europe. In Britain, France and Germany, when locomotives are coupled together to form a multiple-unit set for greater power, they usually are of the same class.

A modern variation of multiple-unit control, as practised in America, is the remote-control (radio) system in which one or more units are placed in the centre or rear of heavy freight trains. They, too, are controlled from the leading cab; their location eases the strains which would otherwise be imposed on the couplings of the leading vehicles.

Traction motors These are similar to those of electric locomotives.

Steam, electric or diesel?

The steam locomotive has a low thermal efficiency; it has low availability because of the need to clean away ash, soot, and boiler deposits; it is associated with the emission of sulphurous fumes, although this depends largely on the type of coal used. Its performance is not quite predictable, depending on so many variables like coal quality, ability and mood of the enginemen and other factors. When the wheels are rotating fast, considerable 'hammerblow' stress is placed on the track. On the other hand, it is very cheap to build and does not demand knowledge of high technology from those who operate and maintain it. It is therefore the most suitable form of traction in circumstances where the labour force is unsophisticated (or where skilled labour, like electricians,

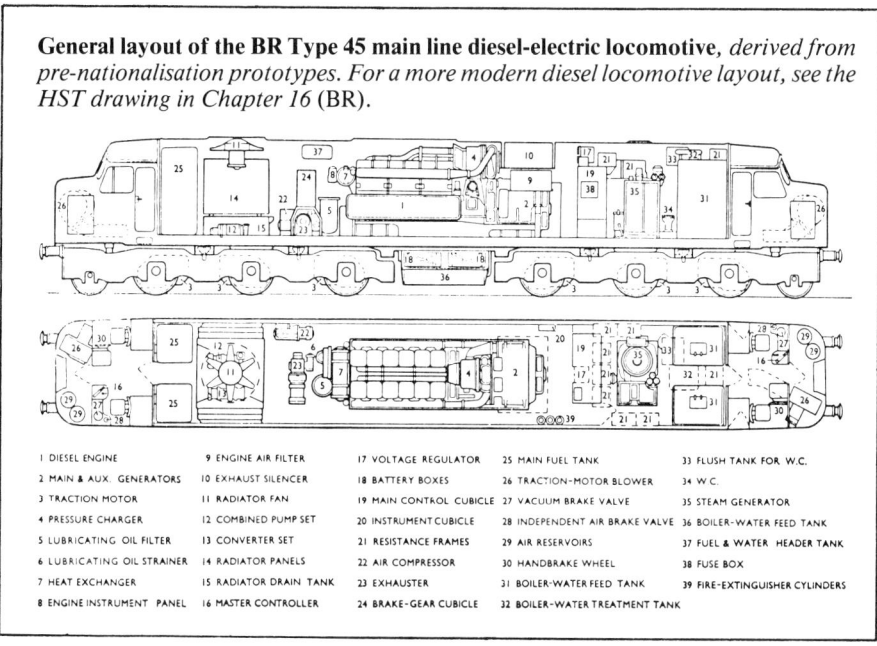

General layout of the BR Type 45 main line diesel-electric locomotive, *derived from pre-nationalisation prototypes. For a more modern diesel locomotive layout, see the HST drawing in Chapter 16* (BR).

1 DIESEL ENGINE	9 ENGINE AIR FILTER	17 VOLTAGE REGULATOR	25 MAIN FUEL TANK	33 FLUSH TANK FOR W.C.
2 MAIN & AUX. GENERATORS	10 EXHAUST SILENCER	18 BATTERY BOXES	26 TRACTION-MOTOR BLOWER	34 W.C.
3 TRACTION MOTOR	11 RADIATOR FAN	19 MAIN CONTROL CUBICLE	27 VACUUM BRAKE VALVE	35 STEAM GENERATOR
4 PRESSURE CHARGER	12 COMBINED PUMP SET	20 INSTRUMENT CUBICLE	28 INDEPENDENT AIR BRAKE VALVE	36 BOILER-WATER FEED TANK
5 LUBRICATING OIL FILTER	13 CONVERTER SET	21 RESISTANCE FRAMES	29 AIR RESERVOIRS	37 FUEL & WATER HEADER TANK
6 LUBRICATING OIL STRAINER	14 RADIATOR PANELS	22 AIR COMPRESSOR	30 HANDBRAKE WHEEL	38 FUSE BOX
7 HEAT EXCHANGER	15 RADIATOR DRAIN TANK	23 EXHAUSTER	31 BOILER-WATER FEED TANK	39 FIRE-EXTINGUISHER CYLINDERS
8 ENGINE INSTRUMENT PANEL	16 MASTER CONTROLLER	24 BRAKE-GEAR CUBICLE	32 BOILER-WATER TREATMENT TANK	

Left *One of the very numerous Type 47 diesel-electric locomotives of British Rail. Over 500 units of this 2,600 hp design have been built* (BR).

Right *The latest BR freight locomotive design, the 3,330 hp Type 58. The layout combines the British-style full-width cab at each end with the US road-switcher feature of walkways on each side of the engine compartment* (BR).

requires high rates of pay). It is economially advantageous where a sparse train service means that it will be out of use for much of the day in any case (for example, on a remote branch line). And, in countries where coal is abundant and oil is not, it may also have advantages. New unorthodox types of steam locomotive (see chapter 15) may overcome some of its traditional disadvantages.

The electric locomotive has great advantages of power output (with good adhesion to make that output real) and acceleration. It is also fume-free. It is much cheaper than a diesel locomotive, much more expensive than a steam locomotive, although it has a longevity comparable with the latter's. It is exceptionally valuable, therefore, for high-density services, with fast trains, difficult gradients and heavy loads. Its advantages in long tunnels are obvious, even though several railway administrations have persuaded themselves (but not their passengers) that diesel locomotives are virtually fume-free. Its operating costs are also lower than those of a steam or diesel locomotive.

However, to those costs have to be added the capital and running costs of substantial networks of transmission and conductor wires conveying the power from powerplant to locomotive. This means that electrification demands a minimum traffic density to make it worthwhile; but it has been found that electrification, with its accompanying improvement of speed, reliability and cleanliness, actually calls forth new passenger traffic. This was discovered by the Paris£ Orleans Railway before 1914, was rediscovered by Britain's Southern Railway between the wars, but nevertheless tended to be ignored by economists examining proposed electrification schemes.

The diesel locomotive has a thermal efficiency at least double that of the steam locomotive, and high availability. It is not surprising that its early success came in yard work, where it could be worked round the clock with no need to return to its locomotive depot between shifts. Potentially, it has always promised a reduction of labour expenses through the elimination of the fireman. In practice, this halving of the locomotive crew has been a long process, although in most European countries, including Britain, considerable mileages are now run with single-manned diesel locomotives and trains.

In the USA, costly strikes persuaded the railroad administrations to relax

their pressure for an end to firemen, so this potential economy has hardly been realised in that country. A 1937 agreement with the trade unions did, however, allow small diesel locomotives to operate with driver only, provided they weighed less than 45 tons on their driving wheels; hence the longstanding popularity of the General Electric 44-ton switch locomotive in the USA.

Finally, even with large-scale production, the diesel locomotive costs more than double a corresponding steam locomotive. However, it is a flexible unit in traffic, with a reliable power output. It is more agreeable to drive than a steam locomotive, an important factor at times when skilled labour is hard to attract. For the majority of those duties which cannot be handed to electric traction, it is the most suitable form of power.

Unfortunately, the reputation of diesel traction has suffered because it has often not seemed to bring the advantages claimed for it. The blame for this may be shared between the diesel locomotive industry's salesmen and the railway managements which initiated dieselisation. Too often, weak and incompetent railway managements regarded the diesel locomotive as a transforming agent which would change their deficits into profits. Many, for this reason, dieselised too fast, jettisoning steam locomotives which had not been fully depreciated and often buying their new units on credit; in America those railroad managements which were not considered good risks by their bankers could usually lease diesels from other corporations, while many third-world managements, tempted by easy-interest foreign loans or downright grants, bought diesel locomotives which they were unable to use effectively. Some railways, like the French SNCF and the German DB, reduced the need for diesels by keeping steam locomotives in service while electrification continued, and did not seem to suffer either economically or in public esteem.

In the USA, the coal-hauling Norfolk & Western was the last major railroad to dieselise. Possibly its careful conservation of capital in this matter was a factor in the subsequent financial strength which enabled it to absorb progressively or merge with neighbouring railroads to become the most powerful of the eastern railroads.

World Diesel Locomotives by K. Harris (1982) is a useful source of information about locomotives currently in service.

Chapter 15

Unorthodox locomotives

During its long life, railway transport has witnessed the appearance, and usually disappearance, of a wide range of unconventional motive power. The list which follows concentrates on those innovations which were successful in a limited foreseen field, or which seem to have been worth pursuing further than they were.

Geared steam locomotives
Locomotive tractors The firm of Aveling and Porter in England specialised in these and they had a limited success; a handful have been preserved. They have a flywheel as well as geared transmission and their advantage lies in the very high tractive effort smoothly applied. They were very suitable for heavy slow-speed work.

Sentinel locomotives Built by the Sentinel Wagon Company of Shrewsbury, these box-like yard locomotives were of the 0-4-0T and 0-6-0T arrangement. They had a vertical watertube boiler, often automatically fired with oil, which could raise steam from cold in less than an hour. The engine had two 2-cylinder units, vertically arranged and with poppet valves. The cylinders were small — about 7 in (18 cm) diameter and 9 in (23 cm) stroke — and drove through reduction gearing to a shaft connected by chains and sprockets to the wheels. These locomotives carried sufficient fuel and water for 16 hours' work. They were quite widely used by industrial lines both in Britain and the Commonwealth, and some common-carrier railways also used them. A main line version was built for the Egyptian State Railways.

Shay locomotives The invention of the American, Ephraim Shay, these locomotives were intended mainly for the lightly-laid and curving forestry lines of North America. The boiler is offset from the centre line, giving space on one side of the locomotive for two or three vertical cylinders. These drive a horizontal driving shaft along the side of the wheels, which is jointed so as to conform to the movement of the wheels, which are in pivoted trucks. Bevel gears convey the drive from this shaft to the wheels. When a tender is included, the tender wheels are driven from the same shaft. In general, a Shay locomotive can go over any track negotiable by a freightcar. Hundreds were built by the Lima Locomotive Works, and some were exported.

Climax locomotives These were later competitors of the Shay in America. Like the Shay, they had widely-spaced trucks driven by gears, but one driving shaft could cross another, thanks to the use of skew gears,

Unorthodox locomotives

Heisler locomotives These were also of American manufacture, and directly competitive with the Shay; the main difference from the latter was that the gears connected with the axles rather than with the wheel rims.

Direct-drive multi-cylinder steam locomotives

The Leader locomotive Possibly the best-known example of this idea, the 'Leader' locomotive was conceived by O. V. Bulleid of the Southern Railway on the eve of British railway nationalisation, and its trials were carried out under the new regime. The locomotive was double-ended and was carried on two six-wheel power trucks. Each of the two engine units was of three cylinders supplied by a novel kind of sleeve valve, with the valve gear being driven by chains, as was the drive to the axles and the coupling of the axles. Being a single unit, water and coal were carried on the same frame. Bulleid described it as a 'total adhesion' locomotive, since all wheels were used to transmit power. After trial this project was abandoned, by which time Bulleid was building a somewhat similar peat-burning prototype for Ireland.

The Paget locomotive This 1908 locomotive was built by the Midland Railway and was a 2-6-2 powered by two blocks of four cylinders, so arranged that the middle axle was powered by four cylinders and the outer driving axles by two cylinders each. Steam admission was controlled by rotary valves driven through a gearbox. This very novel locomotive had all the ingredients of success except the one which is most essential, a management which would continue to give

Right *A British locomotive tractor, now preserved in working order.*

Below *The tram locomotive, a tank locomotive enclosed in rectangular bodywork, was rare in Britain but was favoured in countries having unfenced roadside light railways. This example still works at Prien in Bavaria.*

financial support long enough for manufacturing and design faults to be found and remedied.

The Henschel project This 2-8-2, completed by Henschel in 1941 and taken to the USA after the war, was a streamlined unit. Outside one wheel of each driving axle, on alternate sides of the locomotive, were two-cylinder steam engines in V-form, with their crankshafts in line with the axle.

High-pressure steam locomotives

The conventional railway boiler permits steam pressures only up to a maximum of about 300 lb per sq in (22 kg per sq cm), which is below the pressures used in marine and stationary engines, which are therefore more efficient in fuel economy and power for space and power for weight. In the inter-war period, several railways experimented with high-pressure locomotives with watertube boilers. Among these were LNER, No 1000 (450 psi or 32 kg boiler, marine type watertube boiler, 4-6-4 compound arrangement); Delaware & Hudson, *L. F. Loree* (watertube firebox but firetube boiler, 500 psi or 35 kg, triple-expansion 4-8-0); LMS 4-6-0, *Fury*, Canadian Pacific 2-10-4, No 5905, and Paris–Lyon–Mediterrance 4-8-2, No 241B-1.

These last three worked according to the Schmidt–Henschel concept, in which there were three pressure circuits within the one locomotive. (One was a steam generating circuit of over 1,000 psi (70 kg) pressure and another was a steam generating circuit in which steam at about 850 psi (60 kg) was raised by means of heat transferred from the watertubes of the first-mentioned circuit, this steam being used for the high-pressure cylinders of the locomotive. The third was a conventional low-pressure boiler supplying steam, which might be mixed with high-pressure steam exhausted from the high-pressure cylinders, to the low-pressure cylinders.) These locomotives did not prove immediately successful and were eventually converted into conventional locomotives. A variation was the Löffler locomotive built in Germany, a three-cylinder compound locomotive in which steam was raised not in a boiler but in tube circuits. This, too, proved unsatisfactory.

Turbo-mechanical locomotives

Steam turbine locomotives were once the subject of considerable interest because they promised improved thermal efficiency, elimination of the hammer-blow (dynamic augment), inflicted on the track by reciprocating steam locomotives, and because they imparted a smooth turning effort (torque) to the driving wheels, unlike the steam reciprocating engine. Several were built, including the following:

Ramsay Macleod locomotive This 1924 British machine was of 4-4-0 + 0-4-4 wheel arrangement, each power truck having a 500 hp turbine driving through gearing. Steam was recycled by means of a condenser. The locomotive worked fairly well, but had a low power/weight ratio.

Ljungstrom locomotives Four of these were built in the 1920s (two for Sweden, one for the British LMS Railway and one for Argentina). They had a single turbine driving three axles through gearing. Having condensers, they used

Background photograph *A Shay locomotive.*
Inset *The steam-turbo-electric locomotive built for the Norfolk & Western RR.*

Above *Condenser locomotives of the South African Railways. These units have recently been rebuilt as orthodox locomotives, following the dieselisation of waterless lines.*

Left *A 'Camel' or 'Mother Hubbard' locomotive, a type favoured by some North American railroads in the 19th century. The driver rode in the elaborate cab while his fireman toiled on the unprotected footplate.*

Below *A cab-in-front locomotive of the Southern Pacific RR. By placing the chimney behind the engine-crew, the asphyxiation of the latter in steeply graded tunnels was rendered unlikely.*

very little water, but showed few other advantages. In 1932 a 2-8-0 design was built for the Swedish Grangesburg–Oxelosund Railway. This had gearing, jackshaft and coupling rod transmission, and was said to be reliable, cheap to maintain, and with about ten per cent fuel economy. The turbine locomotives supplied to the Swedish railways were, in general, regarded as successful

LMS Railway turbomotive Designed by Stanier, this had a boiler and some other parts of this designer's 'Princess Elizabeth' Class. Like the latter, it was a 4-6-2 intended for fast passenger trains. It had two turbines, one of 2,600 hp for forward movement and a much smaller one for reverse. It remained in service and was generally successful, although spending much time out of operation awaiting spare turbine parts. It ran from 1935 to 1951.

Pennsylvania RR 6-8-6 This (type S2) was built in 1946. It had main and reverse turbines and a mechanical stoker. It successfully hauled fast heavy passenger trains but suffered from spare-parts problems which, alone, meant that it could not compete with diesels.

Steam-electric locomotives

Heilmann locomotives In many ways anticipating the diesel-electric locomotive, this type, which appeared on the French Ouest Railway in the 1890s, used six-cylinder steam engines to drive generators supplying current for traction motors.

Reid–Ramsay locomotive Similar in principle to the Heilmann, this British machine appeared in 1910 and included a condenser. The Ramsay locomotive of 1920 was a further development. Both differed from the Heilmann in having steam turbine rather than reciprocating engines. Both had a poor power/weight ratio.

Union Pacific RR turbine-electric locomotives These two 4-8-0 units, which could be operated back-to-back as a single locomotive, had watertube boilers of very high pressure (1,500 psi or 105 kg), powering high-pressure and low-pressure turbines which drove generators for the traction motors. Trials were run on several railroads and showed promise but the Second World War cut short further development.

Chesapeake & Ohio RR passenger steam-turbine-electrics These three units, built by Baldwin in 1947–48, had a conventional boiler powering a 6,000 hp turbine which drove two generators. There were eight traction motors. Intended to provide a coal-burning alternative to diesels, they were unsuccessful.

'Jawn Henry' This, No 2300 of the Norfolk & Western RR, was a steam-turbine-electric completed in 1951 for freight service. It had a watertube boiler and was the biggest single-unit locomotive in the world, weighing 586 tons, all of which was adhesive weight, each of the 12 axles having a traction motor. It was said to be very economical in fuel, but teething troubles with various components and the spare-parts problems suffered by one-off designs meant that it was withdrawn after several years service.

Combined diesel and steam locomotives

These were intended to combine the flexibility of the steam locomotive with the thermal efficiency of the diesel.

Kitson-Still locomotive This appeared in Britain in 1927. It was a 2-6-2 with eight opposed cylinders. The latter worked on a four-stroke diesel cycle but, at

A Franco-Crosti locomotive of the Italian State Railways.

times of heavy power demand, steam supplied from the boiler was applied to the otherwise passive side of the pistons. Trials on the LNER showed high thermal efficiency but many detail problems and the Depression ended this experiment.

Teploparovozy These were three units built for Soviet Railways in the 1930s and 1940s which were a development of the Kitson-Still. The cylinders worked on a steam cycle at slow speeds, but at higher speeds the central part of the opposed-piston cylinders was reserved for diesel combustion. Thus, steam impelled the pistons on their inward stroke and diesel combustion on their outward stroke. Despite lengthy trials and expensive tinkering, these were all failures. The second unit was a cab-in-front 2-10-2 with condenser, a pulveriser of anthracite to supply the firebox with powdered fuel, and a producer-gas installation so that the diesel cycle could work on coal gas instead of oil.

Other unorthodox steam locomotives

Condenser locomotives In the inter-war period these were a speciality of the Henschel Locomotive Works. They were intended for lines where water supplies were short or of poor quality. The condenser was mounted in the tender. Exhaust steam from the cylinders was first used to power a turbofan in the smokebox, intended to provide a draught for the fire, and then led to the condenser elements in the tender, en route powering other turbofans which drew cooling air to the condenser. As the condensate was warm when re-passed to the boiler, a small improvement in thermal efficiency was obtainable. Argentina, South Africa and the USSR used these locomotives, as did the *Wehrmacht* in its Russian campaign. High maintenance costs and frequent malfunctioning of the smokebox fans were the main disadvantages. In Britain, a number of tank locomotives were fitted with pipes which took their exhaust steam into the water tanks, where some condensation took place; these semi-condensing locomotives were used on certain underground lines in London.

Fireless locomotives Although spark arrestors fitted to the chimney are effective, an absolute elimination of sparks and hot ash is required sometimes,

Unorthodox locomotives 149

especially in certain industrial sites. The fireless locomotive is a yard unit whose 'boiler' is actually a steam reservoir, being charged from time to time with steam from a stationary boiler. It resembles a tank locomotive minus chimney, firebox, tanks and bunker.

Franco-Crosti locomotives In these, which were quite popular in the last steam decades in Italy, the exhaust steam passed through two drums to heat the boiler feedwater, the drums being usually below the boiler. They brought a marked improvement in thermal efficiency but also high maintenance costs. Experimental examples were tried by German and British railways, but only in Italy, where coal was expensive, were they adopted in significant numbers.

ACE 3000 This was scheduled for construction in the early 1980s, being a new endeavour to provide a coal-burning locomotive competitive with the diesel. (ACE stands for 'American Coal Enterprises'.) It was to be a condensing compound 4-8-2 with a cab in front and another cab at the back of the permanently attached auxiliary unit. The fire was to be a result of coal gasification, reducing smoke, ash and soot emission, and the combustion rate and other variables were to have microprocessor control. Thermal efficiency was expected to be about 15 per cent.

South African Railways No 3450 L. Porta, of the Argentinian Railways, adopted Chapelon's ideas and carried them a stage further. Among his innovations was an improved blastpipe arrangement and his 'gas producer' firebox, in which the fuel was kept at a relatively low temperature, with most combustion taking place above it. His ideas were incorporated in a 4-8-4 of South African Railways, No 3450, which was rebuilt in 1980 and began trials in 1981. A substantial improvement in economy and power output was expected from this innovation.

Gas turbine locomotives

The gas turbine costs less than a diesel-electric power unit and, because it has no reciprocating parts, has lower maintenance costs than both steam and diesel

No 18000, a gas turbine locomotive ordered by the GWR from Brown Boveri and delivered in 1949 (M. Deane).

power. Its big disadvantage is that its efficiency is low when not working at full power, moreover, its efficiency falls at high altitudes and high temperatures and there are not many railway routes where constant full output is required and altitudes are low.

The Swiss Federal Railways tried a gas turbine in the early 1940s and Britain's Great Western Railway ordered two on the eve of nationalisation. All these were technically successful but could not produce a clear-cut economic advantage. However, in the 1950s the Union Pacific Railroad acquired 25 4,500 hp units and went on to order 15 8,500 hp locomotives. All these performed well in freight service on the UP main line up to the Rockies, but the type was not perpetuated. All the types mentioned here had turbine-driven generators, powering traction motors; on the UP units the electrical equipment was standard with diesel-electric designs.

Chapter 16

Self-propelled trains and multiple units

The conventional locomotive-hauled train, whose motive power and composition can be varied according to traffic demand, is a very flexible concept, but it is not always the most economical way of providing a service. One of its drawbacks is the time and space required to turn it round at each end of its runs; this disadvantage becomes greater on the shorter runs where a disproportionate number of locomotive-hours and train-hours may be spent in remarshalling a train. The idea of a double-ended train, which can be driven from either end without a shift of traction unit, was therefore most consistently applied for short-distance passenger service, beginning, of course, with the simple electric tramcar. In such systems peak traffic demand is met, not by adding an extra vehicle here and there, but by coupling one train to another or by increasing the frequency of service. In more recent decades, the use of self-propelled trains has been found advantageous for long-distance services. For really high-speed trains, the multiple-unit train (with traction motors powering all or most axles) is the best configuration for spreading the high tractive effort and engine weight over a sufficient number of axles.

Rail motors This idea appeared in the 19th century and was designed to reduce the working expenses of lines where passengers were few enough to be handled by a single vehicle. Essentially the rail motor consisted of a small steam locomotive whose wheels provided support for one end of the passenger vehicle, of which it was a constituent part. The other end of the vehicle rested on a conventional truck, but there was a driving cab here. There was a somewhat primitive, but nevertheless effective, arrangement of wires between this cab and the locomotive so that, when running with the engine at the rear, the driver in the front cab could pass appropriate signals to his fireman. In some countries, notably Australia, the term rail motor was later applied to diesel railcars.

Auto-trains Known simply as push-and-pull units on many railways, these were a development of rail motors. The same idea of a driving cab with communication to the engine was retained, but the locomotive was separate and coupled in the normal way, while the passenger cars, or trailers, had conventional trucks at each end. In England the Great Western Railway used auto-trains, especially for the branch lines, and they were reputed to be very cheap to operate. Often they had two trailers, and sometimes four; in the latter case the locomotive was sandwiched mid-way between the vehicles.

Push-and-pull trains This term, though technically applicable to the above-mentioned categories, usually refers nowadays to trains of considerable length

A push-pull train of the East German DR. Trains of similar concept are widely used in France and Italy.

with a locomotive at one end and a driving cab in the vehicle at the other end. French railways were particularly original in applying this concept, and the long suburban trains out of the Gare du Nord in Paris to the suburbs and outer suburbs, pushed and pulled by massive tank locomotives, were one of the last steam operations of the SNCF. Since the end of steam traction, new doubledeck push-and-pull trains, powered by electric locomotives, have taken over these and similar services in France.

An interesting variant in Britain is the diesel locomotive equipped with controls for push-and-pull workings between Bournemouth and Weymouth. The trains are electrical multiple units which run as conventional trains from London to the limit of electrification at Bournemouth and then become push-and-pull trains powered by diesel locomotives. The inter-city service between Edinburgh and Glasgow is also operated by push-and-pull trains powered by Type 47 diesel locomotives. These are equipped with a two-wire control system in which messages, in the form of coded pulses, are passed through the train by the two wires which control the electric lighting of the vehicles. Such wires are standard equipment for passenger stock, so no modifications are required to fit the intermediate vehicles for push-and-pull service, making the conversion of such trains considerably cheaper than with the older system of multi-way cables and jumpers passing from the locomotive right down to the second driving cab.

In France, push-and-pull trains operate between Paris and Orleans and Tours, while others connect Le Havre with Paris. In Germany, too, such trains have become popular while, in the Low Countries, the Amsterdam–Brussels service is now operated by such trains, which have largely replaced the electric multiple-units previously used.

Railcars These are in direct line of descent from rail motors, although they tend to serve longer distances than the former. In this category belong the gas-electrics of the inter-war USA, the various types of *autorail* used by the French railways and the very numerous diesel railcars put into service in Germany between the wars. Britain was represented in these pioneer days by the GWR, which built 38 diesel railcars for medium and long-distance services, two of which were parcels-only vehicles. Meanwhile, the LNER was experimenting with a modern version of the rail motor, in which the engine part was provided by a 'Sentinel' high-pressure steam unit.

Self-propelled trains and multiple units 153

In North America the Budd-built RDC (Rail Diesel Car) became very popular in the 1950s and many are still in service in some parts of that continent, as well as in several countries to which it was exported. It came in four versions (RDC1, RDC2, RDC3 and RDC4), according to the proportions in which the space was divided between passenger seats and baggage, mail and parcels accommodation. These cars could be joined together to form multiple-unit trains. Their successor is the Budd SPV2000, which has been purchased by a number of state passenger railway boards for commuter service.

Railbuses These are used for that rapidly diminishing number of services which do not justify the provision of a railcar, and notably for branch line service. Perhaps because it was Germany which refrained the longest from the wholesale closure of branches, the concept has been most widely used in that country and in Austria. A few vehicles were purchased by British Railways but were not perpetuated. A railbus is what its name implies. It runs on a four-wheel rigid chassis and its driving controls usually resemble those of a bus. It tends to be an uneasy rider. The German firm of Uerdingen made a speciality of this kind of vehicle.

The idea of simply taking a bus and replacing its rubber tyres with flanged

Below *One of the GWR diesel railcar fleet, built in the 1930s and representing the first successful application of diesel traction for passenger services in Britain.*
Bottom *A Budd RDC. This unit, unusually, is hauled by a conventional train, presumably in a peak-period when the latter has replaced the limited accommodation RDC.*

wheels has on many occasions been tried, with limited success. The main difficulty has been that railway service puts excessive strain on bus engines and transmissions. However, recently in Britain a mating of the Leyland bus body with flanged wheels has been quite successful, resulting in the Leyland railbus which has been in experimental service.

Electric multiple units (EMUs) These are the best-known form of self-propelled train, being the basis of electric commuter railways as well as underground lines. They are built in large numbers and most railways adopt standard configurations. For example, the Southern Railway's electrified lines out of London used two-car and four-car trainsets. The former consisted of a motorcoach (a passenger car with powered axles and cab) and a driving trailer (a passenger car, unpowered, but with a driving cab at the outer end). Four-car trainsets had, at each end, a motorcoach equipped with a driving compartment with two trailers (unpowered and cabless) in the middle. The more modern Type 508 trainsets are also of four-car configuration. In service, two-car and four-car sets are joined into a single train of whatever length is required. A characteristic of most EMUs is the high power/weight ratio; the Type 508 trainsets, for example, have 120 hp traction motors, which means 960 hp devoted to the powering of just four vehicles; such power ensures the rapid acceleration from stations which these trains need.

One problem faced by designers of these trains is how to ensure the greatest possible number of seats while preserving the ability to load and unload passengers rapidly. In Britain, the compartmented layout, with each compartment having its own manually-operated door, still persists, but the latest trains both in Britain and elsewhere have an open layout and wide, power-operated doors. The latter ensure rapid loading while demanding less vigilance from station staff. There still remains the question of whether one, two or three doors per side is best, and different railway administrations have different solutions for this.

With an extended electrification it sometimes became advantageous to

One of several types of electric multiple-unit trains used by the Netherlands Railways, where they provide the majority of passenger train services.

Self-propelled trains and multiple units

introduce EMUs specially designed for long-distance services. In general, where a service was frequent, such trains had the advantage that their faster turnround at terminals enabled fewer trainsets to provide a given service, compared with locomotive-hauled trains. The London to Brighton and London to Portsmouth services in Britain are an inter-war example. Such trains had a lower density of seating than suburban EMUs and usually provided some kind of meal service. On the Brighton line there was, in addition, the long-lived *Brighton Belle*, a Pullman EMU. In more recent times, the *Metroliner* trains between Washington and New York had similar characteristics, as well as being a step towards that latest manifestation of the EMU, the high-speed train, represented by the *Shinkansen* in Japan, the TGV in France and the APT concept in Britain.

Diesel multiple units (DMUs) Where electrification is absent, but traffic too intensive to be handled by single-unit railcars, the diesel multiple-unit train is often a cheaper alternative to the locomotive-hauled train. In North America, the RDC and its successor can be formed into such a train and, in most parts of western Europe, the DMU plays a role, depending on the extent of electrification; in Switzerland, for example, such trains are rare, whereas in under-electrified Britain there is a large number and variety of such trains, used not only in suburban service but also on the so-called cross-country and some inter-city routes. The division of these trains on BR into suburban, cross-country and inter-city is perhaps archaic and is being replaced by the terms, equally apposite, of high-density, medium density and low-density seating.

Although a decision to build many DMUs was taken before the BR Modernisation Plan of 1955, delivery of these trains was concentrated into a fairly short period, so that three-quarters of them were built in 1957–60. This has meant that almost the entire stock reached obsolescence at the same time, in the early 1980s. This presented both a financial and a design problem and the two problems became linked as soon as it became clear that the number of replacements that could be bought would depend on their cost; that is, on the sophistication of the design. By 1982, no firm decision has been reached on

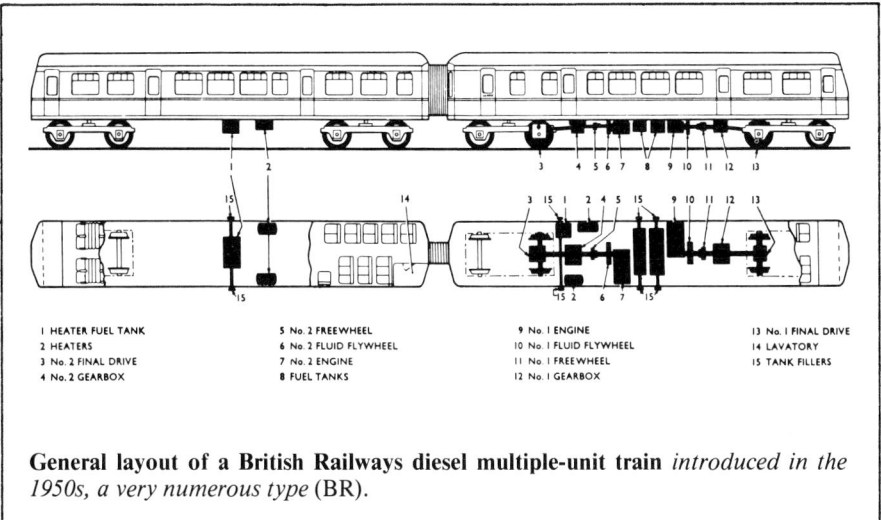

General layout of a British Railways diesel multiple-unit train *introduced in the 1950s, a very numerous type* (BR).

The Type 210 diesel multiple-unit train, a possible replacement for the 1950-vintage dmu trains still working on BR in the 1980s.

replacements, although new prototypes were on trial. One, type 210, provides a quite high degree of comfort and is powerful, so as to make its performance the equal of EMUs, with which it can run in multiple units if required. A cheaper alternative, or supplement, is the type 141, a two-car unit with some of the characteristics of the Leyland Railbus, although considerably more sophisticated than the latter. In the meantime a rehabilitation (called 'refurbishing') of some of the older DMUs is being undertaken.

An unusual type of diesel multiple-unit train is used by the Southern Region of BR. This is the diesel-electric multiple-unit (DEMU); because of the Southern Region's experience with electric traction, it favoured electric transmission, and these trains are virtually EMUs in which the electricity for the traction motors is supplied by an on-train generator instead of by a conductor rail. The generator adds to the weight and cost but the trains have proved reliable in service and, in some ways, superior to DMUs, whose underfloor engines, due to their cramped situation, suffer from design compromises. Type 210 is also a DEMU.

The front end of an APT prototype, the anticipated successor of the High Speed Train (BR).

The power car, or 'locomotive', of the BR High Speed Train (BR).

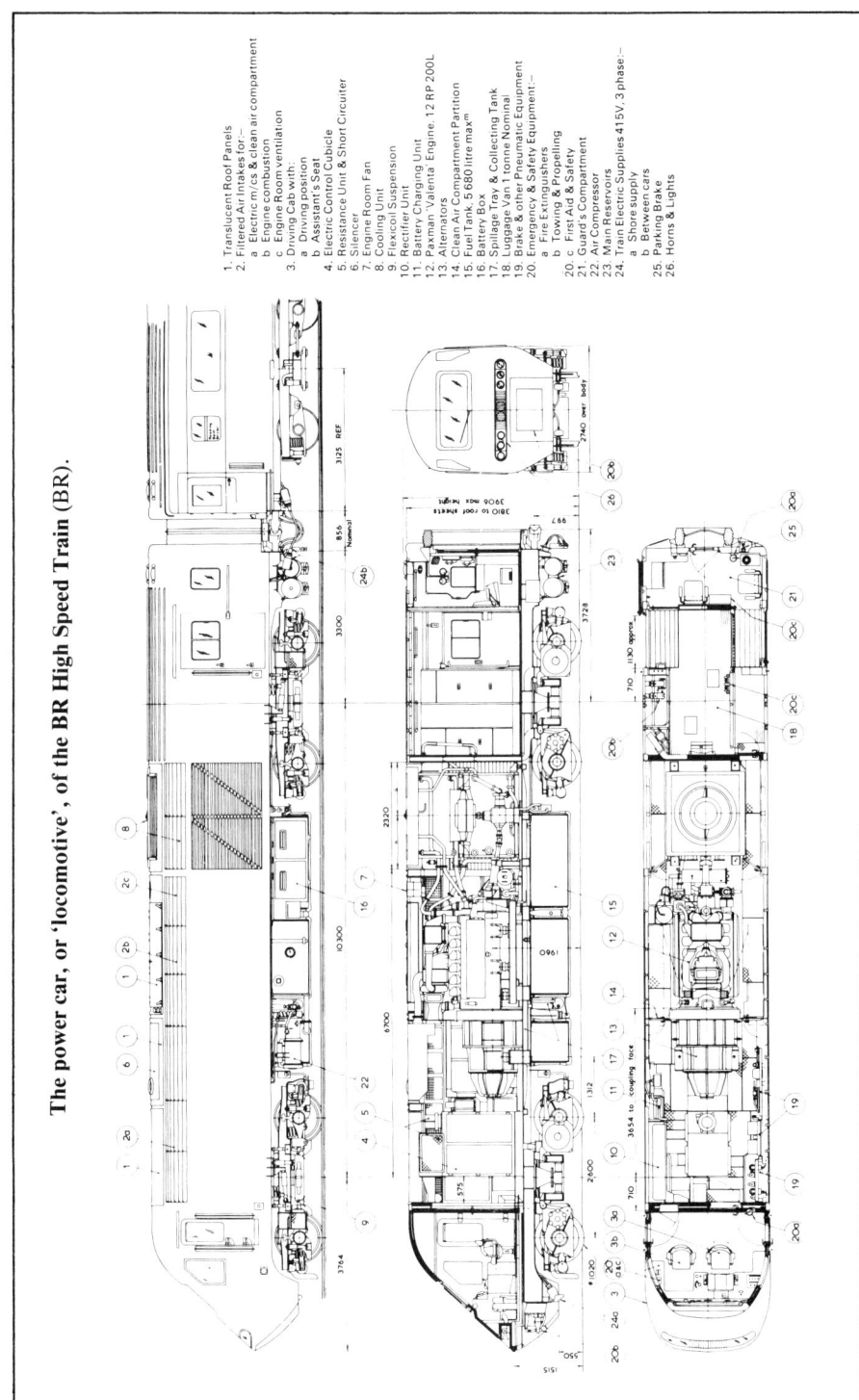

1. Translucent Roof Panels
2. Filtered Air Intakes for:—
   a Electric m/c's & clean air compartment
   b Engine combustion
   c Engine Room ventilation
3. Driving Cab with:
   a Driving position
   b Assistant's Seat
4. Electric Control Cubicle
5. Resistance Unit & Short Circuiter
6. Silencer
7. Engine Room Fan
8. Cooling Unit
9. Flexicoil Suspension
10. Rectifier Unit
11. Battery Charging Unit
12. Paxman 'Valenta' Engine, 12 RP 200L
13. Alternators
14. Clean Air Compartment Partition
15. Fuel Tank, 5 680 litre max'm
16. Battery Box
17. Spillage Tray, & Collecting Tank
18. Luggage Van 1 tonne Nominal
19. Brake & other Pneumatic Equipment
20. Emergency & Safety Equipment:—
    a Fire Extinguishers
    b Towing & Propelling
    c First Aid & Safety
21. Guard's Compartment
22. Air Compressor
23. Main Reservoirs
24. Train Electric Supplies 415V, 3 phase:—
    a Shore supply
    b Between cars
25. Parking Brake
26. Horns & Lights

Diesel trains have sometimes been chosen for high-speed services. The German 'Flying Hamburger' is an outstanding inter-war example. Such trains are not usually multiple units in the sense that the trainsets can be coupled together and operated from one control cab, but they are self-propelled trains and, usually, bi-directional. The five *Blue Pullman* trains, which in the early decades of British Rail provided a hint of luxury for the business traveller, were among these. Their successors, the High Speed Trains (HST) also come into this category even though they are provided with a locomotive at each end. This locomotive is designed as an integral part of the train, and the same applies to the XPT trains of New South Wales, derived from the HST design.

In North America, the Canadian LRC ('Light, Rapid, Comfortable') train is similar in concept but very different in execution. In continental Europe, such diesel trains, of varying designs, were used for the earlier Trans Europ Express services, and there was a tradition in France, dating from the inter-war years, of providing fast and quite luxurious high-speed diesel trains over the key businessmens' routes, access to which required a supplement as well as a first-class ticket. On the modern SNCF, the gas turbine trains are descended from these, although not restricted to first-class or supplement-paying passengers. Turbotrains, of both French and domestic construction, were also seen in the 1970s in North America, where their high fuel consumption and requirement for careful maintenance proved to be their downfall.

Chapter 17

Locomotive manufacturers

The replacement of steam by electric and diesel power was accompanied by an upheaval in the locomotive-building industry. Many old-established firms disappeared, either by merger or dissolution, and there was a growing tendency for locomotives to be built by consortia, typically with one firm supplying electrical equipment, another the mechanical parts, and another, when required, providing the diesel engine.

Britain
The world's first locomotive-building company was Robert Stephenson's, in Newcastle, founded in 1823. Many locomotive-building companies were established before 1850, but only a handful survived to become celebrated names in the history of the steam locomotive. British railway companies, except the very smallest, preferred to design and build their own locomotives in their own workshops, giving orders to outside builders only when their programmes exceeded their workshop capacity. Independent builders were therefore dependent on export trade, which did indeed flourish until the 1950s. By far the largest was North British (NBL), followed by Beyer, Peacock and the Vulcan Foundry. Some companies specialised in the smaller types, while the Bristol firms of Avonside and Peckett were specialists in industrial shunting locomotives.

Of the big three, North British was an amalgamation of three celebrated Glasgow companies dating from the early decades of the railway age (Dübs, Sharp Stewart, Neilson). Its steam locomotives had a high reputation but it was unable to make a successful transition to the new design philosophies required by diesel traction. Beyer, Peacock, whose works were at Gorton, Manchester, had been founded by a German immigrant and a former GWR draughtsman. In the 20th century it acquired the patents for the Garratt locomotive and later made what at first seemed a successful transition to diesel locomotive construction; but it tied itself too closely to British Railways requirements at a time when BR traction policy was incoherent, and this helped to bring its independent existence to an end.

The Vulcan Foundry from the 1960s successfully concentrated on building and assembling the mechanical parts of electric and diesel locomotives, and eventually entered the GEC group. Of the smaller companies, the Leeds firms of Hudswell Clarke and Hunslet (now in association) made a gradual, but successful, change to the construction of diesel yard locomotives. A new name,

Thomas Hill, is also associated with diesel shunting locomotives, combining the railway traction interest of Rolls-Royce with the locomotive experience of the former Sentinel Company.

The British locomotive industry is now dominated by the General Electric group (GEC, which is quite distinct from GE in the USA). Through a series of regroupings, GEC Traction emerged in 1968 as a company embodying the assets of several steam locomotive builders, including Beyer, Peacock; Robert Stephenson and Hawthorn, Leslie (which two had merged to become RSH in 1938); Bagnall; and of electrical engineering enterprises (British Westinghouse; English Electric). The core of this group was English Electric, a company formed in 1918 and incorporating, by the time it was taken over by GEC in 1968, the locomotive builders RSH and Vulcan Foundry (already merged by 1955, when they were taken over by English Electric). English Electric merged with Associated Electrical Industries in 1967, the latter already incorporating British Thomson, Houston and Metropolitan Vickers (Metrovick). English Electric had been building electric and diesel locomotives in the inter-war years and the first version of its successful diesel engine for rail use appeared in 1934.

Another large builder of diesel locomotives is Brush Electrical Machines Ltd of Loughborough. Once a specialist builder of electric trams, Brush entered the diesel locomotive field in 1948; one of its most successful products was the Type 47 diesel locomotive of BR, a 2,750 hp design of which more than 500 were built.

The locomotive works of the former railway companies are now incorporated in British Rail Engineering Ltd (BREL). They are mainly concerned with repair work and most of the locomotive-building facilities have been closed or converted. However, locomotives are still assembled at Crewe and Doncaster. The associated firm of BRE-Metro is an export-sales company jointly owned by BREL and Metropolitan Cammell, the Birmingham manufacturer specialising in passenger rolling stock.

North America

There were three dominant builders of main line steam locomotives. These were the Baldwin Locomotive Works (BLW) at Philadelphia, the American Locomotive Company (Alco) at Schenectady and the Lima Locomotive Works at Lima in Ohio. Alco, with General Electric as its electrical supplier, was a pioneer in diesel-electric traction but, after the post-war boom in diesel locomotive production, it succumbed to the competition of General Motors and left the industry, although its Canadian subsidiary (MLW) remained in business. Baldwin changed over to diesel locomotive production, not too successfully, and then joined with the smallest of the 'Big Three', Lima, and another engineering firm to form Baldwin-Lima-Hamilton. This new company, however, was not successful in the locomotive field.

In the 1930s, General Motor formed its Electromotive Division (EMD) at La Grange (Illinois), and diesel-electric locomotives produced there made GM the world's largest producers of locomotives in the post-war decades. Meanwhile, General Electric of Erie (Pennsylvania), which had been supplying electrical gear for both Alco and GM diesel locomotives, launched its own series of main line diesel locomotives, in 1960. This new entrant into the industry proved to be the final blow to Alco and strong competition for GM.

General electric and GM also produce electric locomotives, when required, and have outdistanced Westinghouse, once an important electric locomotive builder. Fairbanks Morse, a builder of diesel engines, entered the diesel locomotive industry after the war with a series of locomotives based on its opposed-piston engine. However, its prominence as a supplier of main line locomotives was shortlived.

When the early batches of post-war diesel locomotives became time-expired, many railroads decided to have them refurbished, or re-manufactured, rather than order completely new models. This process generally involved the replacement of electrical equipment and engines and the retention of most other parts. The locomotive manufacturers undertook this work, but many locomotives were, and are, remanufactured by the railroads themselves or by independent companies, of which Morrison–Knudsen is the best known.

In Canada, main line steam locomotive construction was undertaken by the Canadian Locomotive Company (CLW) at Kingston, the Montreal Locomotive Works (MLW) and by the Angus workshops of the Canadian Pacific at Montreal. (Few North American railways preferred to build their own locomotives; CP was one, and the Pennsylvania RR at its Altoona Works was another.) CLW briefly changed over to diesel production, in association with Fairbanks Morse, while MLW, in association with Alco, made a more successful transition, MLW continued to build Alco-design locomotives after the demise of its parent firm; it is now a division of Bombardier–MLW and is one of the three big locomotive builders remaining in North America. General Motors has a subsidiary company at London, Ontario.

France
Steam locomotive construction was shared by the railway company workshops and specialised firms. An early example of the latter were the Buddicom works at Rouen, founded by an Englishman. Others were the Batignolles Company (Paris), Gouin (Paris), Cail (Chaillet), Koechlin (Mulhouse) and Corpet Louvet (La Corneuve). However, two dominant companies emerged; these were *Société Schneider* at Le Creusot and the *Société Alsacienne de Constructions Mecaniques* (SACM) at Grafenstaden. The former is now part of Jeumont-Schneider, manufacturing locomotive power equipment, while SACM is a producer of diesel engines for railway locomotives.

The French locomotive industry is now dominated by Alsthom of Belfort, a descendant of the Thomson, Houston Company, which makes both the mechanical and electrical parts for its range of electric and diesel locomotives and multiple units. Another large firm with the same range of activities is MTE, the parent company for Jeumont-Schneider and Creusot-Loire, with several works. Alsthom and MTE jointly own *Traction-Export*, a company devoted to the sale of their products abroad. Brissoneau & Lotz, maker of diesel-electric locomotives, is now part of the Alsthom organisation. Makers of smaller diesel locomotives include Moyse at La Corneuve, and CFD. The latter is historically interesting; the company (*Cie de Chemins de Fer Départmenteaux*) was once important as the owner and operator of metre-gauge local railways and now manufactures a range of locomotives and railcars for light railway use.

Germany
In the 19th century, Germany became the main competitor of Britain in the locomotive export market and many companies flourished. In the hard years

after 1918 the industry was cartelised, with some companies, notably Hohenzollern, voluntarily leaving the business so as to improve the prospects for the remaining companies. The main steam locomotive builders in the 20th century were: Berliner M-A-G, formerly the Schwartzkopff Works (Berlin); Borsig (Henningsdorf), now the Hans Beimler Works in East Germany; Hanomag (Hannover), formerly the Egestorff Works; Henschel (Kassel); Hohenzollern (Dusseldorf); Jung (Jugenthal); Krupp (Essen); Maffei (Munich); Esslingen (Esslingen); Orenstein & Koppel (Babelsberg), now split between the Karl Marx Works in East Germany and O & K in Dortmund; Sächsische Maschinenfabrik (Chemnitz), formerly the Hartmann Works; Vulcan (Hamburg). Henschel, Krupp and Maffei (now Kraus-Maffei) are now the suppliers of main line diesel and electric locomotives to the DB, using electrical equipment from companies including Siemens, Brown Boveri (BBC), AEG and diesel engines from such internationally well-known companies as MAN, Mercedes, Deutz and Maybach. MAK (formerly Deutsche Werk, Kiel) specialises in diesel-hydraulic locomotives.

The Low Countries

Belgium has a long tradition of steam locomotive building, the firm of Cockerill being one of the oldest manufacturers. Cockerill (by then Cockerill-Ougréc) played a large part in the dieselsation of the SNCB and was a licensee of the Baldwin Locomotive Works. General Motors patents were utilised by Franco-Belge and also by La Brugeoise, which merged in 1956 with another company to become Brugeoise et Nivelles. The latter now dominates electric locomotive building in Belgium, in conjunction with the electrical engineering company, ACEC. The Netherlands now imports its locomotives, the Werkspoor plant at Utrecht, once a manufacturer of locomotives, being no longer used for this purpose.

Other countries

Many countries which once imported locomotives now make their own. India's post-war Chitaranjan Works makes electric locomotives and diesel shunters while the Diesel Locomotive Works at Banaras, set up by Alco, concentrates on diesel main line locomotives. In China there are several works. One of these, at Datong, is notable in that it still produces main line steam locomotives. In Japan, locomotive-building branches of conglomerates like Mitsubishi and Hitachi have entered the export market, while Switzerland's SLM works at Winterthur, previously a builder and exporter of steam locomotives, now builds electric units, incorporating equipment from the local firms of Brown Boveri, Oerlikon and Sécheron. Another, though small, exporter is ASEA of Sweden, a company which successfully pioneered diesel traction before the First World War and has more recently been exporting its advanced thyristor-controlled electric locomotives.

A more detailed listing of locomotive (and rolling stock) manufacturers can be found in the current edition of *Jane's World Railways*. For the steam age there are two useful references: *British Steam Locomotive Builders* by J. W. Lowe (1975), and *A Short History of American Locomotive Builders in the Steam Era* by John H. White (1982).

British steam locomotive builders in 1923

Name	Year of last steam locomotive production (or of corporate dissolution)
Armstrong Whitworth	1937
Avonside	1934
Bagnall	1957
Beardmore	1931
Beyer, Peacock	1958
Hawthorn, Leslie	1937*
Hudswell Clarke	1961
Hunslet	1971
Kerr, Stuart	1930
Kitson	1938
Manning Wardle	1926
Nasmyth Wilson	1931
North British Locomotive	1958
Peckett	1958
Robert Stephenson	1937*
Vulcan Foundry	1956
Yorkshire Engine	1955

*The last steam unit came from Robert Stephenson and Hawthorn in 1959.

Railway company locomotive works (British Isles, 1914)

Location	Railway
Ashford	South Eastern & Chatham
Brighton	London Brighton & South Coast
Broadstone	Midland Great Western
Cowlairs	North British
Crewe	London & North Western
Darlington	North Eastern
Derby	Midland
Doncaster	Great Northern
Dundalk	Great Northern (Ireland)
Eastleigh	London & South Western
Gorton	Great Central
Horwich	Lancashire & Yorkshire
Inchicore	Great Southern & Western
Kilmarnock	Glasgow & South Western
St Rollox	Caledonian
Stoke	North Staffordshre
Stratford	Great Eastern
Swindon	Great Western

Chapter 18

Brakes, couplings and lamps

There is little connection between the three topics of this chapter, but it seems right to follow common practice and treat them together as all three are important and visible details of rolling stock.

Brakes
In the early days, brakes were fitted to locomotives only. Then hand-brakes, operated by brakemen rotating a wheel or depressing a lever, were provided for certain vehicles. Such brakes were of little use in an emergency, since they were slow to apply and were not under the direct control of the locomotive crew. The British manually-braked freightcar could be braked only by a man at ground level. The US equivalent was better, having a brake wheel close to the roof, enabling brakemen to scurry down the boxcar roofs to apply the required proportion of vehicle brakes.

In Britain the train guard had his own hand-brake in his brakevan at the tail end of the train, which could be co-ordinated with the locomotive's head-end brake by means of whistle signals. In continental Europe, a proportion of freightcars had a brake, with a brakeman's platform, or miniature cabin, at one end. Brakemen thus distributed along the train could apply brakes in unison in accordance with pre-established routines or, in emergency, at the bidding of the locomotive whistle. Both the British brakevan and the continental brakeman's platform still exist, but are disappearing.

Public opinion and legislatures, often more disturbed by accidents than railway management, took the initiative to compel the introduction of better brakes. What was demanded was a *continuous* and *automatic* brake system. By continuous was meant a system which could be simultaneously applied to each vehicle of a train. By automatic was meant a brake which was both remotely controlled and which would be 'fail safe'. The more farseeing governments and professional associations also required that new brake systems introduced by different railways within a country should be compatible with each other.

A number of inventors patented new brake systems. Eventually, two basic systems emerged as most satisfactory. The first was the air brake associated with the name of the American, George Westinghouse. Westinghouse's first air brake was a 'straight-air' variant, in which a compressor on the locomotive sent compressed air down the train, through the brakepipe ('train pipe' or 'air line') to operate brakes on each vehicle. This is still used as a locomotive brake, but as a train brake it was not fail-safe because, if a coupling parted, the brake was inoperative just when urgently needed.

In 1872, therefore, Westinghouse introduced his 'plain automatic brake'. Successive modifications have improved this, without changing its essentials. Its vital element is the 'triple valve' fitted to each vehicle. This valve is interposed between the compressed air reservoir and the brake cylinder (whose piston actuates the vehicle's brakes). The locomotive carries an air compressor and air reservoirs and, when running freely, the train pipe is used to pass pressurised air to the air reservoirs of the vehicles through the respective triple valves. When the driver operates his brake handle, air escapes from the train pipe and the pressure drop actuates the triple valve, which then admits air from the vehicle air reservoir to the brake cylinder, applying the brakes. This brake, electrically controlled, is also used for multiple-unit trains.

The second brake system was the automatic vacuum brake, in which atmospheric pressure is used instead of compressed air to move the brake piston. A vacuum exhauster on the locomotive draws air via the train pipe from the brake cylinders, until the brake pistons rest in the off position. For a brake application, the driver's brake valve connects the train pipe with the atmosphere, allowing pressure to act on the lower side of the brake piston, whose upper side is still in vacuum. The piston accordingly rises, applying the brake as it does so. The speed with which this brake operates (especially on a long train) can be enhanced by direct-admission valves on each vehicle which enable each vehicle to draw in air, as soon as the 'message' of reduced vacuum in the trainpipe has been received.

In the last decades of the 19th century, when railways, often under government pressure, had to choose one or another system for general adoption, the vacuum and air brakes were evenly matched, the former being a little cheaper and the latter a little more powerful. In North America, and much of the rest of the world, the air brake was chosen. In the British Empire the vacuum brake was usually, though not always, preferred. In Britain itself 'railway politics' resulted in a totally unsatisfactory situation. Some companies, notably the LNWR, had resisted the introduction of automatic brakes until an act of parliament, which followed the 1889 accident at Armagh, made them compulsory. The LNWR, seeing that some of its competitors favoured the Westinghouse air brake, then lobbied in favour of the vacuum brake. The result

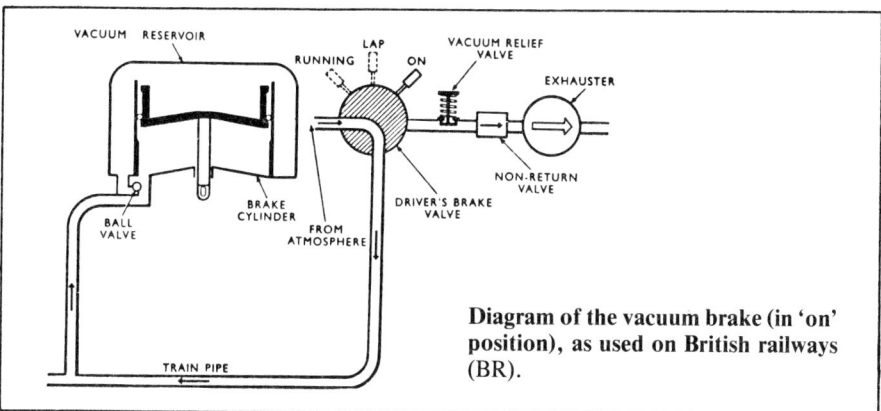

Diagram of the vacuum brake (in 'on' position), as used on British railways (BR).

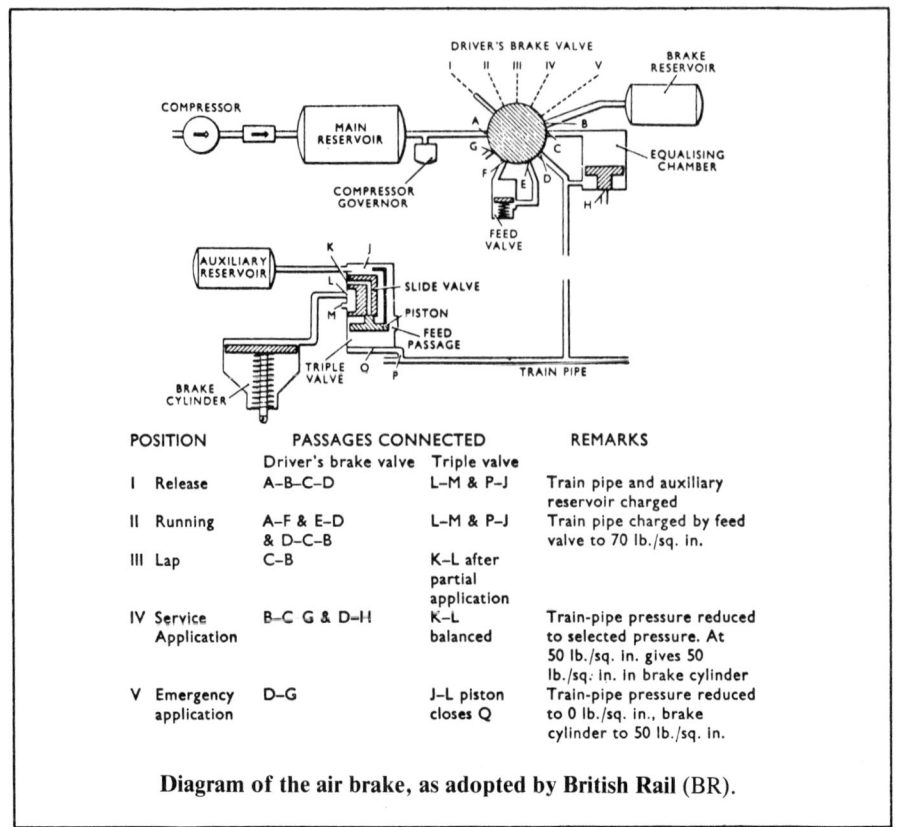

Diagram of the air brake, as adopted by British Rail (BR).

was that some British companies adopted the former, but the majority chose the latter. This meant that through running of passenger cars over several companies' lines was inhibited; for the Anglo-Scottish service, special rolling stock fitted with both brakes had to be built.

Parliament had imposed automatic brakes only on passenger trains. British freight cars continued to have hand-brakes which could be pinned down at the beginning of steep gradients. When fast freight trains became desirable, some freight vehicles were fitted with automatic brakes while some others remained hand-braked but were fitted with the train pipe so that they could take their place in an automatically braked train. The latter were described as 'piped' and the former as 'fitted'. Freight trains were classified (and their maximum running speed limited) by the proportion of vehicles equipped with automatic brakes — such vehicles being marshalled behind the locomotive — as well as by the total of hand-braked cars trailing between the fitted vehicles and the brakevan.

The superiority of the air brake becomes apparent with long, heavy and fast trains; its pressure differential of around 70 lb per sq in (5 kg per sq cm) then becomes crucially superior to the 10–12 lb (.7–.8 kg) of the vacuum brake and also makes it less vulnerable to small air leakages. In particular, even with direct-admission valves, the vacuum brakes take much longer to apply and release at the rear section of long trains. Hence even such long-standing adherents of the vacuum brake as BR and Indian Railways have recently opted for the air brake; both, for some years, will suffer the inconvenience of maintaining two incompatible systems.

In some countries there has been a limited adoption of disc brakes, in place of the conventional brake-blocks. The latter, however, with their frequent grinding action against the wheel tread, keep the metal clean and thereby ensure the good electrical connection so essential for track circuiting devices; in several cases this advantage has ensured their retention. Brake friction surfaces were originally of wood, but cast-iron became standard, followed in recent years by various patented compositions. The smell produced by the latter at high temperatures became a characteristic odour of the first batches of British High Speed Trains, whose air intakes were close to the brakes.

Other kinds of brake include electro-pneumatic, often to be found on electric multiple-unit trains, rheostatic (see chapter 13) and the rather rare rail brake. The latter is a brake shoe which is brought down to bear on the top surface of the rail, usually by electromagnetic force. It has long been normal for a train to have several types of brake. A British steam freight train, for example, had the locomotive's steam brake, it had vaccum brakes on its leading vehicles, manual brakes on the 'unfitted' vehicles and the guard's powerful hand-brake in the brakevan.

Locomotive brake controls were typically designed so as to blend the actions of the locomotive brake and the train's automatic brake. This situation is still general. British diesel locomotives are fitted with an air brake and this is applied simultaneously, through the same brake handle, with the train's vacuum or air brakes. The French TGV trains have three brakes. At speeds over 125 mph (200 km/h) rheostatic brakes are applied (together with a slight tightening of the brake blocks in order to clean the wheel treads). As the speed drops below 125 mph, the air brake is slowly blended in, with the rheostatic brakes being progressively phased out. The TGV also has a 'parking brake', which is held off by the trainpipe pressure when the train is in use.

Couplings

The connections in a train have two main functions; they transmit traction forces and absorb impact ('buffing stress'). Modern types of coupling seek to perform both these functions, whereas most of the older types rely on side buffers to absorb impact. Typical of the old type, and still surviving, is the three-link-and-hook loose coupling used on British freightcars. Trains made up of such vehicles are called loose-coupled, because the cars are not held rigidly together but can bunch up or stretch apart as the train accelerates or decelerates. Coupling and uncoupling with such vehicles is usually done by a shunter, provided with a long shunter's pole; lifting the link off and on to the hook during shunting operations was one of the most dangerous jobs offered by the British railways. Similarly, the old American link-and-pin coupler was lethal for many switchmen, who had to get between moving cars to guide the link into the slot and then drop the pin to lock it.

Several Americans invented automatic couplers, and the most successful of these was Janney's, now known as the buckeye coupling and used by American and several other railways; it was standardised in the USA in 1885 by the Car Builders' Association. This coupler has a movable jaw; when two are pushed together one rides into the other and the two jaws close behind each other.

Top left *The British 3-link coupler. This picture also shows the vacuum reservoir, which is usually positioned beneath the floor.*
Top right *Buckeye coupler, and automatically-opening electric and air connecting box, as fitted to modern BR electric multiple-unit sets.*
Above *The hinged buckeye coupler, as used on many BR passenger coaches, shown in the dropped position, beneath the central drawhook.*

British Rail use this for much of their passenger rolling stock; one of its advantages is that, in derailments, it usually holds firm. Some British passenger cars have interchangeable couplers, with the hinged buckeye coupling dropping down to permit the use of a screw-link coupling when necessary.

An improvement of the Janney coupler was Willison's, a version which is now standard in the USSR and has been adopted by some other railways. In this the jaws are fixed; when they slide over each other a locking claw on each coupler engages the opposing jaw. Both the Janney and the Willison are really semi-automatic because they have to be set manually to the ready-to-engage position (usually by a lever on the side of the car).

Most common in Europe is the screw-link coupler, used in association with buffers. In this the link is placed over the opposing hook and then the coupling is tightened by a screw action, keeping the buffers tightly together. With this,

Brakes, couplings and lamps

trains are close-coupled, but the process is time-consuming and not entirely safe, even though rigorous rules are laid down for the staff performing this duty. Moreover, link couplings are less strong than automatic, which means their use prevents the running of heavyweight trains.

A third coupler is the so-called Colonial type which is a centre buffer combined with a coupling arrangement which has features of the link-and-hook and the American coupler. It is commonly used on the narrower gauges (although not in South Africa, which uses the American coupler). The 'Norwegian' coupling, a central buffer and coupling, is still encountered on some narrow-gauge lines. It consists of a hinged hook which falls downward into a slot in the opposing coupler, the join being effected by both hooks falling into place and being locked by a retaining device.

Front end of a BR Type 50 diesel locomotive. **1** *Air horns.* **2** *Control ('jumper') cable for multiple-unit operation.* **3** *Receptacle for multiple-unit control cable.* **4** *Red rear lights.* **5** *Headlight.* **6** *Multiple-unit compatibility code (orange square).* **7** *Electric train heating cable (receptacle for the cable is at left, obscured by buffer).* **8** *Air brake pipe.* **9** *Screw-link coupling.* **10** *Vacuum brake pipe.* **11** *Running ('marker') lights.*

Changing from one type of coupling to another is an expensive and complex procedure, resisted by railway managements. In the period when both old and new couplings are in use, special devices are used to maintain interchangeability. It took the USSR decades to make the changeover and, until the process was complete, all cars continued to be fitted with buffers. This is one reason why the European railways which, in addition, have to agree among themselves to make a change-over, have hesitated so long in moving away from the screw coupling. On multiple-unit stock, which has to be connected only with similar units, the change is easier; this is why the 'multi-function' centre coupler is used on much modern European multiple unit rolling stock, including trainsets recently built for British Rail. Such couplings connect the brake air-pipes and any necessary electrical contacts at the same time. The coupling and uncoupling is effected solely by vehicle motion, together with the movement of one control lever (which can be mounted in the cab or at the side of the vehicle). The Scharfenberg coupler is the most commonly used multi-function coupler, although the International Union of Railways has specified for eventual all-Europe standardisation a modified form of the latter which is additionally compatible with the 'Intermat' Willison-type coupler standardised by the East European Railway Collaboration Organisation (OSJD), as well as with the existing screw-link couplers.

American couplers are also used on BR iron-ore cars in certain unit trains.

Below right *A few British steam locomotives were fitted with electric lights, but these could not fulfil the function of train-description codes in daylight; hence traditional white oil lamps were mounted above them, appropriate to the class of train.*

Below left *A Canadian Pacific locomotive carrying white flags to indicate that it is an extra train.*

Brakes, couplings and lamps 171

These have each a rotatable and a fixed coupler, enabling them to be tipped upside-down without being detached from the train during the mechanised unloading process.

Lamps

In Britain (except on the SR) a system of front lamp arrangements served as train description codes both at night and in the day; the lamps were painted white (occasionally, at one period, red) and so were easily visible to signalmen and other operating staff. Having no illumination role, and being oil-burning, they were easily shifted from lamp-iron to lamp-iron in accordance with the locomotive's duties. There were four lamp positions (in front of the chimney and, left, right and centre of buffer beam). All of the ten codes utilised no more than two lamps (except the four-lamp Royal Train indication). Two of the most common were express passenger (left and right buffer beam) and ordinary passenger (in front of the chimney).

The Southern Railway (and, for a time, the LNER) used white disc codes in daylight. Such codes are no longer used; modern locomotives carry a pair of electric lights simply as markers, plus a small headlight; although the additional bright left-hand warning light of High Speed Trains may also be regarded as an identification. Southern Region electric trains still use route-identification numbers.

In North America the traditional head-end flags are still used; two white flags on the smokebox (with two white lights at night) denote an extra train, while two green flags, with green lights at night, indicate that there is a following section of the train to come.

In all countries the tail lamp retains its significance. It is still the most immediate assurance that a passing train is entire, and has not left some of its vehicles behind in the section, due to a mishap unnoticed by the locomotive crew. In Britain, the lamp serves this purpose both by night and day. In central Europe, a red and white plate is attached at each side of the rear end of a train in daytime; at night two lamps are used in the same position. In North America, rear lights may have green as well as red lenses, with the green showing in different directions according to whether the train is on or off the main track.

Chapter 19

Locomotive inscriptions

The quantity of information written on the outside of locomotives varies from railway to railway and from decade to decade. The following notes are intended only as an introduction.

Britain

Except on a few very small railways, all British locomotives carry a running number. In addition, works plates (builder's plates) are fitted at the time of building; these usually give the year of construction (sometimes of reconstruction), the builder and, usually, the builder's works number. Due to irregularities, evidence of a locomotive's identity presented by its works plate is not always reliable. Selected British steam locomotives carried names, usually having a cast nameplate on each side mounted on a splasher or, sometimes, the smokebox. A few modern locomotives also carry nameplates. Numbers were, and are, painted on the cabsides, although the GWR and a few pre-1923 companies used cast brass numberplates. Steam locomotives also carried their number on the front buffer beam or (in the case of the LMS and BR) on a plate fixed to the smokebox door.

On the GWR, standard locomotive classes were numbered in blocks of one hundred and an attempt was made to convey, by means of the second digit of the four-figure number, the type of locomotive (for example, four-cylinder 4-6-0 types were numbered in the 4000, 5000, 6000 and 7000 series) but there were too many exceptions in this scheme. After nationalisation, GWR units retained their old numbers, LMS locomotives had 40,000 added to previous four-digit numbers and 30,000 to five-digit numbers, LNER numbers were increased by 60,000, and SR by 30,000. BR standard types then took blocks of numbers from 70,000 upwards. With modernisation, electric and diesel locomotives at first took four-digit numbers, preceded by an E or a D so long as steam traction survived.

In the mid-1970s the present numbering scheme was introduced, more suitable for computer use. In this five-digit system the first two digits give the locomotive class (01-60 are reserved for diesel classes, 80-89 for ac electrics and 70-79 for dc electrics and electro-diesels). The third digit indicates the sub-class (this being determined by such facts as the type of train heating equipment, brakes and control equipment). Often an 0 here denotes the basic design. The last digits constitute the running number. Most British locomotives of the 20th century were renumbered at least once, only GWR units being relatively

Locomotive inscriptions

untouched in this way. The *Flying Scotsman*, to take a perhaps extreme example, began as No 1472, was renumbered to 4472 by the LNER, was then changed to 103 in a 1940s renumbering scheme before becoming 60103. Then, in preservation after withdrawal, it reverted to 4472.

Near the number is now placed a panel of basic data which (as the accompanying illustration shows) is self-explanatory and intended for the guidance of railway operating staff. The old companies varied in their presentation of such data. The GWR had a route restriction system in which lines were classified as red, blue, yellow and uncoloured in descending order of permissible axle weight, and an appropriately coloured disc on the cabside indicated the lowest category of line that a locomotive could use — that is, an uncoloured locomotive could work anywhere (the heavy 'King' Class was

Above *The brass nameplate favoured by the GWR. More frugal managements, especially in Scotland, preferred painted to metal names.*

Above right *Number and data panel of a BR locomotive. Sometimes the depot of the locomotive is indicated by an abbreviation of 2-4 letters placed close to the data panel.*

Right *Front end of a BR (former LMS) steam locomotive. The smokebox numberplate is prominent. The oval plate bears the shed code (Bristol), while SC indicates a self-cleaning smokebox.*

specially restricted and carried double red discs). A letter superimposed on the disc (A to E) indicated, in ascending order, the tractive capacity of the locomotive. The locomotive depot to which a GWR unit was allocated was indicated by an easily comprehensible letter code (CDF for Cardiff, CHR for Chester, etc) painted above the cylinders.

On the LNER, routes were classified by number in accordance with their weight restrictions and the appropriate route availability code (RA 1, RA 2, etc) was painted on the buffer beam. Here too, the name of the locomotive depot was painted. The LMS had a locomotive classification system code painted beneath the cab window. In this P and F represented passenger and freight, and numbers (1 to 8) showed the haulage capacity in ascending order. Thus the famous mixed traffic 4-6-0 was classified 5P5F. The 'Jubilees' were classified 5XP to show that 5 was a slight understatement of their power. BR continued this system, with MT replacing PF for mixed traffic types. Locomotive sheds were indicated by a plate on the smokebox door, carrying a digit (for the area) and a letter (for the shed) — 17A for Derby, 17B for Burton, 63A for Perth etc. This system was later extended to the locomotives of the other companies after nationalisation.

A route availability system, similar to the old LNER scheme, is used by BR. The higher the RA number, the more restricted is the locomotive, the appropriate number being included in the unit's data panel. Because BR diesel locomotives are not fully compatible, symbols have been adopted to show which units may be matched with others for operation under multiple-unit control. These symbols, painted above the buffers, are a blue star for units having compatible electro-pneumatic controls and a red circle for electro-magnetic controls. Class 50 (orange square) and Classes 56 and 58 (red diamond) can be matched only with the few units having the same symbol.

Other countries

French locomotives do not now carry much information externally. As in the steam days, the first letters of the locomotive number indicate the wheel arrangement (axles rather than wheels being counted, 'B' signifying two and 'C', three). Tri-current electrics are numbered in the 30,000 series and quadricurrent in 40,000, while most bi-current types are numbered in the 20,000 series. Diesel locomotives are numbered above 60,000. Yard locomotives have a four-digit number preceded by a Y.

SNCF steam locomotives had cast metal number plates, the number consisting of three digits showing the axle arrangement, then the class letter, followed by the locomotive's running number. The locomotive depot name appeared in a window placed at the top of the plate. The numbers 1 to 6 carried on the plate (and also on the buffer beam, like the number) indicated to which of the six regions the locomotive belonged. A small TIA sign on the cabside meant that the locomotive was fitted for chemical water treatment on the Armand system, while a red disc indicated that a steel firebox was fitted (and a red circle meant a steel tubeplate).

The German steam locomotive number was carried on a cabside plate and on a smokebox plate, and consisted of five digits, of which the last three were the running number and the first two showed the class of the locomotive (and also the category, for classes up to 19 were for fast passenger service, 20–39 for slower passenger service, 40–59 for freight service, while 60–96 were reserved

Locomotive inscriptions

for tank locomotives and 99 for narrow-gauge units). Small plates indicated the locomotive's district (*BD*) and its depot (*Bw*). As in France, a red disc indicated a steel firebox. After computerisation a seven-digit number became standard for all types of traction. First comes a prefix number (0 for steam, 1 for electrics, 2 for diesels, 3 for small shunters, 4 for EMUs, 6 for DMUs). Then come two digits showing the class, followed by a three-figure group denoting the running number and, finally, a computer check number which is calculated by a formula involving each of the preceding digits.

In Switzerland, where locomotives are classified with a combination of letters and figures, the first numeral indicates the number of driving axles and the second the total number of axles.

In North America, the steam railways each had their own system (usually no system at all) for locomotive numbering, and this situation continues with modern traction. Most locomotives carry only their running number and the name of the railway, with perhaps a crest or logo and sometimes a slogan. If a class indication is carried, it is almost always the manufacturer's catalogue serial for that particular product.

Chapter 20

The freight train

Most railways handle considerably more freight than passenger traffic, although this pattern is changing in some of the more highly-developed smaller countries. In Britain, the Southern Railway was alone among the inter-war companies in deriving most revenue from passenger traffic, but, over the last decade, British Rail as a whole has seen the outpacing of freight by its passenger revenues. In North America, on the other hand, passenger traffic has fallen even further behind freight since the Second World War. On all systems there has been a reshaping of freight operations and an introduction of more specialised and effective techniques, the main influence being road transport competition.

Types of freight traffic

Bulk traffic This is regarded as being the most suited to rail transport and, on most railways, is the predominant freight. It includes coal, oils, ores, grain and building materials. Latterly roadstone and urban refuse have advanced within this category. These shipments are carried at low charges and their costs per ton are low. They usually move direct from shipper to receiver in the same vehicle and can be loaded and unloaded mechanically. They are fairly safe from highway competition. More often than not they move by the *trainload*, the most cost-effective form of rail transport.

Left *An LMS branchline coal train of the 1940s. Coal concentration schemes have since almost eliminated such short-distance services.*

Right *'Piggyback' in the 1950s, just as this type of operation was being adopted in North America.*

The freight train

Merchandise This consists mainly of manufactured goods and is 'high-value' freight; that is, it is of high value itself, and it is charged a fairly high tariff. For this reason, and because clients require a fast, reliable and prompt service, it is very vulnerable to highway competition. It may move as a *carload* or in smaller shipments. In America the term MM & P ('Manufactured, Merchandise and Perishables') is used to describe this traffic.

Package freight Sometimes known as *less-than-carload* (lcl), this consists mainly of merchandise. Because it needs much handling, its costs are high, and so are the charges. In some countries independent agencies (forwarders or, in America, 'pool car operators') handle this traffic, consolidating it into carloads which are sent at carload rates. Many, if not most, railways now discourage this traffic which, after all, is conveniently conveyed either as passenger train or Post Office parcels.

Freight trains

Freight train operations have traditionally been based on the running of trains of different speeds. Thus, in North America, high-value freight is sent by 'hotshot' fast freight train, usually running to a regular schedule, while low-value freight moves in a 'drag' train. In Britain, freight trains are similarly divided, with the added distinction that fast freights (Class I) are composed of fully-fitted (with automatic brakes) rolling stock, semi-fast of partially-fitted stock, and slow freights (Class 9) of vehicles fitted with hand-brakes only, with a brake van at the end of trains containing unfitted vehicles. These divisions are currently changing with the advent of new techniques and rolling stock. In France there is a clear and logical distinction; two types of train are offered to shippers. The fast service has somewhat higher rates, but offers scheduled fast 'RA' (*Régime Accéléré*) trains. Other traffic moves in 'RO' (*Régime Ordinaire*) trains.

Within, or additional to, these divisions are specialised trains. Many of these carry perishables. The refrigerated car train is still used for the transport of perishables, although it had been circumscribed by road transport competition. The Pacific Fruit Express trains, painted bright orange and owned by two US western railroads, used to carry all the Californian fruit crop to eastern markets,

with trains dispatched to no fixed destination being routed, while in transit, to one urban area or another according to market demand.

The scale of operations of American refrigerator car trains has been severely limited by competition over the last two decades but, in Europe, international traffic is still handled by such trains. One large fruit-despatching agency is the Spanish Transfesa company which undertakes the international carriage of Spanish fruit in vehicles with adjustable axles. The European railways have their own organisation, Interfrigo, for administering international refrigerator car movements.

A special category of perishable traffic is livestock. This, too, has virtually disappeared from European railways, and in America the procession of solid livestock trains from the prairies to the Chicago meatpackers belongs to the past. In Australia and certain other pastoral countries this traffic is still considerable, however. Because of the cleaning and watering required, it is a labour-intensive traffic and not always welcomed by the railways.

In recent decades new types of train have been introduced, while others have disappeared. A need to compete with the door-to-door convenience of highway transport, and a realisation that conventional freight services make very poor use of rolling stock, have been the main motives for this change. On most railways, the fastest-growing freight sector has been the movement of road trailers on flatcars ('piggyback' or TOFC), and of containers on flatcars (COFC). Both these are 'intermodal', combining the long-haul speed and economy of rail transport with the terminal convenience of the road vehicle. A door-to-door transit is obtained without time-consuming loading and unloading operations at the beginning and end of the rail part of the haul. All that needs to be done is to transfer the containers or trailers between road and flatcar. Most railways not only carry their own trailers or containers, but also those of highway firms, their nominal competitors, as well as containers owned by shippers, agencies and shipping companies.

In North America, unlike Europe, TOFC is much more important than container traffic. The diadvantage of TOFC is that the trailers' chassis adds a considerable weight to the train, and is aerodynamically deficient. In Europe, additionally, the trailers are often too high for the railways' height limitations. This problem is solved, at a cost, with flatcars which have a pouch in their floors into which the trailer wheels are put (known as *'Kangarou'* cars in France). But

A BR Freightliner depot (BR).

even so, this mode is limited to a few routes with suitable clearances. Also encountered in Europe are flatcars built with an abnormally low floor; these serve the same purpose.

The TOFC and container revolution in America was not accompanied by a strict standardisation policy which would have assured common equipment among all the railroads. Thus in the 1950s, when the revolution started, different railroads had different tie-down systems. But the dominance of flatcar leasing corporations, and especially of the Trailer-Train Corporation, has since remedied this. In Europe, standardisation has been imposed on container traffic, thanks to the unified dimensional standards and handling characteristics agreed by the international shipping companies, who are the railways' biggest clients in this field. Both in Europe and America there are variations, of no operational significance, in the equipment provided for transferring containers between flatcar and road vehicle. Gantry cranes have proved the most effective, but are too expensive for the smaller container depots.

Several railways have established networks of regular container trains. The British Freightliner system is one of the oldest and most developed of these. Freightliners Limited is a subsidiary of British Rail, contracting with the latter for the rail haulage component of its activities; it owns containers, flatcars, road vehicles and most of the container terminals. Spain also has a very developed system.

In continental Europe, Trans-Europ-Container-Express (TECE) trains are organised by the Intercontainer organisation, which is jointly owned by the railways, including BR and several eastern bloc railways. In America, TOFC cars are frequently hauled in ordinary freight trains and subjected to delay in intermediate sorting yards. However, there is an increasing number of all-TOFC trains. One, run by Conrail and the Santa Fe RR, was introduced in 1979 and provided a five-day transit between New York and Los Angeles. Some shorter inter-city TOFC trains have also appeared. Among the pioneers was the 298-mile (480 km) Chicago£ St Louis 'Slingshot', which is interesting because the railway unions allowed it to be manned by one two-man crew, instead of the three shifts of four men which would have been the normal manning level.

To secure better utilisation of freightcars, and to improve the service offered marginally, railways have recently introduced many unit trains which are reserved ('in captive service') for fixed transits between the same points with the same traffic. The term 'block train' is sometimes used to describe these trains, but is more

A private-owner train consisting of 100-ton tank cars operated by Shell BP (BR).

A Burlington Northern RR unit coal train, hauled by a 5-unit set of road-switchers (Burlington Northern RR).

properly employed to mean simply a train running without change of composition between origin and destination. Unit trains are block trains but block trains may not be unit trains, although both have the great advantage of avoiding time-consuming processing at intermediate marshalling yards. Block trains composed solely of one client's private-owner vehicles are known in Britain as 'company trains'. A technologically advanced variation are the 'merry-go-round' (mgr) trains which circulate between colleries and power stations. These are hauled by locomotives specially equipped for very slow speeds and are loaded and unloaded while moving slowly through the highly mechanised terminals. Thus there is none of the terminal standing time which, in conventional operations, takes up so much of the average freightcar working day.

In order to meet highway competition on international routes, the European railways introduced, in 1961, the fast TEEM (Trans-Europ-Express-Marchandises) trains. These run to regular schedules and arrangements are made to keep frontier delays to a minimum. Only freightcars carrying the symbol 'S', meaning that they are designed for 100 km/h (62 mph) running, are admitted to these trains. To hold and regain merchandise traffic, BR has established its network of 'Speedlink' services. These are formed of high-capacity vehicles, air-braked and capable of 75 mph (120 km/h) running, which are formed into regularly scheduled (usually overnight) trains for movement between selected terminals.

Economies in locomotive and labour costs can be obtained by the operation of heavier trains, although the combining of two trains into one may, by reducing service frequency, actually increase the transit time of freight. This is one reason why heavyweight trains are typically those carrying low-value traffic. The world's heaviest trains are operated in North America. The Burlington Northern's coal unit trains normally consist of 110 100-ton cars, representing a gross weight of 12,500 tons and a payload of 11,000 tons (13,250 and 9,975 tonnes). The Canadian Pacific's coal trains from the Kootenay River to Vancouver, cover the 4,400 mile (7,080 km) round trip in about 90 hours with a gross weight of 12,700 tons (11,520 tonnes). British and continental trains are considerably lighter than these. For Britain, exceptionally heavy are the iron ore trains between Port Talbot and Llanwern. These, when hauled by three locomotives, have a gross weight (including locomotives) of 3,300 tonnes.

The heaviest regular trains on BR; tripleheaded, an ore train arrives at Llanwern in South Wales (BR).

Freight vehicles

In most countries there is a trend away from the old general-purpose type of freight vehicle towards the highly specialised car. At the same time, a greater proportion of cars are owned, not by the railways but by shippers and car-lessors. Freightcar builders strive to increase the carrying capacity (payload or net weight) while keeping the empty (tare) weight to a minimum, so that net weight forms as large a proportion as possible of gross (tare weight plus payload) weight. Gross weight has also crept upwards, aided by increases in the permissible axleweights of cars. In the USA, 30-tonne axle weights are permissble, in Britain 25 tonnes, but in Ireland only 15½ tonnes.

In the past, railways relied on three or four basic cars to carry almost all of their traffic. British and continental railways used two-axle vans (covered, with sliding side doors) and open cars (sometimes provided with tarpaulins) and these were supplemented by flatcars and tank cars. In America the situation was similar, except that cars were four-axle, being mounted on pivoted trucks, and were much larger, with the van-type boxcar carrying a very high proportion of the traffic. The argument in favour of general-purpose vehicles is that they are more likely to find a load for the return trip. On the other hand, more specialised vehicles are usually suited to mechanical loading and unloading. They often have a higher maximum speed and therefore make their return trips so much faster than conventional cars that their high empty mileage is more than fully compensated. An ordinary American boxcar makes only about 12 trips each year, whereas TOFC flatcars average 51 trips and coal hoppers, 37.

British freight cars are traditionally smaller than those of continental Europe and, in the past, this has not been because of size restrictions (although the hopelessly inefficient 10- and 12-ton mineral car was kept in service because some collieries could not handle larger vehicles). In recent decades an effort has been made to increase the capacity of British vehicles, a notable technical change being the widespread use of long wheelbase cars and an increase in the number of four-axle cars. Possibly the most significant technical improvement, in Britain and elsewhere, has been the widespread equipment of freight cars with roller bearings in place of the primitive oil- or grease-lubricated frictional axlebox, whose overheating was a cause of the vast majority of freight train delays and, not infrequently, of fires and derailments. In a new category of specialised car are the purpose-built container and TOFC vehicles. In Britain the Freightliner trains are composed of 'Lowliner' cars of two types; inner (which can be coupled only among themselves) and outer, which couple both to the inner cars and to conventional rail vehicles. Containers and trailers are often loaded on ordinary or slightly modified flatcars in many countries, but the trend is towards purpose-built vehicles. Several varieties have appeared in the USA, and the 'Ten-Pack' TOFC sets, which are highly skeletal in design and are of exceptionally light weight, have made a good impression on operators. A vehicle which promises to supersede the container in domestic service is the 'RoadRailer'. This is a modern variant of an old idea, a covered vehicle with two easily-switched sets of wheels, one for rail use and the other for highway use. A freight agency, Inter Rail Express (IREX), was planning to introduce (in 1983) a 30-hour Florida–New York service with these vehicles; the agency was to provide the locomotives and vehicles, paying the railroads for the use of their tracks and enginemen. Another design of the lightweight flatcar is the 4-Runner, introduced by the major car lessor Trailer-Train. Unlike the Ten-Pack and RoadRailer, 4-Runner sets can be included in trains of conventional vehicles.

Thanks to high utilisation, many railways expect a reduced requirement for freightcars, which they reckon to have a 30-40-year life. (US railroads regard 25 years as the useful life of a freight car.) A greater proportion of private-owner cars also contributes to this. In Britain, private-owner cars were a prominent feature of pre-nationalisation railways. British Railways initially eliminated them, but subsequently changed its mind. In the late 1960s, BR possessed about 500,000 freightcars, which were reduced to 150,000 by the early 1980s; an additional 20,000 were owned privately. By the end of the decade BR is hoping to reduce its holding to only 31,000.

Private-owner cars are owned partly by freight forwarders, but largely by big shippers, among the latter being oil companies and stone-quarrying companies whose products are distributed by regular trains composed of their own rolling stock. This practice not only relieves BR of considerable capital investment, but ensures that the clients, in order to get the most out their investment, load and unload the cars very quickly. A similar situation prevails in several other

A very special specialised vehicle, used by BR to carry nuclear flasks containing spent fuel from nuclear power stations (BR).

countries. The German DB owns about 300,000 cars and German private owners 50,000. Private owners, taking the form of car-lease organisations, are also important in the USA. Cars bearing the symbol GATX, rather than the initials of a railroad company, belong to one of the biggest lessors, General American Transportation Corporation. Trailer-Train (TTX), which specialises in TOFC flatcars, but has subsidiary companies operating other cars, is said to be the biggest freightcar owner in America, with about 120,000 vehicles.

Freight stations

Until the reorganisations of recent decades, a freightcar started its journey either on a private siding (that is, it was loaded on the premises of the shipper) or at a freight station (where either the shipper or the railway's pick-up and delivery service would bring and load the shipment). Freight stations were numerous, being attached to most passenger stations, and so were factory sidings. Individual cars would be picked up at these points by a pick-up train (known as a way-freight in America) and taken to a main sorting yard where they would be marshalled with other cars to form trains to the main destinations. En route, the main line freight train would pass through intermediate sorting (marshalling) yards where cars would be added or subtracted.

The main change over the last decades is that all railways, to varying degrees, have embarked on freight concentration schemes. Local freight stations have been closed, so the pick-up freight has virtually disappeared. Shipments now tend to move a greater distance over the highway at destination and origin; the progress of container and TOFC service has both facilitated and resulted from this. The road segment of the haul may be handled either by the railways' own road transport organisation, or by private contractors, or by the clients themselves.

Most railways have tried to discourage less-than-carload business; in Britain this sector was more or less taken over by the National Freight Corporation following the 1968 Transport Act. This corporation uses the highway services of National Carriers and the latter may use the railway for trunk haul business when this is commercially desirable.

Marshalling yards may be divided into the mechanised, automated and non-mechanised varieties. The mechanised type are of the gravity, or 'hump', configuration, in which uncoupled vehicles are pushed over a hump and allowed to run into the tracks reserved for each group of destinations and on which complete trains are thereby formed. The speed of the cars in this process is controlled by remotely controlled retarders, which momentarily grip the wheel flanges to slow cars down. Yardmasters supervise from the control tower.

Automated yards, which are still quite rare, incorporate various electronic devices, the most important system of which estimates the speed of cars and actuates the retarders accordingly, without human intervention. In France, marshalling yards are divided into RA and RO categories; the former tend to be mechanised, perhaps automated, and deal with the fast trains. With the increasing use of block trains, designed to speed up traffic flows by avoiding intermediate marshalling yards, most railways now find themselves in possession of vast acreages of unwanted yards. This problem was first realised in America in the 1950s, but the American experience was ignored, until it was too late, by other railway administrations.

On several railways a computerised car control system aids improved vehicle utilisation while providing a better service to the customer. The TOPS (Total Operations Processing System), originally devised for the Southern Pacific Railroad, has been adopted by a number of railways, including the British and the Spanish. The TOPS centre keeps a record of each vehicle, its location and its routing. This enables the management to provide empty vehicles for new traffic promptly and economically, and clients can telex in to find the position and probable arrival time of their shipments. Some of the larger companies have their own terminals directly connected to the system and can in this way monitor not only the progress of their own cars but also, indirectly, the quality of the railway management.

British freight car inscriptions

With the introduction of the TOPS system, new identification codes for rolling stock were introduced. Freight cars now carry, on each side, a data panel containing three lines of information. The top line is a three-letter type identification code. The middle line gives the maximum payload and the empty weight of the vehicle, while the last line contains the vehicle's individual running number.

The last letter of the identification code indicates the type of brake fitted:

A   Air brake   R   Piped for air and vacuum
B   Air brake and vacuum pipe   V   Vacuum brake
O   Unfitted   W   Vacuum brake and air pipe
P   Piped for vacuum   X   Dual fitted (ie, air and vacuum)
Q   Piped for air

The first letter of the code indicates the broad vehicle type:

B   Four-axle (ie, bogie) steel cars   F   Flatcars
C   Covered bulk carriers   H   Hopper cars

Data panel of a BR vacuum-braked 21.5 tonne coal hopper. The builder's plate can be seen just above the leaf spring; apart from the works number, this indicates the builder, Cravens, the year of building, 1958, and the lot, or batch, number.

The freight train

Continental freight vehicles, some of which enter Britain by train ferry, have standard inscriptions. In this picture the first item of the number (on the right) is two digits denoting both the gauge and the class (normal- or high-rate) for demurrage charges; 01 signifies normal rate and standard gauge. Second item of the same top line is RIV, indicating registration with the Regolamento Internationale Veicoli. The addition of EUROP to this line means that the vehicle, under an agreement made by nine West European administrations, can be used in the internal services of the host administration if one of those nine. A similar agreement has been reached among Eastern Bloc countries, whose vehicles may carry the addition OPW instead. On the second line are the computer and traditional symbols of the owning railway (see Chapter 2). The third line begins with the four-digit code describing the category of vehicle; the series 103 0 to 174 5 is for standard vans. Then comes the running number, followed by the computer check number. The letter symbols on the bottom line are the owning railway's codes, and often repeat as well as add information; G, for example, signifies a standard van. Some vehicles in this location bear, inside a rectangle, a small anchor (signifying suitability for train-ferry operation) or a P (signifying a private-owner vehicle). Interior length and length over buffers are shown towards the left, and below them, enclosed in a rectangle, is the empty (tare) weight. The grid at the extreme left shows the permissible weight of load. The letters denote the three categories of track (A is for lines accepting 16-tonne axleloads, B for 18, and C for 20 tonnes); the permissible loading is written beneath each letter. The bottom line, prefixed by an S, shows the permissible loads if speeds up to 100 km/h (62 mph) instead of the normal 80 km/h (50 mph) are envisaged. An additional line (SS) on modern vehicles gives the same information for speeds up to 120 km/h or 75 mph.

I	Train-ferry cars		S	Two-axle steel-carrying cars
J	Four-axle steel coil cars		T	Private-owner tank cars
K	Two-axle steel coil cars		U	Open cars for bulk traffic
M	Mineral cars		V	Vans
O	Open cars		X	Special service cars
P	Private-owner cars (except tank)			

'Q', 'Y' and 'Z' are reserved for service vehicles, 'A' for passenger coaches, 'D' and 'E' for diesel and electric multiple units, and 'N' for parcels and mail cars.

The second letter of the code indicates the precise sub-type. A full list was published in *Modern Railways* (November 1976) and here is given, just as an example, a breakdown of one of the smaller groups (M):

MC-	16.5-tonne mineral car	MS-	26.5 or 27.5-tonne ironstone or stone tippler
MD-	21.5-tonne mineral car		
ME-	25-tonne mineral car	MT-	23.5-tonne stone car
MF-	32-tonne scrap metal car		

Chapter 21

The passenger train

Although the prime function of the passenger train is to convey people, it may also carry traffic for which a fast transit is desirable. Foremost among the secondary traffics are mail and parcels. In the past many railways attached horseboxes to passenger trains and often milk vehicles. In recent decades a number of passenger trains have conveyed passengers' cars.

In Britain the word *express* was usually employed for fast trains making limited stops. However, this term is inappropriate in America, where 'express' means express parcels, while in France a *train express* comes between a *rapide* (fast) and *omnibus* (stopping train). In many countries, brand-names like Inter-City, HST and TEE have, to some extent replaced traditional terminology. This is especially the case in Germany. Here *D-Trein* (meaning corridor train) came to mean fast train (*Schnellzug*) early in this century, but nowadays the *D-Trein* is outpaced by the *IC* (Inter-City) which is a fast regular-interval train, as well as by the TEE (Trans Europ Express), but remains superior to the *E-Trein* (*Eilzug*), which is only a semi-fast.

In Britain, *express* (slowly falling out of use in favour of *fast*), *cross-country*, *stopping* and *suburban* cover most categories. A *mail*, in the English-speaking world, can describe a long-distance passenger train carrying mail (typically the fastest train on the route) or a mail train, carrying mail only. The *mixed train* is still encountered in some countries; it combines the functions of stopping

Mixed trains were rare in Britain, so the 'Hemyock Mixed' in Devon, illustrated here, was quite celebrated (M. Deane).

passenger and pick-up freight train. The slow passenger train, stopping at all or most stations, handling more parcels than passengers, and typically running during the night, is colloquially known as 'the milk' in Britain and more formally as an *accommodation train* in America. In Australia a distinction is made between the few *interstate trains* and the long-distance trains within one state which are known as *country trains*.

Non-passenger traffic

Apart from passengers' baggage, most passenger trains convey parcels. In the USA a special agency, the Railway Express Agency, handled this for many decades. Occasionally, special vehicles, apart from parcels vans, were provided for long-term traffic flows. Horseboxes were common on British railways and so were vehicles reserved for pigeon traffic (station staff would release racing pigeons in accordance with the instructions received from the race organisers). In New South Wales, dog vehicles, converted from passenger cars, still serve the greyhound racing industry. Milk churns were once a common traffic at British country stations.

Mail in most countries is carried in accordance with long-term contracts by which agreed space is allocated on trains. Sometimes the mail contract is sufficient to keep otherwise unprofitable trains in operation; many of the 'train off' petitions made by US railroads in the 1950s and 1960s followed the loss of such contracts. In several countries the railways operate special sorting vehicles, staffed by the postal administration, on which mail can be sorted in transit. Solid mail trains still operate in Britain, although they are now painted in BR livery rather than Post Office red; they consist of sorting cars and storage cars. Apparatus by which mail bags could be picked up or set down en route without the train stopping is now no longer used, but it is still possible to make use of the letter box set in the side of mail trains to post a late letter. In Britain, mail trains are known as Travelling Post Offices (TPO). The expression Railroad Post Office (RPO) is used in the USA, for the compartment reserved for mail on passenger trains. Especially in America, mail and parcels cars were generally marshalled at the front, and passenger cars at the rear; hence the term 'head-end traffic' for the former.

Passenger classes

The provision of different standards of comfort and convenience with corresponding differentiation between the prices charged is generally and misleadingly known as passenger class distinction. A more modern and more accurate term would be market differentiation. Right from the early days it was found commercially expedient to provide a range of services which would cover the needs of the poor and the desires of the rich.

In Britain a three-class system was soon adopted by most railways. Until parliament intervened, the cheapest (Third) class accommodation could be primitive indeed. Parliament also insisted that railways should offer at least one Third class service over each route; in response some companies ran very slow stopping trains with low-grade rolling stock at inconvenient hours, while others, conscious that the sheer numbers of Third class passengers made them a potentially fruitful source of revenue, tried to do better. These obligatory Third class trains soon became known as 'parliamentary trains'. In 1875, the Midland

Railway, preferring to compete with comfort rather than speed, abolished Second class and conveyed Third class passengers at the former Second class standard. With varying degrees of reluctance the other railways followed suit, so that in Britain there were two classes, Third and First until, in 1956, British Railways renamed Third class as Second.

On the continent there were three, sometimes four, classes until 1956, but now there are two. However, the continental practice of levying supplementary fares for superior accommodation or faster speeds means that, in effect, there is a wide range of choice. Supplementary fares (sometimes disguised as compulsory seat reservation tickets) are levied by many railway administrations on passengers travelling by the fastest trains. Limiting such trains to First class passengers, as is common in Italy, has a similar effect.

In Britain, supplementary fares have rarely been imposed, but a form of price discrimination, known as 'market pricing' has been practised by British Rail and, in effect, has superimposed a second form of discrimination across the formal divisions of First and Second. This approach seeks to separate passengers who pay for their tickets themselves from those whose fares are paid, ultimately, by the consumer or taxpayer. The former are price-sensitive while the latter are not. The BR solution has been to offer cheap (approximately half-price) fares for those willing to travel by trains whose timings are unattractive to businessmen and officials on business; so, while speed and comfort are indistinguishable, there are trains which (in effect) require extra fare.

In countries whose size determines that most long-distance passengers spend one or more nights in the train, the standard of accommodation is the determining factor in classifying passengers. In the USSR there are two basic classes, Hard and Soft, which are said to determine the standard of comfort but, in addition, price differentials are in force to separate accommodation in open sleeping cars, and in four-berth and two-berth compartments. In addition, the basic rate per mile is higher for a fast train. In North America, the 'transportation' part of a fare may be for either First class or Coach class accommodation. The latter simply provides a seat (nowadays a reclining seat), while a First class ticket entitles the passenger to a seat in the club car (the modern equivalent of the old parlour car) and to purchase sleeping accommodation. The latter is nowadays a single-berth 'roomette' or a double bedroom, but in the

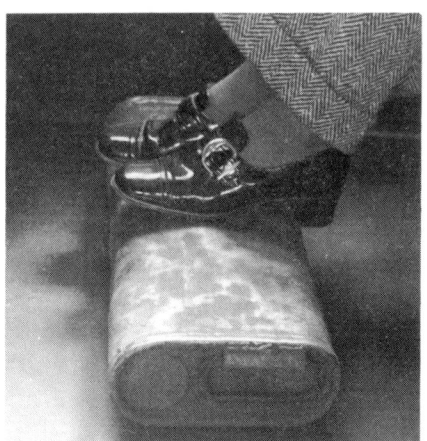

A traditional footwarmer, still in use in New South Wales, where some trains are hauled by diesel locomotives lacking train-heating boilers.

past a wide variety of accommodation has been provided, with timetables detailing the composition of each train and the type of accommodation provided. The old 'section' sleeping car — an open vehicle with curtained upper and lower berths which convert to seats for daytime use — survives in Canada.

Passenger vehicles

Passenger car development has brought progressively greater comfort and convenience for users, and at the same time improved mechanical and structural characteristics. From the safety point of view, the replacement, in the 20th century, of wooden vehicles by wooden-bodied but steel underframed vehicles, then by all-steel construction, was a major improvement. Integral construction is now used, with the body frames welded to the underframe and thereby forming a strong box-type structure. The development of the chassis has been of benefit both to passengers and to the railways.

Four-wheel cars, with their jerky motion contributing both to passenger discomfort and physical wear and tear, are no longer encountered on Western European standard-gauge railways, while the six-wheeler, only a marginal improvement, has almost entirely disappeared from Germany and is not used in France, Britain or the Low Countries. The use of the pivoted truck, or bogie, was exploited first in the USA, which for a period used both six- and four-wheel trucks. Four-wheel trucks are now standard both in the USA and elsewhere, but varying designs are in use; the best arrangement of components, and the amount and type of springing, is still being studied. Trucks which are excellent for ride and stability at medium speeds may be uncomfortable and even dangerous at high speeds.

The bogie, or truck, had its origins in the USA, but its advantages were so obvious that it was soon adopted throughout the world. It improved the riding qualities and, at the same time, enabled longer cars to be built without fear of wheel-grinding, or perhaps derailment, on curves. Six-wheel trucks were once used on the heavier American cars, but four-wheel is now universal. The wheels are set in the bogie frame and are sprung, but the frame is not attached directly to the car body. Instead there is a *bolster*, which is inside and across the frame and suspended from the latter. The bolster can move independently of the frame both vertically and horizontally, has its own springing and is attached to the car body by a pivot.

There are many different designs of bogie and each is a compromise. Design (and maintenance) is of crucial importance for high-speed service; the early TGV trains of the SNCF had bogies which were supremely comfortable at 100 mph (160 km/h) but inferior at the lower speeds. The weight of the bogie forms a high proportion of total weight, and *articulated* vehicles have appeared from time to time as an answer to this problem. In these, a common bogie supports the two ends of adjacent vehicles. Such cars were used successfully in suburban service out of Kings Cross (London) for many years and, subsequently, a few US railroads used the idea. The main drawback is that the two or more cars sink or swim together; if one has to be withdrawn for repairs its dependent neighbours have to be withdrawn too.

In the early railway age, trains were not heated; Queen Victoria's vehicle in one of the royal trains had a primitive but effective form of underfloor heating, but ordinary passengers had to be content with nothing, or with a footwarmer. The latter was a metal canister containing soda acetate. Heated in special installations, this could give out heat for hours, helped by an occasional shake. It was eventually superseded by under-seat radiators, fed by steam conveyed down the train in pipes. Steamheating, though far from perfect, was a great step forward and no improvement was sought until the introduction of non-steam locomotives presented an obvious problem. A number of railways, notably those in North America, attached steam-heating vans (containing an oil-fired boiler) to their trains in winter. Others, including British Railways, mounted the boilers in selected locomotives (where they were a frequent source of technical trouble).

However, the present-day trend is towards electrical heating, usually in association with air-conditioning. Power for this may be from diesel generators provided on each vehicle (as on post-war American vehicles) or from a special diesel generator van (as on French TEE trains), or from the locomotive itself. During the transition period, some vehicles may be dual-heated, steam or electricity being used in accordance with the motive power provided. British Rail expects to eliminate steam heating by the mid-1980s. By 1982 Amtrak was operating only one steam-heated train (the Florida-New York *Silver Star*).

There are several variants of rolling stock, and variants of terminology, which are unfamiliar outside a particular country or continent. Among these are the *slip coach*, which was used by certain British railways, notably the Great Western. The slip coach had its own brake system and a small cab at the end, and a coupling which could be released at speed. Non-stop trains could detach this car to set down passengers on the approach to an intermediate station, an extra guard being entrusted with its detaching and the run, under its own momentum, to the platform.

Dome cars were widely used by American railroads after the war. They had a part- or full-length upper deck with a mainly glass roof through which passengers could enjoy the scenery. In the early 1980s, Amtrak was operating one regular train with domes, and some were still in transcontinental service in Canada. In Europe, dome cars were used for some years on the 'Rheingold' train and the SNCF still has some railcars with the same feature.

A Talgo train of the Spanish National Railways. This is one of the latest batch, which incorporates a tilting mechanism. This is the rear end, the last vehicle being used for baggage and air-conditioning plant.

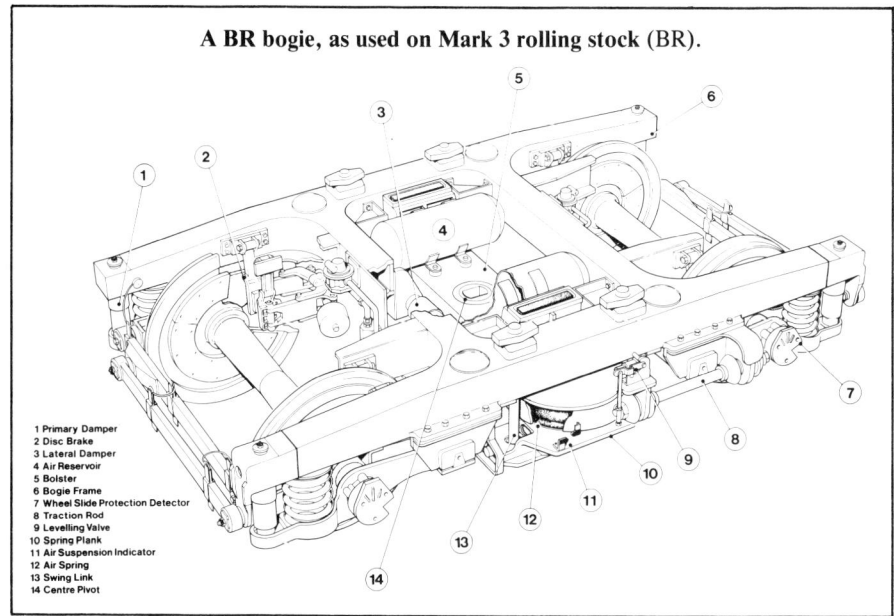

A BR bogie, as used on Mark 3 rolling stock (BR).

1 Primary Damper
2 Disc Brake
3 Lateral Damper
4 Air Reservoir
5 Bolster
6 Bogie Frame
7 Wheel Slide Protection Detector
8 Traction Rod
9 Levelling Valve
10 Spring Plank
11 Air Suspension Indicator
12 Air Spring
13 Swing Link
14 Centre Pivot

The *couchette* car is unknown in Britain and America but is standard equipment in continental Europe. It has compartments which provide seats by day and three-tier berths by night; there is a supplementary fare in addition to the normal Second class fare. The nearest British equivalent is the four-berth Second class sleeper, which is less spartan and more expensive.

The *Talgo* train is a Spanish development and is a lightweight train with a low centre of gravity, whose vehicles are in effect carried on one axle each, the non-axled end resting on the axled end of the adjacent vehicle. Talgo trains, with axles adjustable for the different gauge, operate beyond the Spanish frontier to Paris and Geneva, while a Talgo train was among the several light-weight trains tried, but not adopted, by US railroads in the 1950s.

Finally, *composite* is used in Britain to describe a car which is divided into sections for different uses; a Brake Second Composite, for example, is a vehicle which provides Second class seats at one end and the guard's brake compartment at the other.

In America the open car with a central aisle was favoured, but, in Britain and continental Europe, the compartment was preferred. Recently, and with considerable controversy, British Rail has moved to the American layout, except that seats are arranged in bays, facing each other, whereas American practice has been to have all seats facing forward (the seats being reversible). With its latest rolling stock, French Railways provides both styles, as does the DB.

The 1970s and 1980s witnessed the introduction of new ranges of passenger car in Britain, Western Europe and the USA. A wide variety of layouts were used, within a standard bodyshell. In Britain the Mark 3 coach was a development of the later varieties of Mark 2. It is of 32 tons and 75 ft (22.8 m) long. It is open-plan with centre aisle, although the latter is slightly offset in the First class layout (48 seats) because the seats are arranged as 2 × 1 (two on one side, one on the other). The Second class vehicle offers 72 seats in a 2 × 2 layout, with tables in the bays of facing seats. It is air-conditioned, the three-phase power being supplied from its own alternator, itself taking current from the locomotive. (HST Mark 3 cars take three-phase current direct from the power car and therefore are not compatible with the locomotive-hauled vehicles.) Air-conditioning was first introduced on British Rail in 1971, the Mark 3 cars being the first to have it.

The French 'Corail' cars, which have been appearing since the mid-1970s, were designed to provide the ordinary passenger with the comforts hitherto reserved for just a few travellers in the *Grand Confort* vehicles built for the TEE services. They are somewhat longer than the corresponding British Mark 3 cars, being 87 ft (26.4 m). They are built in ten air-conditioned varieties. The open First seats 58 passengers, while the open Second is built in two seat densities; for internal services an 88-seat variant is used, while international trains have cars with only 80 seats so as to provide extra leg-room. The Second class couchette cars have ten compartments which can seat six in daytime and can be rearranged to provide two sets of three-tier berths at night. 'Corail' cars are classified VU (compartment) and VTU (open plan). In the same period, the SNCF received some VSE vehicles. These are built to a European standard design, sponsored by the UIC, and are identical with units supplied by several builders to the German, Belgian, Swiss, Italian and Austrian railways.

The American railways re-equipped their long-distance passenger trains in the 1950s with smooth-riding, rather heavy, rolling stock. When Amtrak took over surviving passenger services, these vehicles were ready for replacement. For its western services, where height restrictions are generous, Amtrak has acquired a series of doubledeck cars, called 'Superliners'. Those providing coach class accommodation have 78 or 62 seats, depending on whether they are intended for long or intermediate distance passengers; with the lower density, it is possible to provide leg-rests as well as foot-rests. The medium-distance version has all its seats on the upper deck, the lower deck being used for toilets, washrooms and baggage. In the dining cars, the upper deck provides seats for 72, with the kitchen being placed on the lower deck. Each sleeping car has a mix of First class and 'economy' bedrooms, including a bedroom for the physically handicapped.

Amtrak 'Superliners', doubledeck vehicles used on western routes, where clearances are generous (Amtrak).

The latest British vehicles have wide doors, a partial move towards Continental standards. However, British car designers have a great advantage over American and Continental in that all British stations have raised platforms. In other countries, designers have to arrange doors and steps to suit both the high platforms of main stations and the low platforms elsewhere.

Design requirements for suburban trains are very different from those of long-distance stock. Seating density has to be high, and doors must be sufficient to allow prompt loading and unloading of passengers. In the steam age, the six-a-side compartment became standard, each compartment having its own pair of doors. (There was no corridor; British regulations do not require on-train toilets on stopping trains.) Several countries, in order to increase train capacity without investing in longer platforms, use doubledeck rolling stock. The British Southern Railway experimented in this direction, but the height restrictions made it impossible to design a really satisfactory vehicle.

Liveries

The passenger trains of the very early railways were typically painted in bright colours but, as the decades passed, an increasing number of railway administrations began to favour a dull, though varnished, livery. In the steam age, bright paintwork was expensive to maintain as well as being more costly to apply, but many railway companies made the effort. In Britain, attractive and distinctive liveries remained general, but in North America the duller shades of maroon or green became characteristic.

After the British railway Amalgamation, the new companies maintained, to varying degrees, the old traditions. The LMS adopted a maroon livery reminiscent of (but less striking than) that of its constituent company, the Midland Railway. The LNER continued with the 'teak' (unpainted varnished wood) finish of the Great Northern. The GWR continued with a two-colour livery (chocolate lower panels and cream uppers), while the Southern introduced an eye-catching green for both locomotives and passenger vehicles. After nationalisation, a succession of colour schemes were adopted and then abandoned by British Railways, including LMS maroon and maroon and cream. Finally, the blue and grey scheme was adopted for both vehicles and locomotives but BR then decided, for safety reasons, to paint yellow the noses of its locomotives and multiple-unit trains.

In the USA, dieselisation and the demands of competition persuaded many railways to introduce striking, sometimes garish, liveries. The widespread use of stainless-steel unpainted cars gave additional opportunities, and stainless steel, with some red, white and blue additions, is the livery adopted by Amtrak.

In continental Europe, subdued colours were the general rule until the end of the steam era. France preferred olive green, although its railcars were brightly painted in red and cream. Germany, Austria, Switzerland and Belgium favoured dull shades of green, the Netherlands used a pleasing dark blue for locomotive-hauled stock and green for electric multiple units, while Italy used a brown of indeterminate hue. Nowadays, there is much more variety and gaiety. The Netherlands' Railways have changed to yellow. Eurofima (UIC) cars in international service are usually painted orange and grey. French *Grand Confort* cars are red and stainless steel, while the 'Corail' vehicles in internal service are in two-tone grey with bright orange doors. So-called ambulance cars (vehicles adapted for invalids but often used in ordinary service) retain the grey and green which, for a time, was the SNCF livery for long-distance trains.

In the early days of railways, many administrations, aware of general illiteracy, used different colours to distinguish the several classes of vehicle. In India and Russia this practice survived into the 20th century and lately has been revived (presumably for different reasons) by the DB, whose IC trains have First class cars in red and cream, Second class in blue and cream. Other railways, including the French and the British, place a colour band running below the eaves. On 'Corail' vehicles, a green band denotes Second class, and yellow First class. In Britain, Second class is uncoloured, First class has yellow, while red denotes a dining or buffet car.

Pullman and wagons-lits

George Pullman, in the 1860s, introduced on American railroads a series of sleeping car which became immediately popular. The design depended on longitudinal upper and lower berths which could be folded to form seats for daytime use. These cars transformed long-distance travel for those willing to pay the First class fare, plus the Pullman supplement. Pullman was responsible for the internal management of these vehicles, with the railroads responsible for their running. Some railroads preferred to operate their own sleeping cars, but often purchased the vehicles from Pullman's works.

After the Second World War, the US government — under anti-monopoly legislation — obliged Pullman to abandon either the car management or the car-building business. The company continued with car-building, but built its last railway passenger car (for Amtrak) in 1981. The Pullman company also built and operated both sleeping and parlour cars on Britain's Midland Railway in the 1870s. Later, the Pullman subsidiary company in Britain operated on board a number of 'Pullman' day trains, of which the 'Brighton Belle' and 'Golden Arrow' were the best-known. For a supplementary fee, passengers enjoyed low-density seating, waiter service and other comforts. The Pullman organisation in Britain was acquired by British Railways in 1962, which then began to eliminate Pullman-operated catering, despite its consistently high standards.

The International Sleeping Car Company (wagons-lits) was established in Belgium to provide Pullman-style facilities. Wagons-lits (sleeping cars) and restaurant cars were the nucleus and often the entirety of a series of famous trains like the *Blue Train* and the *Orient Express* which criss-crossed the Continent. Most of these trains have either succumbed to air competition or have been outclassed by other trains, but wagons-lits vehicles of modern design are still in use on many routes.

Both wagons-lits and Pullman faced competition, not only from railway-operated services, but also from rival companies. In the USA, Wagner's Palace Car Company was eventually forced out of the business, but the Berlin-sponsored Mitropa organisation, originally established as a deliberate competitor of wagons-lits, lives on in the German Democratic Republic.

Named trains

In most countries, although not in Britain, a passenger train's number is printed in the public timetable. According to a 1981 poll in Germany, one in three of passengers know the number of the train in which they are travelling. Many railways give their better trains a name; in Germany the IC trains are named

The 'Scarborough Flyer', an LNER train whose title has since been used for a BR regular steam excursion train from York.

and, according to the same poll, half of the passengers know the name of their train. Train names are less for convenience than for public relations and they are most generously distributed in North America and Germany. In Britain, they were used sparingly to denote trains which, for one reason or another, were counted as very superior although, after the Second World War, some British trains were named not so much because they were superior as because it was hoped that, being named, railway staff would give them extra attention so that they would indeed become superior. The name 'Inter-City', subsequently used as a generic name by BR and then by other railways, was originally carried by one such train, connecting London and Birmingham over the former GWR.

British long-distance trains used to carry long wooden destination boards midway along, or below, the car roof eaves. These were eliminated by British Railways in favour of sticky paper labels which might, or might not, be affixed to windows. In continental Europe it is usual for destination plates to be hung beside the entrance doors or to be presented as illuminated signs in the same vicinity. American trains may display the train name or number but, in any case, it is usual for the conductor or another member of the train staff to stand beside each entry door to tell passengers where the train is going.

Some of the best-known train names are given below. The word 'Limited' was meant to give an air of exclusivity, but was said to indicate either that the number of stops was limited, or that the number of passengers would be limited (that is, extra vehicles would not be added, although one or more duplicate trains, 'extra sections' or 'second parts', might be run at peak periods).

Some notable named trains
Britain

Name	Route	Railway
*Aberdonian**	London & Aberdeen	LNER
Atlantic Coast Express	London, Ilfracombe & Padstow	SR
Bournemouth Belle	London & Bournemouth	SR
Brighton Belle	London & Brighton	SR
Bristolian	London & Bristol	GWR
Cheltenham Spa Express	London & Cheltenham	GWR

Britain (cont'd)

Name	Route	Railway
Cornish Riviera Express*	London & Penzance	GWR
Coronation	London & Edinburgh	LNER
Coronation Scot	London & Glasgow	LMS
Devonian	Bradford & Paignton	LMS/GWR
Flying Scotsman*	London & Edinburgh	GNR and LNER
Golden Arrow	London & Dover	SR
Hook Continental*	London & Parkeston Quay	LNER
Irish Mail*	London & Holyhead	LMS
Merseyside Express	London & Liverpool	LMS
Midday Scot	London & Glasgow	LMS
Night Ferry	London, Brussels, Paris	SR/SNCB/SNCF
Pines Express	Manchester & Bournemouth	LMS/SDJR
Queen of Scots	London, Harrogate & Glasgow	LNER
Royal Highlander*	London & Aberdeen	LMS
Royal Scot*	London & Glasgow	LMS
Scarborough Flyer†	London & Scarborough	LNER
Silver Jubilee	London & Newcastle	LNER
Sunny South Express	Liverpool, Manchester & Brighton	LNWR/LBSC
Thames-Clyde Express	London (St Pancras) & Glasgow	LMS
Torbay Express*	London & Paignton	GWR

Overseas

Name	Route	Railway
Avrora*	Moscow & Leningrad	SZD
Blue Train*	Cape Town & Johannesburg	SAR
Broadway Limited*	New York & Chicago	PRR
Canadian*	Montreal & Vancouver	CPR
Capitol Limited	New York & Chicago	BO
City of San Francisco	Chicago & San Francisco	UP
El Capitan	Chicago & Los Angeles	Santa Fe
Empire Builder*	Chicago & Portland	Burlington/GN
Frontier Mail*	Bombay & Amritsar	BBCI/NWR
Grand Trunk Express*	Madras & Delhi	SIR/GIP
Indian Pacific*	Sydney & Perth	ANR/NSWGR/WAGR
Mistral*	Paris & Nice	SNCF
North Coast Limited	Chicago & Portland	Burlington/NP
Punjab Mail*	Bombay & Firozpur	GIP/NWR
San Francisco Chief	Chicago & Oakland	Santa Fe
Southern Aurora*	Sydney & Melbourne	NSWGR/VR
Sunset Limited*	New Orleans & Los Angeles	SP
Train Bleu*	Paris (formerly Dover) & Nice	SNCF
Twentieth Century Limited	New York & Chicago	NYC

The passenger train

Name	Route	Railway
International		
*Nord Express**	Paris & Stockholm	SNCF/DB/DSB/SJ
Orient Express†	Paris & Bucharest	SNCF/DB/OBB/MAV/CFR
*Puerta del Sol**	Paris & Madrid	SNCF/RENFE
*Rheingold**	Hook of Holland, Geneva, Milan	NS/DB/SBB/FS
*Simplon Express**	Paris & Belgrade	SNCF/SBB/FS/JZ
*Sud Express**	Paris & Lisbon	SNCF/RENFE/CP

*Name still in use (note that routes may change over the years, especially with international trains).
†Name still in use for tourist operation.

The first named train was probably the *Granville Express* between London and Ramsgate (1877). Two useful references are *Titled Trains of Great Britain* (1953) by C. J. Allen and *Grand European Expresses* (1962) by C. Behrend, the latter dealing with the wagons-lits operations.

In the 1950s, the western European continental railways combined to establish the Trans Europe Express (TEE) concept. This was aimed at the international business traveller who was leaving the railways in favour of the airliner. TEE trains were First class, supplementary fare, trains painted in a distinctive red and cream livery, provided with extra comforts and conveniences, and circulating across the frontiers between the main European cities. A number of distinctive and varied trainsets were provided and the services, all named, won considerable prestige, although it is doubtful whether many of them paid for themselves. TEE trains still exist but have lost some of their glamour in the light of later developments.

The 'Gottardo', a TEE train linking Basle and Genoa.

Passenger vehicle inscriptions

Britain The scrapping of pre-nationalisation rolling stock has meant a reduction in the number of type identification codes in Britain. On the other hand, with the current co-existence of different systems of heating and braking, vital information has to be provided for the use of railway operating staff. BR locomotive-hauled main line passenger vehicles carry a running number on each side, close to the end of the vehicle, and a panel of technical information at each end, beside the gangway. Vehicle numbers have a letter prefix ('M', 'E', 'W', 'S', 'SC') to indicate the region to which cars are allocated. Among the information provided at each end is the maximum permitted speed and the *eth* rating. The latter indicates the load imposed by the vehicle's electrical train heating; in train formation the *eth* ratings of the vehicles are added together and they are not permitted to exceed in total the locomotive's *eth* potential (which is indicated on the locomotive's data panel).

The most prominent symbols (a letter and a digit) relate to the vehicle's route restriction. Unlike locomotives, whose axle loadings determine route availability, passenger vehicles are usually restricted by width (which also involves length, since the greater the length the greater the overhang on curves). In principle, the route restriction symbols which were adopted in the 1950s are based on the standard BR coach of that time, whose profile was designed to fit the standard loading gauge. To this profile, Restriction C1 was allocated, with non-standard profiles given other Restrictions.

Each category of passenger-carrying vehicle has its own type code, of which the most common are given below. It should be noted that these relate to locomotive-hauled stock. Multiple-unit train vehicles (including HST cars) have a prefix 'T' (trailer), or 'M' (motored) or 'D' (driving). Also, vans included in

BR coach-end inscriptions. The prominent 'C1' is the route-availability code. Beneath it is a dimensions plate, and then a record of recent repairs. Then, below these, come the heating and braking details. Finally there is the code indicating the configuration of the vehicle, in this case BSO (Brake Open Second), and the maximum permitted speed.

The passenger train

passenger trains are coded according to the TOPS system of identification, as described in the previous chapter.

BCK	Brake Corridor Composite	SLF	Sleeping First
BFK	Brake Corridor First	SLC	Sleeping Composite
BG	Brake (with gangway)	SLS	Sleeping Second
BSK	Brake Corridor Second	RB	Buffet with Kitchen
BSO	Brake Open Second	RBR	Refurbished Buffet
CK	Corridor Composite	RF	Restaurant First with Kitchen
FK	Corridor First		
FO	Open First	RK	Kitchen Car
SK	Corridor Second	RKB	Kitchen and Buffet
SO	Open Second (other than TSO)	RMB	Open Second with Buffet
		RSO	Restaurant Second
TSO	Tourist Open Second (62 or 64 seats, with 72 in Mark 3 vehicles)	RU	Unclassed Restaurant Car
		RUB	Unclassed Restaurant with Buffet

In multiple-unit stock, the letter indicating open or corridor layout is omitted.

The Continent European practice is now to present the vehicle number as numerator and denominator (see the accompanying illustration). The top line is a computer-usable series of five number-groups, plus a computer check number. The first two digits are usually either 50 for stock not registered for international service with RIC (see Chapter 2) or 51 for stock which is so registered; 60 signifies a service vehicle and 61 a TEE or similar vehicle. The second pair of digits is the owning railway code (see the table in Chapter 2). The third pair indicates the accommodation provided, common examples being:

00	Mail	82	Second with baggage compartment
06	Sleeping cars		
10-19	First class	88	Restaurant
20-29	Second class	89	Lounge
26	Doubledeck	91	Baggage with mail section
30-39	First and Second	92	Baggage car
50-59	Second with couchettes		
81	First with baggage compartment		

Then follows a dash. The next pair of digits denotes both the type of heating and the maximum speed; for example, the range 70-78 means that the vehicle has electrical heating only and can run up to 160 km/h (100 mph), the precise number in the range depending on the electrical system. After this comes the running number of three digits and the check number. The bottom line, or denominator, presents additional or identical information in the form used by the owning railway. Common codes used by the SNCF include the following:

A	First class	s	Side corridor (in van)	d	Baggage space provided
AB	First and Second	u	Air-conditioned		
D	Baggage	B	Second class	r	Catering facilities
c	Couchettes	C	Train heating van	t	Open seating
j	Stainless steel car	WR	Restaurant		

French passenger vehicle inscriptions. Beneath the SNCF inscription is the computer-usable vehicle number (see text). Beneath this the A4B6u inscription denotes four First and six Second class compartments, air-conditioned. In the centre, almost indecipherable in its rectangular border, is the vehicle's depot (Metz). To the left is the RIC inscription explained in the text.

Small numerals refer to the number of compartments or seating bays. Thus an air-conditioned vehicle with four First and six Second class compartments would be classified A4B6u. On the DB the lower line begins with bold letters indicating the category of vehicle, of which the following are most common:

A	First class	Post	Mail car
B	Second class	PwPost	Baggage with mail section
Bc	Second with couchettes	WL	Wagons-lits sleeper
AB	First and Second	WR	Restaurant
PW	Baggage car	WG	Lounge
BPw	Second with baggage section	DAB	Doubledeck First/Second
		K	Narrow-gauge
BR	Second with buffet		

There then follow small letters denoting details of the vehicle. Among these are:

y	Open car with central aisle	kr	With invalid compartment
m	More than 24 m long	e	Electrical heating
k	With kitchen	bu	With buffet
tr	With hand-baggage section		

Finally, there comes the batch number of the vehicle.

Vehicles in international service also carry an RIC data panel. This begins with a three-digit number which shows the maximum permitted speed (km/h). Then comes 'RIC', followed perhaps by an anchor which indicates suitability for a limited list of train ferries; a following section indicates, by appropriate letters, any other train ferries which may be used (for example, KN means Korsor to Nyborg). The remainder of this panel is occupied by letters indicating which railways the vehicle may move over with, finally, electrical details.

Chapter 22

Speeds and schedules

Train speed, being measurable and accessible to the general public, has always been popularly regarded as an index of excellence. In Britain and America, where there was competition between companies serving the same points, there were sporadic outbursts of competitive schedule-cutting while in those countries and in Western Europe, attempts to break the current speed record have been made from time to time. The latter is assessed as the maximum (peak) speed reached on a run, although the earlier records were in fact averages, being calculated from the passing times at neighbouring points (usually mileposts).

Speedometers were not fitted to British steam locomotives until the final decades of the steam age and, in modern times, the speed recorder of the dynamometer car, used for testing, has been the confirming authority. The 112 mph (180 km/h) claimed for No 999 is open to some doubt, while *City of Truro*'s 102.3 mph (165 km/h), though timed by an expert, may have been slightly overstated.

Some speed records

Year	Speed (mph)	(km/h)	Country	Motive power
1893	112	180	USA	No 999 (New York Central 4-4-0)
1903	130	209	Germany	Electric railcar on test track
1904	102.3	165	Britain	*City of Truro* (GWR 4-4-0)
1931	143	230	Germany	Propeller-driven railcar
1934	124	199	USA	M-10001 (Union Pacific streamline train)
1936	124.5	200	Germany	No 05-001 (streamlined 4-6-4)
1938	126	203	Britain	*Mallard* (streamlined 4-6-2)
1939	133.5	215	Germany	Diesel railcar
1954	151	243	France	No CC-7121 (electric locomotive)
1958	206	331	France	Nos CC-7107 and BB-9004 (separate runs)
1981	236	380	France	TGV train

Mallard—a Gresley Pacific of the LNER—retains the world record for steam traction, although German engineers regard the performance of No 05-001 as more meritorious, since *Mallard* was assisted by a falling gradient and was damaged during its exploit. It has to be remembered, too, that even higher speeds may have been reached in normal service by trains which were not being timed. In the USA, for example, the streamlined steam 'Hiawatha' service regularly ran at over 100 mph (160 km/h) and may well have broken world records, unnoticed, on occasions. On the narrower gauges, the railways of the Dutch East Indies set up some records on the eve of the Second World War, but the present record is held by South African Railways, one of whose 6E1-type electrics reached 159 mph (256 km/h). The fastest speed reached by a Japanese 'bullet train' appears to be 198 mph (318 km/h) which was recorded in 1980.

Absolute speed records, although having great publicity value, are of doubtful relevance. Closer to real life are the records for start-to-stop average speeds. The following runs were achieved by regular fast trains improving on their schedules in the pre-Second World War period:

Notable start-to-stop runs

Year	Distance (miles)	(km)	Speed (mph)	(km/h)	From	To	Motive power
1905	55.5	89.4	78.3	126	Camden	Atlantic City	Reading RR4-4-2
1932	77.3	124.5	81.7	131.5	Swindon	London	*Tregenna Castle* GWR 4-6-0
1935	219	352.6	87.6	141	Paris	Nancy	Bugatti railcar
1936	1,017	1,637.4	83.3	134	Denver	Chicago	*Denver Zephyr* (diesel)
1939	195.8	315.2	102	164.1	Florence	Milan	Electric luxury train

Competitive schedule-cutting had its most dramatic manifestation in the 'railway races' in Britain. In the Race to the North of 1888, the East and West coast consortia of companies made a succession of cuts in the timing of their respective 10 am trains from London to Edinburgh. Then, in 1895, the same groups of companies engaged in the Race to Aberdeen, the climax of which was the West Coast average speed of 63.3 mph (102 km/h) for the 540 miles (869 km) with three intermediate stops. Then, in 1904, the GWR and the LSWR competed for the 'Ocean Mail' traffic between Plymouth and London. Such races were great sporting occasions, but of no benefit to clients, whose lives were put at risk, and who sometimes reached their destination inconveniently early (in the small hours, in the case of 'Ocean Mail' passengers).

In North America there were similar outbreaks. The Pennsylvania and New York Central railroads competed for the New York–Chicago traffic, but soon learned that competition could be expressed better in standards of accommodation and convenience; by 1925 both companies had increased the timing to 20 hours, two hours more than it had been two decades earlier at the height of the competition. In the 1920s the Canadian Pacific and Canadian National competed for the Montreal–Toronto business. In its unsuccessful effort to match the CNR six-hour schedule, the CPR, over its longer route, scheduled a train at 68 mph (109 km/h) over 124 miles, which was a world record for a regular schedule. Soon afterwards this competition was abandoned, the two companies agreeing to operate 'pool trains' jointly over this and other competing routes.

For much of the inter-war period, the world's fastest scheduled train was the *Cheltenham Spa Express* (*Cheltenham Flyer*) of the Great Western, between Swindon and London. In 1932 it was accelerated to an average speed of 71.4 mph (115 km/h) over the 77 miles (124 km). But, in the late 1930s, the LMS and LNER were introducing competitive fast schedules between London and Scotland. Spurred by the success of its *Silver Jubilee* train (London–Newcastle), the LNER introduced its *Coronation* (London–Edinburgh) in 1937 on a six-hour timing for the 393 miles (632 km). The LMS engineers, whose *Coronation Scot* train on trial achieved 114 mph (183 km/h) in 1937 at the expense only of dining car crockery, had similar thoughts, and the LMS responded with its *Coronation Scot*, making six and a half hours over the slightly longer and more heavily graded West Coast route to Glasgow. When the *Coronation* was timetabled to run from London to York (188.2 miles or 303 km) in 157 minutes, the *Cheltenham Flyer*'s 71.4 mph average was surpassed by 0.5 mph. Meanwhile, in the USA, loss of passengers to other forms of transport had stimulated the introduction of fast streamlined trains on many routes.

For the railway passenger, the existence of a crack train is of less benefit than a timetable which offers fast, not necessarily super-fast, trains at frequent intervals. The high speed trains which have appeared in several countries in recent decades do offer a frequency of service unmatched previously, except on a very few routes like the electrified New York–Washington and London–Portsmouth lines. Until the opening of the first Japanese *Shinkansen* line, the world's fastest trains were operated by the French. The *Mistral* of the SNCF, running from Paris to the Mediterranean over a route which was being progressively electrified, averaged — between Paris and Dijon, — 84 mph (135 km/h) over the 195½ miles (315 km). However, the other trains on this route were neither frequent nor especially fast. For a short time, after further electrification, the world's fastest trains ran between Paris and Lille.

The new high speed trains

The new era of fast passenger train services, running at very high speeds, at close regular intervals, and open to all classes of passenger, began in 1964 with the opening of the first Japanese *Shinkansen* route, the New Tokaido Line. This first line now runs to Hakata, with the better trains covering the 661 miles (1,064 km) in six hours 45 minutes, an average of 98 mph (157.6 km/h) with six intermediate stops. Between Nagoya and Yokohama (196 miles or 316 km) the trains average 112 mph (181 km/h). The top running speed of the trains, electric multiple-units, is 130 mph (210 km/h). Rolling stock for later lines has been engineered for 162 mph (260 km/h), but the extra stresses caused by high speeds and other disadvantages may result in the retention of the old 130 mph.

The *Shinkansen* network is completely new, the old narrower-gauge lines being retained for freight service and night trains. The French Paris–Sud Est scheme, with its electric TGV trains, is also purpose-built, although the trains utilise the old tracks for the approaches to the city terminals and for service extensions to cities like Geneva; unlike the *Shinkansen*, the new line is of the same gauge as the old. Service frequency is less dense than on the *Shinkansen*, being (at the start of the service in 1981) 13 trains a day in each direction

An APT prototype, with tilt mechanism in action. In 1983 the future of this concept was still in doubt (BR).

between Paris and Lyons (the New Tokaido Line offers six departures every hour for most of the day). With its maximum running speed of 162 mph (260 km/h), the TGV provides faster transits than any other of the world's trains.

Locomotive-hauled high speed trains are also offered by the SNCF. In the early 1970s the *Etendard* and *Aquitaine* were timed to run at speeds up to 125 mph (200 km/h) on the Paris–Bordeaux run. These were TEE trains but, in 1980, the first of several orthodox services on a similar schedule was introduced, the *Montaigne*. The latter can carry up to 1,130 First and Second class passengers, compared to the 450 First class supplement-paying passengers of the TEE versions.

In Britain, the aim has been to introduce high speed services over existing track, and the diesel High Speed Train (HST) has, since 1976, successfully achieved this. Initially, the HST services were over the London–Bristol and London–South Wales routes, but they were later extended to Penzance, to the East Coast route, and the south-west to north trunk route through Bristol and Birmingham. With their maximum running speed of 125 mph (200 km/h) these trains have considerably reduced travelling time; in 1982 their fastest schedule averaged 103 mph (166 km/h) between London and Chippenham (94 miles or 151 km). In 1979 one of them covered the 58 miles (93 km) from Reading to Chippenham at an average of 111.6 mph (180 km/h), a British record.

The HST's successor, the Advanced Passenger Train (APT), was designed for high speed services on electrified routes. The trials of three APT prototypes were long drawn-out and somewhat painful, due to frequent failures and mishaps; too many innovations had been incorporated in one design. In 1982 it was decided to build a new prototype (APT-U) which, unlike its predecessors, would not have articulated suspension and hydrokinetic brakes. It would, however, retain the novel aluminium body and the vehicle-tilting concept. (Tilting cars are intended to enable trains to pass over curves at speeds higher than the superelevation of the rails would normally permit; the tilt is intended to eliminate passenger discomfort caused by centrifugal forces. Passive, or 'pendulum', tilting, in which the vehicle body itself swings under the influence of centrifugal forces, has been tried in several countries. Active tilting, in which electronic and electro-hydraulic systems push the vehicle body to the appropriate angle, was chosen for the APT, but may be abandoned.)

In the USA, an attempt at a high speed service was made with the electric *Metroliner* trains over the North Eastern Corridor (Washington–New York–Boston). Initially, speeds of 160 mph (257 km/h) were envisaged, but a succession of technical difficulties brought this down. The original *Metroliner* trains have now been relegated to local services, being replaced by locomotive-hauled trains which can run up to 125 mph (200 km/h) and average 75 mph (121 km/h) between New York and Washington. In Canada, turbotrains brought the Montreal–Toronto timing down to four hours 30 minutes, but they experienced sporadic technical troubles. The new Canadian-built LRC ('Light, Rapid, Comfortable') trains, built for speeds up to 125 mph (200 km/h), were later ordered for this route.

The German Federal Railways (DB) have not offered schedules comparable to those of France, Britain and Japan, but plan to do so. The absence of long stretches of route suitable for high speed running is a handicap and a number of new or reconstructed high speed lines are in hand, suitable for 125 mph running speeds. By 1981, less than 155 miles (250 km) of route were suitable for such a speed, but a steady extension was under way which would bring this to 1,056 miles (1,700 km) by 1990. Meanwhile, the German IC (Inter-City) trains, running at regular intervals in a carefully co-ordinated timetable, provide well-equipped trains of moderately high speed and good frequency. One of them, the *Ernst Barlach*, in 1982, was covering the Hanover–Hamburg run at an average speed of 83 mph (134 km/h).

Chapter 23

A note on statistics

'Figures can't lie, but liars can figure' is perhaps too harsh a saying in this context, but it should be borne in mind when dealing with railway statistics. To make the jump from statistical data to opinion or judgement is perilous and a prerequisite is to know not only what each figure describes, but also how it was obtained. The following are some statistical terms which are frequently encountered.

Gross revenue is the total receipts over a given period. *Net revenue* is gross revenue less operating costs. *Operating costs* are the expenses of all the factors employed in running the trains and exclude capital charges. *Capital charges* are the amounts payable for the use of the money invested in fixed railway facilities, and interest on certain debts. The financial relations between governments and state railways are so complex that the ascertainment of capital charges is usually an exercise in unreality. However, it follows that the achievement of a net revenue does not necessarily mean that a railway is profitable; there has to be a surplus to cover the capital charges as well. The *operating ratio* (net revenue divided into operating costs, multiplied by 100) is a useful measure of a railway's year-by-year performance; an operating ratio above 100 indicates an operating loss, below 100 an operating surplus.

Railway mileages are usually expressed as *route miles* or route kilometres; these represent rail distances. *Track miles*, or track kilometres, are the total length of all tracks, including yards and sidings as well as both tracks on double-track lines. Tariff mileage is the mileage attributed to a movement between any two stations for the purpose of calculating a fare or tariff. It is usually identical to the route mileage but not always. For example, the tariff distance between Paris and Lyon is 317 miles (this being the mileage via the traditional route) whereas most passengers travel by the TGV route, whose route mileage is 279 miles.

Train miles (or train kilometres) express the total mileage of all trains (sometimes excluding non-commercial trains) in a given period (usually the accounting year). It is a good indication of the volume of service offered to the public and an approximate indication, over several years, of the volume of business. However, the latter function is best performed by the figure for passengers carried (usually revenue passengers; that is, excluding passengers travelling on free passes) and for freight tonnage.

Freight traffic can be measured in tons originated (that is, loaded) or in *ton miles* (or ton kilometres), which is the tonnage originated multiplied by the *average length of haul*. The latter is the distance travelled by the average ton of freight, and is a statistic often misused. For most railways, the higher the length of haul the better, because net revenue is almost always greater on the long-distance shipment or passenger. But some railway systems, like that of the USSR, which are overloaded, seek to reduce the average length of haul as a means of relieving pressure. Soviet Railways has a habit of carrying trees from the Baltic to the Pacific, and other trees from the Pacific to the Baltic; it also carries many cabbages from village to city. The first traffic increases the average length of haul, while the latter decreases it; in other words, even more than most averages this statistic has to be carefully interpreted. Both in America and Russia the number of *carloadings* is a carefully gathered index. Indeed, at the height of the railway age, American presidents studied monthly carloading figures as a guide to the economic health of the USA.

Some indicators of locomotive performance are given in Chapter 9. In addition, locomotive utilisation figures are regarded as important. These can take the form of *average annual mileage, average ton miles (or ton km) per locomotive, average mileage between repairs*, and *locomotive miles (or km) per locomotive failure* (but different railways define differently a failure). In obtaining these statistics, some administrations exclude locomotives employed in yard work (for example, by including only locomotives above 1,000 HP).

Similar figures are derived for the utilisation of rolling stock. The utilisation indices for labour are a sensitive issue. *Labour productivity* is the amount of traffic (ton miles or km) added to passenger miles (or km) and divided by the total number of railway workers. Some railways exclude non-operating workers from this, others exclude those employed in railway works. It is rare for total working hours to be used as the denominator instead of total number of workers.

More refined indices include *train control personnel per route mile or km* and *permanent way staff per track mile or km*. Particular care has to be exercised in using utilisation and efficiency indicators for the purpose of making comparisons. Always, the saving phrase 'all other things being equal' must be kept in mind. Efficiency comparisons should never be regarded as comparisons of managerial competence; a railway carrying coal from a colliery to a power station is bound to appear statistically more efficient than one carrying general freight in a rural region, but the latter may be operated more efficiently than the former (and probably is, insofar as smart management is a product of necessity).

Appendix 1

Preserved steam railways

What is briefly known as the railway preservation movement embraces three distinct activities: the running of steam-hauled or 'vintage' trains over main line tracks; the restoration and operation, usually with steam traction, of lines abandoned by the various railway administrations; and the establishment of railway museums.

In Britain, after a complete ban on steam traction by British Rail in the years immediately following dieselisation, there has been a reversal of policy, with several main lines being opened for steam-hauled excursions. Moreover, such excursions are no longer organised only by enthusiast organisations, but on some routes by BR itself, with the co-operation of private organisations which provide the steam locomotives. BR excursions, which run regularly in the summer, are notably on the Leeds–York–Scarborough lines and in Cumbria, the Carnforth Steamtown Railway Museum being responsible for the locomotives. These, as well as the privately organised steam excursions, are well-publicised in the railway monthly press and by SLOA (Steam Locomotive Operators Association). For a detailed reference guide to both preserved lines and railway museums and relics, there is a book by R. Crombleholme and T. Kirtland, published annually by Allen & Unwin with the title *Steam '82, Steam '83,* etc. Smaller but cheaper is the annual *Railways Restored* (Ian Allan), while the Association of Railway Preservation Societies publishes an annual leaflet, *Guide to Steam Trains in the British Isles*, which can be obtained by sending an SAE to the ARPS (Sheringham Station, Norfolk, NR26 8RA).

The operation of abandoned lines had its beginnings with the resuscitation of the Talyllyn Railway in Wales. This was a narrow-gauge line which had fallen on hard times. It was transformed into a flourishing tourist railway, using original locomotives, by a volunteer organisation especially created for the purpose. This was in the early 1950s; in the late 1950s a start was made on the transformation of an abandoned standard-gauge line in Sussex. This became the Bluebell Railway, which showed that standard-gauge lines were capable of rehabilitation and financial viability. Since then, many other ventures have been begun and proved successful. They tend to rely heavily on volunteer labour, and sometimes the combination of a preservation society and an operating company is uneasy, since the former provides unpaid labour from which the latter may draw financial benefit. In the circumstances, it is creditable that so few lasting quarrels have disturbed the work of preservation. In contrast, notably with the USA and France, argument has usually not led to continued dissension.

The list which follows omits many of the smaller or beginning ventures and is confined mainly to lines which are at least open at weekends and weekdays in summer. Although it is steam locomotives which are the great attraction of these lines, it should not be forgotten that they possess old rolling stock, often superbly restored, and make an effort to preserve the old style and atmosphere of their stations and installations.

Steam tourist railways in Britain

(The dates and frequencies given in this list should only be regarded as a guide which the reader is advised to check before visiting any of these lines.)

Bala Lake Railway, Llanuwchllyn, near Bala. This is a 4½-mile (7-km), 1 ft 11½ in gauge line operating from Easter to autumn. Laid on former GWR trackbed, it is one of the newest of the Welsh narrow-gauge lines.

Bluebell Railway, Sheffield Park, Sussex. A 5-mile (8-km) standard-gauge line, open on winter Sundays, weekends in the warmer months, and daily in summer. Its large locomotive stock includes many Southern Railway types.

Brecon Mountain Railway, Pant, Merthyr Tydfil. A new 2-mile (3-km), 2-ft gauge line featuring overseas locomotives and fine scenery. Open daily in summer and at certain other holiday periods.

Dart Valley Railway, Buckfastleigh, Devon. Part of the former standard-gauge GWR Totnes–Ashburton branch, reduced to 7 miles (11 km), and providing a daily service in summer.

East Somerset Railway, Cranborne, Somerset. A short standard-gauge track offering trains on summer Sundays and certain other days, with the locomotive depot open daily in summer and at weekends in winter. The locomotives include BR standard 2-10-0 and 4-6-0 units.

Ffestiniog Railway, Portmadoc, Wales. This 12-mile (19-km), 1 ft 11½ in gauge line, a former slate railway, is notable for its use of Fairlie-type locos.

Great Central Railway, Loughborough. Part of the former Great Central main line, consisting of 5½ miles (9 km) of standard-gauge track with a train service at weekends all the year, with Wednesday running in the summer. The locomotive stock consists largely of medium-size tender locomotives.

Isle of Man Railway, Douglas, Isle of Man. Not a typical preserved line, this 3-ft gauge railway is the surviving 15 miles (24 km) of the once extensive Isle of Man Railway. Owned by the local government, the line provides daily summer services, hauled by the original 2-4-0 tank engines (the oldest was built in 1874).

Isle of Wight Steam Railway, Haven Street, near Ryde. A standard-gauge 1¾-mile (3-km) line perpetuating the old island railway and operating a passenger service on summer Sundays and certain other days.

Keighley & Worth Valley Railway, Keighley, Yorkshire. A 5-mile (8-km) standard-gauge line in picturesque hilly terrain. A large and varied locomotive stock hauls the passenger trains at weekends in winter and daily in summer.

Kent & East Sussex Railway, Tenterden, Kent. A former standard-gauge light railway, of which 4 miles (6 km) have been rehabilitated. Passenger services run daily in the summer holidays and certain weekends at other times.

Lakeside & Haverthwaite Railway, Haverthwaite, Cumbria. Operating daily in summer, this 3-mile (5-km) standard-gauge line connects with the Lake Windermere steamers.

Leighton Buzzard Narrow Gauge Railway, Leighton Buzzard, Bedfordshire.

This 2-ft gauge, 1¾-mile line operates on summer Sundays and at certain bank holidays. Its locomotive stock includes some exceptionally interesting types.

Llanberis Lake Railway, Llanberis, Gwynedd. A 2-mile (3-km), 1 ft 11½ in gauge line, which uses former quarry locomotives. Open daily in summer.

Middleton Railway, Hunslet Moor, Leeds. A 1½-mile (2½-km) standard-gauge line with passenger service on summer weekends and commercial freight service at other times.

Mid-Hants Railway, Alresford, Hampshire. This line was once a LSWR route. It operates on summer weekends and its original 3-mile (5-km) run is being progressively extended.

Nene Valley Railway, Wansford, near Peterborough. This 5½-mile (9-km) standard-gauge line operates on weekends and three days midweekly in summer. It includes continental European locomotives in its stock.

North Norfolk Railway, Sheringham, Norfolk. This 3-mile (5-km) standard-gauge line preserves the Great Eastern Railway style, and operates on summer weekends and certain other days.

North Yorkshire Moors Railway, Pickering, Yorkshire. This is a substantial line of great historic interest. It operates trains daily in summer from Grosmont with steam (sometimes vintage diesel) traction. The length of this standard-gauge line is 18 miles (29 km).

Severn Valley Railway, Bridgnorth, Shropshire. This is another of the big tourist lines, with 12½ miles (20 km) of standard-gauge track, and a large stock of locomotives, mainly of GWR and LMS origin. Services operate at weekends for half the year with daily service at the height of summer.

Sittingbourne & Kemsley Light Railway, Sittingbourne, Kent. A 2 ft 6 in gauge, 2-mile (3-km) line open on summer weekends and some days in August.

Snowdon Mountain Railway, Llanberris, Gwynedd, Wales. An old-established 4¾-mile (7½-km) Abt rack railway up Snowdon. Of 2 ft 7½ in gauge, it is open daily from spring to autumn, using Swiss-built locomotives.

Strathspey Railway, Boat of Garten, Highlands. A 5½-mile (9-km) standard-gauge section of the former Highland Railway near Aviemore. It operates at weekends in summer with additional days in July and August.

Talyllyn Railway, Tywyn, Gwynedd. A historic and charming 7-mile (11-km) line, of 2 ft 3 in gauge and providing daily services from spring to autumn.

Tanfield Railway, Marley Hill, near Gateshead. A 1-mile (1½-km) standard-gauge line with undistinguished steam locomotives and operating only on Sundays in July and August and at certain bank holidays. Its attraction is that it is being extended along the route of the old (1725) Tanfield Waggonway.

Torbay & Dartmouth Railway, Paignton, Devon. A 7-mile (11-km) standard-gauge line preserving the Great Western atmosphere of the original owner.

Vale of Rheidol Railway, Aberystwyth. A former Cambrian Railway tourist line, operated daily in summer by British Rail, using the original steam locomotives. Of 1 ft 11½ in gauge, it runs for 12 miles (19 km) in scenic terrain.

Welshpool & Llanfair Light Railway, Llanfair Caereinion, near Welshpool. A charming 5½-mile (9-km), 2 ft 6 in gauge line using not only the original locomotives but also some brought from overseas. It operates at weekends from spring to autumn, and daily in the summer.

West Somerset Railway, Minehead, Somerset. This 20-mile (32-km) line operates a daily steam service in summer from Minehead over a 10-mile (16-km) section.

Preserved steam railways 211

Whipsnade & Umfolozi Railway, Dunstable, Bedfordshire. Part of Whipsnade Zoo, this 2ft 6in gauge line is 2 miles (3-km) long and operates daily in summer.

Although this list has deliberately excluded 'miniature' railways, there are three steam-worked 15-in gauge lines whose extent and maturity qualify them for inclusion:

Fairbourne Railway, Fairbourne, near Barmouth, Gwynedd. This 2-mile (3-km) line runs among sand dunes, using some attractive locomotives, daily from spring to autumn.

Ravenglass & Eskdale Railway, Ravenglass, Cumbria. This is a former iron ore railway, progressively transformed into a very picturesque scenic steam line of 7 miles (11 km).

Romney, Hythe & Dymchurch Railway, New Romney, Kent. This is the most substantial of the minimum-gauge railways, (almost 14 miles (22 km) long). It connects south coast holiday resorts and provides a daily service in summer.

A handful of the tourist railways operate main line diesel locomotives, the dates usually being advertised in the railway press. In addition there are two electric railways of considerable interest:

Manx Electric Railway, Douglas, Isle of Man. This is a 3-ft gauge trolley-pole electric light railway, extending for 18 miles (29 km) to Ramsey. It was 'nationalised' by the local government in 1956. It connects at Laxey with the 3 ft 6 in gauge electric Snaefell Mountain Railway.

Volks Electric Railway, Brighton. Owned by the borough of Brighton, this 2 ft 8½ in gauge, 1¼-mile (2-km) line is a third-rail electric system and the oldest (1883) electric railway in Britain. It runs daily from spring to autumn.

Tourist railways in North America

In North America a number of main line steam locomotives haul excursions, but these are irregular; *Trains Magazine* usually provides advance information about these. A regular (summer) steam excursion is that of the Province-owned British Columbia Railway, which runs a weekly train northwards out of Vancouver, using an ex-Canadian Pacific 'Royal Hudson' locomotive.

The following list of American steam tourist lines is highly selective. A much more detailed survey can be obtained from the current edition of the *Steam Service Passenger Directory*, published by the Empire State Railroad Museum (PO Box 666A, Middleton, NY 10940).

Arcade & Attica Steam Railroad, Arcade, NY. Steam operations at summer weekends.

Cass Scenic Railroad, Cass, West Virginia. A former logging railroad, with Shay and other geared locomotives.

Cumbres & Toltec Scenic Railroad, Chama, New Mexico. One of the 3-ft gauge Rocky Mountain lines resurrected for tourists with steam traction.

Edaville Railroad, South Carver, Massachusetts. A museum, together with 2-ft gauge steam operations.

Silverton Railroad, Durango, Colorado. A Rocky Mountain 3-ft gauge line of the former Denver & Rio Grande RR, offering long steam trips between Silverton and Durango.

Steamtown, Bellows Falls, Vermont. Many US and Canadian steam locomotives, with trains at advertised weekends. Transfer expected to Scranton, Pa.

Strasburg Railroad, Strasburg, Pennsylvania. A charming steam railway through Pennsylvania's 'Dutch Country'.

Tennessee Valley Railroad, Chattanooga, Tennessee. Trains hauled by steam and elderly diesel locomotives.

In Canada there are two especially interesting tourist lines:

Cape Breton Railway, Glace Bay, Nova Scotia. Several steam locomotives are used here, including a British (SR) 'Schools' 4-4-0.

Prairie Dog Central Railroad, Winnipeg, Manitoba. Trips in wooden rolling stock behind a centenarian ex-CPR 4-4-0.

Steam tourist railways in continental Europe

Most of the west European countries, and Scandinavia, have tourist railways, but their number and operating frequency tend to fluctuate. The lines listed below are relatively long-established and may therefore be expected to operate every summer. Frequencies are lower than in Britain, Sundays-only operations being quite common. French trains sometimes make a single return trip, with a long lay-over for gastronomic purposes at the outer terminus.

A volume of timetables for European tourist lines is published by Schweer & Wall, Postfach 1586, D-1500 Aachen (the 1982 edition was priced at DM.15). Somewhat larger, detailing also museums and being a general survey of accessible steam and old electric and diesel locomotives, but not including timetables, is *LOK Report Reisefuhrer* (Postfach 1280, D-4400 Munster; the 1982/83 edition costing DM.18). In addition, a trilingual folder detailing French tourist lines is distributed by the *Féderation des Amis des Chemins de fer Secondaires* (134, Rue de Rennes, 75006, Paris). An annual list of Swiss steam operations can usually be obtained from offices of Swissair.

Baie de la Somme Railway, Noyelles (near Abbeville). Within easy reach of southern England, this metre-gauge line runs to St Valery and Le Crotoy.

Blonay-Chamby Railway, Blonay (near Montreux). This is the largest of the Swiss tourist operations and features metre-gauge steam and electric traction.

Chinon-Richelieu Railway, Richelieu. This is a standard-gauge line, using ex-SNCF steam locomotives.

Goes-Borsele Railway (near Flushing). This is a Dutch standard-gauge line using small tank locomotives.

Hoorn-Medemblik Railway, Hoorn. A standard-gauge line, perhaps the most interesting of the Dutch steam railways.

Pithiviers Transport Museum, Pithiviers. A museum offering a 5-mile (8-km) trip. The gauge is 2 ft; the line is a remnant of a Décauville agricultural railway.

Trois Vallées Railway, Mariembourg, near Charleroi, Belgium. This is a standard-gauge line from Mariembourg to Treignes, and is the most developed of the Belgian lines.

Vivarais Railway, near Valence. This picturesque metre-gauge line is one of the longest-established French tourist railways and is notable for its Mallet-type tank locomotives. It runs from Tournon to Lamastre.

Germany was a little late in resurrecting lines for steam operations. In order to run main line steam power, despite the DB's reluctance to co-operate, a weekend summer steam train runs over the harbour lines at Bremen. There is a standard-gauge line from Achern to Ottenhofen (near Baden Baden), and the metre-gauge Mockmuhl Eisenbahn (Schontal-Dorzbach).

Appendix 2

Major railway museums

The following list excludes many more museums than it includes because there are so many small museums, often of local or specialised interest. Many of the tourist railways listed elsewhere could also be regarded as museum lines, since so many have made a point of preserving the style of the former operating companies. The division between a tourist railway and an operating museum is ill-defined but, in general, a site where trains move but have no real destination may best be regarded as an operating museum. Some static museums, it should be noted, occasionally loan their stock for operation on tourist lines. The York Railway Museum makes a regular practice of this.

Britain
Britain is especially rich in carefully preserved railway relics and there are many small specialised museums not mentioned here. A good reference to these is the Crombleholme and Kirtland book mentioned in Appendix 1.

Public museums (open most days of the year)
National Railway Museum, York. Opened in 1975 in the premises of the former York locomotive depot, this is Britain's main railway museum. Only part of its holdings are on exhibition at any one time, although some favourite items, like the record-breaking *Mallard* steam locomotive, tend to be permanently on display. Apart from steam, electric and diesel locomotives, it has a large collection of rolling stock, equipment and 'railwayana'

Science Museum, London. This has a relatively small collection which, however, includes three very early locomotives, the *Puffing Billy* of 1813, Stephenson's *Rocket* and Hackworth's *Sanspareil*.

London Transport Museum, Covent Garden, London. This museum of London's transport includes steam and electric locomotives as well as Underground rolling stock.

Glasgow Museum of Transport This displays one locomotive from each of the five main pre-grouping Scottish railway companies.

Great Western Railway Museum, Swindon. Apart from smaller exhibits, this museum contains five Great Western Railway locomotives, including *City of Truro, Lode Star* and a 'Dean Goods'.

Belfast Transport Museum This exhibits locomotives which operated on the broad and 3 ft gauges in Northern Ireland as well as early railcars and a railway horse-tram.

North of England Open Air Museum, Beamish, County Durham. Part of this operating museum is a reconstructed station. The locomotives include an 1822 Stephenson product and a working replica of *Locomotion*. There is a good collection of early 20th century North Eastern Railway passenger stock.

Darlington Railway Museum This is situated at the 1842 North Road Station in Darlington and is devoted to the Stockton & Darlington Railway. Exhibits on loan from the National Collection include the original S & D *Locomotion*.

Bowes Railway, Springwell, near Gateshead. An operating museum working on advertised summer weekends and demonstrating a very old colliery railway, including rope-haulage inclines.

Private museums (limited opening, at weekends and holiday periods)

Birmingham Railway Museum An operating museum based on the former GWR locomotive depot at Tyseley. Its loco collection, mainly GWR and LMS types, provides motive power for certain main line steam excursions on BR tracks.

Bressingham Steam Museum, Diss, Norfolk. An operating museum with a large locomotive stock of four gauges.

Bulmer Railway Centre, Hereford. This centre, alongside Bulmer's cider factory, usually houses, among other exhibits, three large locomotives used on main line excursions, *King George V, Clan Line, Princess Elizabeth*.

Didcot Railway Centre Based on the former GWR locomotive depot at Didcot, this is an operating museum run by the Great Western Society with a representative selection of Great Western rolling stock.

Dinting Railway Centre, Glossop, Derbyshire. An operating museum on Sundays (except winter) and a static museum on most other days. Its stock includes *Blue Peter*, the 4-6-2 of television fame, and one of the few preserved LNWR locomotives.

Midland Railway Centre, Butterley, Derbyshire. Open daily, and as an operating museum occasionally, this possesses a representative stock of MR locomotives and vehicles.

Narrow Gauge Railway Centre, Blaeneau Ffestiniog, Wales. Open daily in summer, this museum has over 40 locos plus many other vehicles.

Penrhyn Castle Museum, Bangor, Wales. Open daily in summer, portraying the industrial railway with locomotives and stock of four different gauges.

Port Erin Railway Museum, Isle of Man. Open daily in summer, this museum houses exhibits, including locos, relating to steam railways in the Isle of Man.

Quainton Railway Centre, near Aylesbury. An operating museum with a very varied locomotive stock.

Southport Locomotive and Transport Museum An operating museum based on the former LMS locomotive depot at Southport.

Steamtown Railway Museum, Carnforth. One of the biggest operating museums, this is based on the former LMS Carnforth locomotive depot. Its stock includes French and German locomotives, as well as British main line locomotives which are regularly used in excursion service over BR track; among these are *Flying Scotsman, Leander* and *Lord Nelson*.

Whitehead Excursion Station, County Antrim. An operating museum maintained by the Railway Preservation Society of Ireland which, among other things, provides steam locomotives of the former Irish companies for its regular steam excursion trains over CIE and NIR tracks.

Museums outside Britain

Because the British locomotive builders were primarily exporters, overseas railway museums often have a wide range of British-built locomotives. Perhaps the best, from this point of view, is the Indian Railway Museum at New Delhi. The largest collection of Beyer, Peacock locomotives is to be found among the numerous exhibits of the New South Wales Railway Museum at Thirlemere, not far from Sydney. Other Australian Museums with British-built holdings are the Redbank Museum near Brisbane, with its Queensland Government Railway exhibits, the Mile End Museum at Adelaide, which covers the South Australian railways, the North Williamstown Railway Museum near Melbourne, which does the same for the Victorian Railways, and a museum covering the Western Australian Government Railways, close to Perth. The Netherlands Railway Museum at Utrecht has some early British-built locomotives, and so will the Belgian railway museum, which is not yet properly established.

The national French railway museum is at Mulhouse, in eastern France. The corresponding institution in Germany is at Nuremberg, but the latter is supplemented by the Deutsches Museum in Munich. There is also the Deutsches Dampflok Museum at Neuenmarkt-Wirsberg with its expanding collection. Other European railway museums include the Lucerne museum of transport, the Leonardo da Vinci Museum in Milan, and there are several others.

In the USA it is harder than elsewhere to distinguish between tourist railways—which often have large static exhibitions and operate trains only on a few days each year—and true museums. Among the institutions which it seems safe to categorise as museums are the Baltimore and Ohio Railroad's museum at Baltimore, which may be regarded as the prime North American railway museum. The Smithsonian Institution in Washington owns, among others, the Stephenson locomotive, *John Bull*, and also exhibits a more modern Pacific of the Southern Railway System. Another large railway museum forms part of the Henry Ford Museum at Dearborn, near Detroit.

The Museum of Science and Industry at Chicago has two of the earliest American-built locomotives. At St Louis, under the auspices of that city's parks department, is the National Museum of Transport, which has a large and varied collection of locomotives. Like other US museums, its holdings include diesel as well as steam locomotives. The East Broad Top Railroad in West Virginia is a museum with a particular flavour. Based on an old 3-ft gauge system, it is unique in that it preserves a turn-of-the-century locomotive running and repair facility, including machine shops and foundry. At present, these are only open to the public on advertised days in February.

Other local museums include the recently opened California State Railroad Museum at Sacramento, whose exhibits are spectacularly displayed, and the Pennsylvania State Museum at Strasburg. The Colorado Railroad Museum at Golden is an operating museum. There are many others, and four which should perhaps not be left out are the museum devoted mainly to the Norfolk and Western Railroad at that company's headquarters town of Roanoke, the Ohio Railroad Museum at Worthington (Columbus), the Lake Superior Transportation Museum at Duluth and the Illinois Railroad Museum at Union.

In Canada the efforts of organised railway enthusiasts have created the Canadian Railway Museum at St Constant, near Montreal, and there is a large railway display at the National Museum of Science and Technology at Ottawa.

Appendix 3

Railway enthusiast societies

In Britain, the oldest established of the larger railway societies are the Railway Correspondence and Travel Society (160, Hillend Crescent, Clarkston, Renfrewshire G76 7XY), the Railway Club (112, High Holborn, London WC1) and the Stephenson Locomotive Society (34, Durley Avenue, Pinner HA5 1J2). These vary in their activities. They all hold regular meetings and all have libraries; the RCTS has a reputation for its intensively-researched publications; the SLS and the RCTS have their own journals (*SLS Journal* and *Railway Observer*) and have branches throughout Britain.

Of more recent origin, but big, is the Locomotive Club of Great Britain (8, Lovatt Close, Edgware HA8 9XG). Semi-specialised clubs include the Continental Railway Circle (1, Magenta Close, Bletchley MK2 3NE) and the Industrial Railway Society (13, Heathgate, Yatton, Bristol). Both of these have high-quality publications. A relative newcomer to this group is the Diesel and Electric Group (21, Oakcroft Court, Liskeard Gardens, London SE3 0PL). In addition to these there are numerous smaller societies, typically single-interest groups or localised general-interest societies. These are publicised in the *Railway Magazine* and *Railway World*. These two magazines should, ideally, be consulted before approaching the societies whose addresses are given above, as such addresses may change.

In France the senior society is the *Association Francaise des Amis des Chemins de Fer* (Gare de l'Est, Paris). For short-line and narrow-gauge enthusiasts there is the *Fédération des Amis des Chemins de Fer Sécondaires* (134, Rue de Rennes, 75006 Paris).

There are three large German societies: *Eisenbahn-Kurier GmbH,* D-7800, Freiburg, PO Box 5560; *Bundesverband Deutscher Eisenbahn-Freunde EV*, 3, Hanover 1, Viethof 3, Postfach 1163 and *Deutsche Gesellschaft für Eisenbahngeschichte EV,* D-7100 Heilbronn, PO Box 1627. The second of these is closest to an enthusiasts' association, while the last-named specialises in history.

In the USA is the Railway and Locomotive Historical Society (133, Kresge Hall, Harvard Business School, Boston). The RLHS has branches nationwide and its *Railway History* is a journal which resembles a learned publication and contains the biggest and deepest book reviews to be found anywhere. There is also the National Railroad Historical Association (PO Box 2051, Philadelphia, 19103). In Canada there is the Canadian Railway Historical Society (PO Box 148, St Constant, Province of Quebec, H3C 1C5) and the Upper Canada Railway Society (PO Box 122, Terminal A, Toronto).

Further reading

Magazines

The senior British railway monthlies are the *Railway Magazine* and the *Railway Gazette*, both published by IPC Transport Press (The Quadrant, Sutton, Surrey SM2 5AS) and both having their roots in the 19th century. The *Railway Magazine* is intended for railway enthusiasts and provides a mix of modern and historical articles and features. Its regular 'Locomotive Practice and Performance' article has a distinguished past and an interesting present. The *Railway Gazette* is for professional railwaymen, is rather expensive, and is not sold at station bookstalls; its coverage is concentrated on the present day, and is worldwide.

Ian Allan Ltd (Shepperton, TW17 8AS) publish *Modern Railways*, which is devoted to present day developments, not always British, and is very mature in its approach, as well as *Railway World*, directed towards the railway enthusiast, and especially the steam enthusiast. It also publishes, at two-month intervals, *Locomotives Illustrated* and *Trains Illustrated*. Its new monthly, *Modern Railways Pictorial*, is exactly described by its title. Like the *Railway Magazine*, these can be bought from station bookstalls.

Not so long established are four magazines which, however, seem to have made a good start: *Rail Enthusiast* and *Steam Railway* (both EMAP National Publications, Bushfield House, Orton Centre, Peterborough), *Steam World* (an IPC publication) and the quarterly *Locomotives Large and Small* (Bardonela, Adgestone, Sandown, Isle of Wight). A useful 'newsletter' kind of periodical is *World Steam* (124, Wendover Road, Stoke Mandeville, Allesbury, HP22 5TE). This details current steam operations as reported by its correspondents throughout the world.

Another enthusiasts' periodical is the quarterly *Continental Railway Journal* (1, Magenta Close, Bletchley, MK2 3NE). This has worldwide coverage, leans towards steam operations and has a correspondence column filled by highly knowledgeable readers. *European Railways* (Evelyn Way, Cobham, Surrey KT11 2SJ) covers current events on continental railways. *The Continental Modeller* (Peco Publications, Beer Seaton, Devon, EX12 3NA) also makes a contribution, many of its articles being about railways, as distinct from model railways. From the same address can be obtained one of the oldest French periodicals, *Loco Revue*, which is also for modellers but of interest to non-modellers. Among other French magazines are *Rail Magazine* (28, Rue des Petites Ecuries, 75010 Paris), which has coverage of both modern and historical aspects of French railways, *Trains* (34 Boulevard du Général de Gaulle, 78700 Conflans Ste Honorine), and *La Vie du Rail* (11 Rue de Milan, 75440 Paris). The latter is the weekly SNCF employees' magazine, but it has much space devoted to railway equipment and operation, both modern and bygone. *Voie Etroite* (Box Postal 106, 30001 Amiens) concentrates on the narrow gauge.

German railway magazines include *Eisenbahn Magazin* and *Lok Magazin*, both of which are obtainable through *European Railways* (see above). For Dutch speakers, there is *Op de Rails* (Meppelweg 299, 2544 AG The Hague).

The major US railway magazine is the monthly *Trains Magazine* (1027, N Seventh Street, Milwaukee WI 53233) which caters for a very varied railway enthusiast readership. The railways' trade magazine, *Railway Age*, is readable but offers little. Smaller circulation magazines include the *Passenger Train Journal* (PO Box 397, Park Forest, ILL 60466) and *The Short Line* (PO Box 587-T, Pleasant Garden, NC27313) which specialises in industrial and local railways.

Books

New railway books appear so fast that many worthy publications are not even reviewed. The majority of titles are never reprinted, although there are some reference books which are revised and reprinted at frequent intervals. An enthusiast wishing to build up a library should therefore see what is on offer at station bookstalls and large booksellers and then refer to the advertising pages of the *Railway Magazine* and *Railway World*. For out-of-print books recourse has to be made to libraries (including those of the railway enthusiast societies) and to second-hand booksellers specialising in railway books. The latter tend to advertise themselves in the classified columns of the *Railway Magazine*. In addition, it is useful to obtain booklists, both from publishers and large booksellers.

Among publishers, Ian Allan Ltd (Shepperton, TW17 8AS) is the most prolific publisher of books for British railway enthusiasts. Bradford Barton (Trethellan House, Truro) specialises in picture albums and railwaymens' reminiscences. Oxford Publishing Co (Link House, West Street, Poole, Dorset) has a rapidly growing list of well-produced books, with the emphasis on steam locomotives and branch-line or small company histories. David & Charles (Newton Abbot, Devon TQ12 4PU) is a general publisher which has always had a strong interest in railways.

Other publishers with smaller, though good, railway lists are Allen & Unwin (45, Museum Street, London WC1) and Patrick Stephens Ltd (Bar Hill, Cambridge CB3 8EL). In addition, there are several small publishers supplying the needs of the specialist reader. One of the oldest of these is the Oakwood Press (distributor: Element Books, The Old Brewery, Tisbury, Wiltshire SP3 6NH) which specialises in the history of small railway companies and of particular lines. Of more recent appearance are Moorland Publishing Co (PO Box 2, 9, Station Street, Ashbourne, Derbyshire) and Becknell Books (PO Box 21, King's Lynn, Norfolk PE30 2QP).

Large booksellers from whom lists may be obtained include Fleetline Books (186, Victoria Road, Swindon, SN1 3DF), Hambling's Ltd (29, Cecil Court, Charing Cross Road, London WC2N 4EZ), Motor Books (St Martin's Court, London WC2N 4AL), Fox's Railway Books (30, Princes Street, Yeovil, Somerset), Great Western Book Service (Keegan's Bookshop, Harris Arcade,

Further reading 219

Friar Street, Reading RG1 1DN) and the Baker Street Bookshop (33 Baker Street, London W1M 1AE). The latter two also deal in second-hand titles.

Continental railway books are reviewed and sold by *European Railways* (Evelyn Way, Cobham, Surrey KT11 2SJ) and the *Continental Railway Journal* (whose address for this purpose is 25, Woodcock Dell Avenue, Kenton, Harrow, HA3 0PW). For American books, there are at least two dealers in Britain — Clyde (Box D, 6, The Mount, Ewell, Epsom, Surrey KT17 1LZ) and Willen (Howard House, Howard Road, London E11 3PL). Alternatively, lists might be requested from one of the large American railway booksellers (for example, Kalmbeach Publishing Co, 1027 N Seventh Street, Milwaukee, WI 53233, or Rails 'N' Shafts, PO Box 300, Laury's Station, PA18059). Booksellers and publishers advertise regularly in *Trains Magazine*.

Timetables

Timetables deserve a section of their own for they are perhaps the most essential item of a railway enthusiast's equipment. Traditionally, they are issued both by railway administrations and by private publishers. In Britain, *Bradshaw's Railway Guide* was published up to the 1950s, and contained the timetables of all the British railway companies. The latter also published their own timetables, usually twice a year as winter and summer editions. After nationalisation, BR followed traditional practice insofar as it issued its timetables in regional volumes, but nowadays it publishes an all-system timetable instead. The BR timetable is in two volumes, one for internal services and a thinner and slimmer volume for international services; several continental railways also follow this practice. Unfortunately BR has not yet succeeded, as *Bradhsaw* succeeded with its monthly publication, in getting its timing perfect. It publishes new editions annually, but newly-issued volumes tend to be overtaken by schedule changes within weeks of publication, necessitating the preparation and distribution of timetable supplements which are entirely unloved by those who have to use them. BR also publishes free timetable leaflets for most lines, but their availability (especially in the first half of the timetable-year) is not generous.

A surviving, indeed flourishing, privately-published timetable is *Cook's Continental Timetable* which expanded in 1976 and, since 1981, has appeared in two volumes, *Cook's Overseas Timetable* having been introduced to detail services outside Europe. The *Continental Timetable* covers all major routes, some secondary, and the occasional minor line. It is published monthly and includes BR as well as local passenger shipping. It is obtainable from branches of Thomas Cook.

In North America the passenger-carrying railway companies used to issue their own (free) timetable folders, while the weighty *Official Railway Guide* (formerly, *The Official Guide of the Railways*) was a private monthly publication combining railway timetables of all the companies with additional sections for shipping and air services. This picture is now changed. Amtrak and Via Canada publish their own timetable folders (still free) while the *Official Railway Guide* still appears ten times annually, a little emaciated perhaps, and is largely devoted to regular freight train schedules, although it has a separate passenger edition. It covers Canada and Mexico as well as the USA. (The address is: National Railway Publications, 424, West 33 Street, New York, 10001.)

Timetables can be of great historic interest, for they provide, directly or indirectly, a great deal of information in addition to performing their main task.

Old timetables can be acquired through second-hand railway booksellers. A few libraries also keep them; the British Library (British Museum) has a good stock, including long runs of *Cook's Continental Timetable*. The larger public libraries in Britain often keep some of the current overseas railway timetables. The latter can also be purchased through a London specialist in these publications (BAS Overseas Publications Ltd, 48-50 Sheen Lane, London SW14 8LP).

All the above are what are known as *public* timetables (often called *timebooks* by railwaymen). There are also employees' timebooks, known in Britain as *working timetables*. These are not available to the public, although old copies sometimes find their way into specialist booksellers' hands. They include regular freight services, give passing times for stations at which stops are not made, and provide a good deal of operational information. The times they give for passenger trains may not always match those given in the public timetables (the 'advertised' time). For example, an advertised arrival time may be later than the actual schedule time, in order to discourage passengers from attempting to make a too-tight connection.

Index

Abbots Ripton accident, *63*
Absolute permissive block, *58*
Abt system, *39, 210*
Adhesion, *38, 39, 84-85, 104, 106, 143*
Albania, *25*
Alco, *134, 160*
Allport, J., *27*
Alsthom, *161*
Alternators, *138*
Amalgamation, Railway, *12, 108, 121, 193*
Amtrak, *19, 192*
APT, *155, 204*
Articulated locomotives, *89, 106-108, 142-143*
Ashfield, Lord, *27*
Ashpan, *93*
Aspinall, J., *27*
ATC *see* AWS
Atmospheric railway, *44*
Australia, *8, 26, 45, 50, 51, 52, 60, 151, 158, 215*
Austria, *24, 25, 44, 114, 116, 119, 153, 193*
Automatic signalling, *57-60, 81*
Automatic warning system, *59, 72, 74-75, 79, 81*
Auto-trains, *151*
AWS *see* Automatic warning system
Axle counters, *57*
Axleweight, *31, 86, 106*

Baldwin works, *104, 160*
Ballast, *34, 41*
Barlow, P., *43*
Barry Railway, *12, 16*
Beeching, R., *17*
Belgium, *9, 24, 25, 27, 28, 66, 76, 103, 120, 126, 131, 135, 162, 193*
Belpaire, A., *27, 93*
Blanketing, *34*
Blastpipe, *99, 102*
Block system, *54-61, 80*
Block trains, *180*
Boiler, *82-83, 91, 93, 108*
Boiler pressure, *82-83, 91, 93, 103, 145*
Bousquet, G. du, *105*
Brakes, *57, 92, 99, 126, 129, 164-167*
Brassey, T., *43*
BREL, *160*
Bridges, *41, 43, 44, 45*
British Rail (BR), *13, 17, 25, 26, 35, 41, 54, 56, 61, 64, 66-72, 86, 111, 115, 116, 117, 121-124, 135, 136, 153, 155, 166, 168, 172, 174, 176, 179, 182, 184, 193, 198, 208*
British Railways Board, *13*
British Transport Commission, *13*
Brunel, I., *12, 33, 43, 47*
Bulleid, O., *111*
Bury, E., *102*

Cab signalling *see* Automatic warning system
Caledonian Railway, *12, 15, 163*
Cambrian Railway, *12, 16*
Camelback locomotives, *104*
Canada, *8, 21, 29, 43, 44, 48, 52, 113, 124, 158, 161, 215*
Canadian National Railways, *21, 28, 44, 113, 134, 202*
Canadian Pacific Railway, *21, 29, 44, 113, 145, 161, 180, 202*
Cant, *38, 205*
Catchpoints, *35*
Catenary, *117, 128*
Centralised train control (CTC), *57*
Chapelon, A., *113*
Check rails, *37*
Cheshire Lines Committee, *11*
China, *52, 114, 162*
Chopper control, *126*
Churchward, G., *108*
CIE *see* Ireland
Climax locomotives, *142*
Collett, C., *108*
Common carrier railways, *7*
Compounding, *94, 104-106*
Condenser locomotives, *148*
Connecting rods, *95*
Conrail, *19, 125, 179*
Containers, *178*
Contractors, railway, *43, 45*
Couplings, *167-171*
Crampton locomotives, *103*
Crewe, *163*
CTC, *57*
Cubitt, W., *44*
Curves, *37, 38, 205*
Cut-off, *94, 113*
GWR, *33*
Cylinders, *94, 95, 102, 103, 143*

DB *see* Germany
Denmark, *25, 119, 134*
Despatchers, *53, 65, 80*
Detonators, *53*
Diagrams, locomotive, *100*
Diesel engine, *137*
Diesel locomotive, *83, 86, 87, 89-90, 120, 133-141, 147-148, 172, 174*
Dimensions, locomotive and car, *47, 86-87, 102, 104*
Distant signals, *66, 73, 76, 81*
DMU, *155-158*
DR *see* Germany
Drivers, locomotive, *101, 105, 129, 140, 151*
Dynamometer cars, *86, 201*

Electric locomotives, *83, 86, 87, 89-90, 119, 126-132, 140, 172, 174*
Electrification, *114, 115-125, 154*
EMU, *154-155*

Facing points, *35*
Fairlie locomotive, *106*
Fay, S., *27*
Fell system, *39*
Field weakening, *131*
Finland, *25, 119*

Firebox, *84, 92-93, 103, 108, 111*
Fireless locomotives, *148*
First Class railroads, *20*
Fishplates, *31*
Flaman recorder, *75*
Flying Scotsman, 110, 173
Footplate, *91*
Fowler, J., *44*
Frames, locomotive, *98, 102*
France, *22, 23, 25, 28, 37, 43, 50, 56, 62, 72-75, 86, 88, 95, 104, 105, 113, 116, 120-121, 126, 135, 141, 152, 161, 174, 178, 186, 192, 193, 199, 203, 212, 215*
Franco-Crosti locomotive, *149*
Freight trains, *166, 176-184*
Freight vehicles, *178, 181-185*

Garratt locomotive, *89, 107*
Gauge, *42, 46-52*
General Electric, *134, 160*
General Motors, *134, 160, 162*
Germany, *22, 24, 25, 28, 33, 50, 59, 62, 76-79, 88, 107, 113, 114, 116, 119, 120, 127, 133, 135, 136, 141, 153, 158, 161-162, 174, 183, 186, 193, 200, 205, 212, 215*
Glehn, A.de, *105*
Gooch, D., *27, 103, 104*
Goss, Professor, *86*
Gould, J., *27*
Gradients, *37, 44*
Great Central Railway, *12, 15, 27, 29, 108, 163, 209*
Great Eastern Railway, *12, 15, 28, 163*
Great Northern Railway, *11, 12, 15, 104, 110, 163*
Great North of Scotland Railway, *12, 15*
Great Western Railway, *12, 13, 16, 42, 43, 47, 63, 72, 85, 96, 103, 106, 108, 110, 135, 150, 151, 152, 163, 172, 173, 174, 193, 213*
Gresley, H.N., *12, 108, 201*
Guard rails, *37*

Hackworth, T., *102*
Hammerblow, *87*
Headcodes, *171*
Heisler locomotives, *142*
Heywood, A., *48*
Highland Railway, *15, 53*
High Speed Train (HST), *70, 157, 158, 167, 171, 192, 198, 204*
Hill, J., *27*
Horsepower, *83-84, 87*
Hudson, G., *28*

Ignitrons, *126*
India, *26, 46, 49, 51, 52, 84, 162, 166, 193*
Indicator diagram, *86*
Indonesia, *25, 114, 202*
Industrial railways, *8, 17, 117, 125, 142*
Injectors, *91*
Interlocking, *56-57, 64*
International Union of Railways (UIC), *25, 31, 170, 192*
Inter-urban railways, *9*
Invertor, current, *127*
Ireland, *22, 23, 25, 48, 51, 52, 125, 143, 181, 213, 215*
Isle of Man, *39, 49, 52, 209, 214*
Italy, *8, 25, 116, 119, 126, 149*
Ivatt, H., *110*

Japan, *9, 51, 52, 155, 162, 203*
Johnson, S., *104*
Joint railways, *11*
Joy, D., *103*

Kando system, *117*
Kitson-Still system, *147-148*

Lancashire & Yorkshire Railway, *12, 14, 27, 44, 121, 163*
'Leader' locomotive, *143*
Level crossings, *42*
Lickey Incline, *37*
Light Rail Transport (LRT), *9*
Light Railway Orders, *61*
Lima works, *111, 160*
Liveries, *193-194*
Liverpool & Manchester Railway *44, 102*
Loading gauge, *42, 47, 198*

Lock and Block, *57*
Locke, J., *44*
Locomotive see Diesel, Electric, Steam locomotives
Locomotive depots, *100-101, 174*
London & Birmingham Railway, *44, 45, 102*
London & North Eastern Railway, *12, 15, 100, 108-109, 122, 145, 152, 173, 193, 201*
London & North Western Railway, *12, 14, 28, 95, 103, 121, 163, 165*
London & South Western Railway, *12, 16, 116, 121, 163*
London Brighton & South Coast Railway, *12, 16, 45, 121, 163*
London Midland & Scottish Railway, *12, 14, 22, 28, 72, 108, 122, 135, 145, 172, 174, 193*
London Passenger Transport Board (LPTB), *18, 27*
London Transport, *18, 59, 71, 115, 213*
Longmoor Military Railway, *10*
Lubricators, rail, *38*

Mail, *187*
Mallard, 110, 201, 213
Mallet type, *89, 95, 107, 113*
Maunsell, R., *111*
Merry-go-round (MGR), *180*
Meyer system, *107*
Midland & Great Northern Joint Railway, *11, 15*
Midland Railway, *11, 12, 14, 22, 27, 28, 95, 104, 124, 143, 163, 187, 193*
Military railways, *10*
Minimum gauge railway, *10, 48, 60*
Moon, R., *28*
Multiple unit, *87, 119, 138, 151, 154-158, 165, 174, 198*
Museums, railway, *213-215*

Named trains, *194-197*
Narrow gauge, *8, 44, 46-52*

Index 223

Nationalisation, *13*
Netherlands, *24, 25, 44, 50, 114, 116, 120, 126, 162, 193, 212, 215*
New Zealand, *52, 58*
North British Railway, *12, 15*
North Eastern Railway, *12, 15, 121, 163*
Northern Counties Committee, *22*
Northern Ireland Railways, *22, 23, 25*
Numbering schemes, *172-175, 198-200*

OSJD, *170*

Paget locomotive, *143*
Pannier tanks, *110*
Pantograph, *84, 116, 118, 128*
Passenger classes, *27, 158, 187-189, 193*
Passenger services, *17, 22, 122, 154-158, 186-205*
Passenger vehicles, *189-194*
Peto, S., *45*
Piggyback *see* TOFC
Points *see* Switches
Porta, L., *149*
Portugal, *25, 44, 52*
Private owner cars, *182*
Public Transport Executives (PTE), *17*
Pullman, *158, 194*
Push-pull trains, *151-152*

Rack railways, *39, 210*
Radio control, *59, 65*
Rail, *30-33, 35, 40, 86*
Railbus, *153, 156*
Railcars, *135, 152*
Rail motors, *151*
Railway Clearing House, *11*
Railway Executive, *11, 13*
Rainhill trials, *102*
Ramsbottom, J., *103*
Rapid transit, *9, 18, 22*
Rastrick, J., *45*
Rectifiers, *126, 128, 138*
Refrigerator trains, *177-178*
Regions (of BR), *13, 123, 198*
Regulator, *85, 92, 93*
RENFE *see* Spain
Resistance, train, *84*
Reverser, *92*

Rhymney Railway, *12, 16*
RIC, *26, 199*
Riddles, R., *111*
Riggenbach system, *39*
RIV, *26*
Route indicators, *70, 77*
Route restriction, *173, 198*
Running powers, *11*
Russia, *25, 34, 45, 46, 51, 86, 98, 101, 116, 119, 120, 125, 133, 148, 168, 170, 193, 207*

Safety valves, *93, 103*
Sanding, *85, 104*
Schmidt, W., *106, 145*
Semmering Pass, *44*
Sentinel type, *142, 152, 160*
Shay locomotive, *142*
Shinkansen, *51, 155, 203*
Signalboxes, *54, 57, 60, 64, 68*
Signalling, *53-81*
Signals, *57, 62-81*
'Single' locomotives, *104*
Sleepers, *33*
Slip coaches, *190*
Smokebox, *99*
SNCB *see* Belgium
SNCF *see* France
SNCV *see* Belgium
Somerset & Dorset Joint Railway, *11, 16*
South Africa, *46, 114, 117, 149, 169*
South America, *28, 50, 52, 114, 149*
South Eastern & Chatham Railway, *12, 16*
Southern Railway, *12, 13, 16, 28, 110-111, 116, 121-122, 135, 140, 154, 193*
Spain, *9, 52, 88, 116*
Speedlink, *180*
Speed restriction, *38, 74, 77*
Speeds, *98, 103, 104, 180, 201-205*
Sprague, F., *119*
Staff system, *53*
Stamp, J., *28*
Stanier, W., *108, 147*
Statistical terms, *206-207*
Steamchests, *94*
Steam locomotives, *82-89, 91-114, 139-140, 142-149*
Stephenson, G., *45, 47, 102*
Stephenson gear, *96*

Stephenson, R., *45, 102*
Stirling, P., *104*
Streamlining, *108, 134*
Suburban railways, *8, 22, 24, 115, 119, 121-122, 152*
Superelevation, *38, 205*
Superheater, *84, 93, 106*
Surrey Iron Railway, *7*
Sweden, *119, 133, 162*
Swindon, *86, 163*
Switches, *35*
Switzerland, *9, 10, 22, 25, 52, 107, 116, 119, 150, 162, 175, 215*

Taff Vale Railway, *12, 16, 63*
Talgo trains, *191*
Tank locomotives, *100, 110*
Tender, *100*
Terminal railways, *20*
Testing, locomotive, *86*
TGV, *37, 74, 155, 167, 203*
Thermal efficiency, *88, 93, 119, 139-140*
Thompson, E., *110*
Thornton, H., *28*
Thyristor control, *130*
Timetables, *53, 219-220*
TOFC, *178-179, 181*
Token system, *60*
TOPS, *184, 185, 199*
Tourist railways, *10, 208-212*
Track, *30-52*
Track circuits, *57, 61*
Traction motors, *130, 139*
Tractive effort, *82-83, 119*
Trailing points, *35*
Train describers, *59*
Train orders, *53, 65, 79-80*
Trans Europ Express, *158, 186, 197*
Transition curves, *38*
Transponders, *60*
Trevithick, R., *102*
Tubes, boiler, *93, 99, 102*
Turbine locomotives and trains, *145, 147, 149, 158, 205*
Tunnels, *10, 41, 43, 44*
Tyne & Wear PTE, *18*

Underground railways, *18, 22, 24, 27, 43, 59, 71, 115, 148*
USA, *8, 9, 10, 18-21, 27, 28, 31, 34, 44, 45, 48, 52,*

54, 56, 58, 62, 64, 79-81,
84, 86, 88-89, 95, 98,
102, 103, 107, 116, 117,
124-125, 134-135, 138,
140, 141, 142, 147,
152-153, 158, 167-168,
171, 175, 177, 179-181,
184, 191, 202, 205, 211,
215

Valve gear, *92, 94, 96*
Vanderbilt, C., *28*
Van Horne, W., *29*
V1A Rail, *21*
Vignoles C., *45*

Volk's Railway, *52, 119,
211*

Wagons-lits, *194*
Walker, H., *28*
Walker, T., *45*
Walschaert gear, *96, 103*
Water troughs, *103*
Watkins, E., *29*
Webb, F., *104*
Weight, locomotive, *86*
 see also Axleweight
Welded rail, *33*
West Coast Route
 (WCML), *122, 128, 202*

Westinghouse, G., *164*
Wheel arrangement, *87,
88-90, 102, 104, 106, 111,
131*
Wheelbase, *87*
Wheels, driving, *83,
88-90, 95, 97, 104, 111*
Wheelslip *see* Adhesion
Whistler, G., *45*
Whistles, locomotive, *66*
Whitton, J., *45*
Whyte notation, *88-89*
Woodard, W., *111*
Woodhead route, *122*

Yugoslavia, *25, 52, 114*

The best in railway reading

British Locomotives of the 20th Century
Vol 1: 1900-1930
O.S. Nock
The first volume of three describing and illustrating in depth the development, design and mechanical features of all British locomotive types from 1900 to the present day. Containing plans, diagrams and photographs, as well as details of service and anecdotes about the people intimately concerned with British locomotive development, this definitive work will stand as a permanent tribute to the imagination and skill of British engineers.
(*Vol 2: 1930-1960* and *Vol 3: 1960-Present Day* in preparation.)

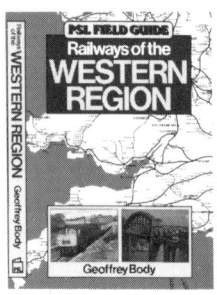

PSL Field Guide
Railways of the Western Region
Geoffrey Body
The first of five gazetteers to the sites and sights of railway significance, historical and modern, within the boundaries of the modern British Rail Regions. Ideal for use on a train journey, enabling details of a route to be followed, for touring in a car or for general reference. Contains many maps and photographs.
(*Railways of the Southern Region* in preparation.)

How To Go Railway Modelling
5th edition
Norman Simmons
Widely accepted as the 'bible' of the hobby, as tens of thousands of satisfied readers will attest, this is a complete introduction to scales, gauges, track, locos, stock, electrification, controllers, signalling, scenery and operating, with many valuable appendices.

Full catalogue available free of charge on request.